MERGERS AND ACQUISITIONS

IN A NUTSHELL®

FOURTH EDITION

JEFFREY J. HAAS
Distinguished Visiting Professor of Law
Southwestern Law School
Professor of Law Emeritus
New York Law School

DALE A. OESTERLE
J. Gilbert Reese Chair Emeritus
Michael E. Moritz College of Law
The Ohio State University

WEST ACADEMIC

860 Blue Gentian Road, Suite 350
Eagan, MN 55121
1-877-888-1330

Published in the United States of America

ISBN: 979-8-89545-005-5

To my amazing children, Sammie and Peter, who keep me young (against my will!)

J.J.H.

To my son William: For showing courage and pluck at a very young age

D.A.O.

PREFACE

The following materials provide a summary of the legal regulation of acquisitions in the United States. Since the legal rules define acquisition structure and procedure in the United States, the materials also provide a snapshot of current acquisition practice.

JEFFREY J. HAAS
RANCHO PALOS VERDES,
CALIFORNIA

DALE ARTHUR OESTERLE
COLUMBUS, OHIO

January 1, 2026

ACKNOWLEDGMENTS

The authors thank Ms. Ebony Mobley for her manuscript assistance and Scott Walker for his research assistance.

OUTLINE

PART II. LEGAL RULES AFFECTING THE CHOICE OF ACQUISITION FORM

TABLE OF CASES

References are to Pages

ABBREVIATIONS

ADSP	Aggregate Deemed Sales Price
AGUB	Adjusted Grossed-Up Basis
APB	Accounting Principles Board
Bankruptcy Code	Bankruptcy Code of 1978 (11 U.S.C. § 101 *et seq.*)
BJR	Business Judgment Rule
CBOE	Chicago Board Options Exchange
CCC	California Corporations Code (Cal. Corp. Code tit. 1, § 100 *et seq.*)
CFIUS	Committee on Foreign Investment in the U.S.
DGCL	Delaware General Corporation Law (Del. C. tit. 8, § 101 *et seq.*)
DOJ	Department of Justice
EBITDA	Earnings Before Interest, Taxes, Depreciation and Amortization
FAS	Financial Accounting Standard
FASB	Financial Accounting Standards Board
FIRRMA	Foreign Investment Risk Review Modernization Act of 2018
FTC	Federal Trade Commission
GAAP	Generally Accepted Accounting Principles
HHI	Herfindahl-Hirschman Index
HSR	Hart-Scott-Rodino Antitrust Improvements Act of 1976

IRC	Internal Revenue Code of 1986, as amended (26 U.S.C. § 1 *et seq.*)
IRS	Internal Revenue Service
M&A	Mergers and acquisitions
MBCA	ABA Model Business Corporation Act (2016 rev., unless otherwise noted)
Nasdaq	National Association of Securities Dealers Automated Quotations System
NJBCA	New Jersey Business Corporation Act (N.J. Bus. Corp. Act tit. 14A, § 14A:1–1 *et seq.*)
NLRA	National Labor Relations Act (29 U.S.C. § 151–169)
NYBCL	New York Business Corporation Law (N.Y. Bus. Corp. Law § 101 *et seq.*)
NYSE	New York Stock Exchange
OGCL	Ohio General Corporation Law (Ohio Rev. Code Ann. tit. XVII, Chpt. 1701, § 1701.01 *et seq.*)
PBCL	Pennsylvania Business Corporation Law (Pa. Stat. Ann. tit 15, Part II, § 1101 *et seq.*)
Rel.	(SEC) Release
SA	Securities Act of 1933, as amended (15 U.S.C. § 77a *et seq.*)
SA Rules	Rules promulgated by the SEC under the SA (17 C.F.R. Part 230)
SEA	Securities Exchange Act of 1934, as amended (15 U.S.C. § 78a *et seq.*)
SEA Rules	Rules promulgated by the SEC under the SEA (17 C.F.R. Part 240)
SEC	Securities and Exchange Commission

SOX	Sarbanes-Oxley Act of 2002 (Pub. L. 107–204, 116 Stat. 745)
UFCA	Uniform Fraudulent Conveyance Act
UFTA	Uniform Fraudulent Transfer Act
UVTA	Uniform Voidable Transactions Act

MERGERS AND ACQUISITIONS

IN A NUTSHELL®

FOURTH EDITION

PART I

THE BASICS OF A CORPORATE ACQUISITION

CHAPTER 1

THE PRIMARY TYPES OF CORPORATE ACQUISITIONS

Corporations are artificial legal entities. They must be created and empowered by legislative authority. In the U.S., unlike most other countries of the world, individual states charter corporations at the request of groups of one or more individuals, so-called *incorporators.* All states now use a registration system; that is, if the certificate or articles of incorporation (a.k.a. the "*charter*") filed by an incorporator meets minimal, objective administrative standards, a state official must give official ("*de jure*") recognition to the new corporate entity.

The state corporate codes provide the fundamental authorization for corporations to enter into major corporate acquisitions. Moreover, the state codes specify the internal procedures required for corporations to execute an acquisition. The provisions on acquisitions of our 50 state corporate codes give corporate acquisitions in the U.S. their basic structure and, therefore, their basic legal nomenclature. The statutory definitions depend more on the *procedure* constituent parties use to effect the transaction than the end position of the parties.

Since the beginning of the 20th Century, the tiny state of Delaware has been the most popular jurisdiction of incorporation for large, publicly traded multi-state corporations. Over 66 percent of our 500 largest corporations and almost 80 percent of all publicly traded corporations are Delaware corporations. Relative to most other states, Delaware's basic corporate code, entitled the "Delaware General Corporation Law," gives more leeway to corporate managers in their operation of the firm's business; hence, that leeway is one of the reasons why incorporators prefer to incorporate in Delaware.

Perhaps the most important illustration of Delaware's enhanced flexibility is in its provisions on mergers and acquisitions. Indeed, the differences are so pronounced in the acquisition sections that one often finds large firms changing their place of incorporation to Delaware on the eve of a major acquisition to take advantage of the Delaware provisions. Sections of the Delaware corporate code will be referenced as "DGCL §".

The structure of the DGCL is typical of the structure of most state corporate codes. Both the authority and procedure for effecting a *statutory merger* among domestic entities (corporations chartered in Delaware) are outlined in § 251. A special *short-form* merger procedure for some parent-subsidiary mergers is contained in § 253, while a special *medium-form* merger procedure for second-step mergers that follow friendly first-step tender offers is set forth in § 251(h). There is also an abbreviated procedure for cash mergers in § 251(f). Subsequent sections authorize the merger of a domestic and foreign corporation (a corporation incorporated in another state) (DGCL § 252) and the merger of a domestic corporation with other types of foreign and domestic entities (e.g., a limited liability company or "LLC") (DGCL § 264). The legal effect of a merger is detailed in §§ 259 to 261.

The procedure for a sale of "all or substantially all" of a corporation's assets (an *asset sale*) is contained in § 271. The appraisal rights of dissenting shareholders in statutory mergers and consolidations are outlined in § 262. Delaware regulates single-firm reorganizations of capital structure in § 242, which specifies the requirements for amending a corporation's certificate of incorporation—a procedure often necessary to rejuggle a corporation's capital structure.

The DGCL, in § 123, necessarily grants a Delaware corporation the power to engage in *stock acquisitions* by the simple expedient of empowering a corporation to own stock in other legal entities. The only provision in the DGCL specific to stock acquisitions is § 203—Delaware's anti-takeover statute—that restrains some hostile tender offers.

Delaware also has developed a sophisticated body of judicial precedent on corporate law issues. This is due to the expertise of the judges on a limited jurisdiction trial court, the Delaware Court of Chancery, and of the justices on the Delaware Supreme Court, who hear appeals from the Chancery Court. This body of case law precedent has proven to be particularly important in acquisitions that often cause disgruntled shareholders to take their grievances to court. Delaware case law controls Delaware corporations. It also has significant precedential value to the courts of other states dealing with issues involving their own domestically incorporated firms. As a consequence, this book will often feature and discuss Delaware court cases.

Other states' corporate codes deviate from Delaware in significant respects. California's corporate code features more shareholder protections in acquisitions. For example, its acquisition provisions give shareholders of constituent corporations their strongest set of voting and appraisal rights. The corporate codes of Ohio, Pennsylvania and Virginia, by contrast, feature more protection of management prerogative in acquisitions than does the Delaware code.

The Committee on Corporate Laws of the Section of Business Law of the American Bar Association exerts a very significant influence on the content of many state corporate codes. The Committee has developed and periodically revises a Model Business Corporation Act (hereafter cited as the MBCA). Over 35 states have used one of the versions of the MBCA as a basis for their local codes, and states scrutinize each new revision of sections in the MBCA with an eye toward adopting the most modern provisions. The ABA has made proposed major revisions to the Model Act in 1999, 2010 and 2016 relevant to mergers and acquisitions.

This book will feature the provisions of the DGCL and the MBCA on mergers and acquisitions. Brief mention is also made of the California, New York and Ohio provisions.

§ 1. THE STATUTORY MERGER OR CONSOLIDATION

A. STOCK SWAP STATUTORY MERGER

Diagram 1 shows a *stock swap statutory merger,* also known as a *stock-for-stock* merger or *plain vanilla* merger. Two corporations, A Corp and B Corp, start as separate legal entities with separate owners, their shareholders. In the transaction, B Corp merges *with and into* A Corp. A Corp is the survivor and B Corp ceases to exist.

There are other structural options. A Corp could also merge into B Corp, or A Corp and B Corp could merge into a new corporation formed for the transaction, C Corp, in a *consolidation.*

In the merger in Diagram 1, B Corp shareholders' stock is cancelled and they receive as consideration A Corp shares. It is, therefore, a stock-for-stock merger (or a stock swap merger). A Corp absorbs the assets and liabilities of B Corp "as a matter of law." We will investigate further what this means in Chapter 5 on successor liability.

After the merger closes, only A Corp survives; B Corp is extinguished. The shareholders of A Corp continue to hold their stock as before and the shareholders of old B Corp now hold shares of newly-issued additional A Corp stock; the ownership interests of A Corp and B Corp are pooled in the survivor. A Corp now has added the assets and liabilities of old B Corp to A Corp's original assets and liabilities; the assets and liabilities of both constituent corporations are pooled within A Corp.

Diagram 1.
The Plain-Vanilla Statutory Merger:
Stock-for-Stock*

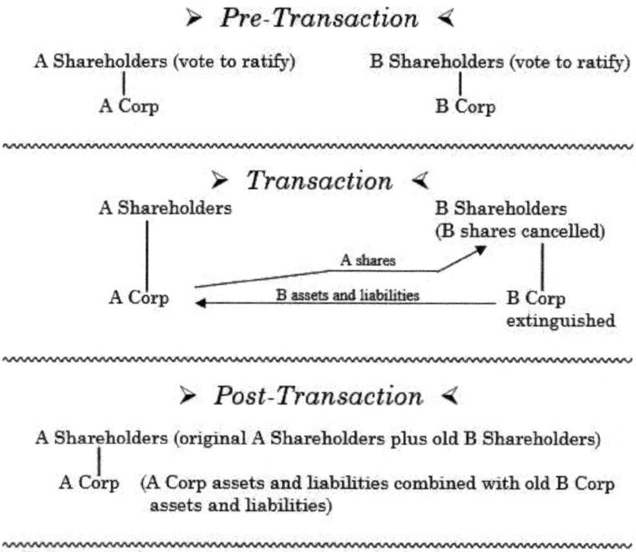

* This is a tax-free merger (an A reorganization).

B. CASH-OUT STATUTORY MERGER

In a *cash-out merger,* the shareholders of the seller do not end up holding voting common stock in the purchaser. The purchaser wants to pay cash for the seller or, if cash is not available, to pay the seller's shareholders in non-voting investments in the purchaser—debentures (debt) or non-voting preferred or common stock (equity). For a cash-out statutory merger, start with Diagram 1 and replace the A Corp shares going to the B Corp shareholders with cash. See Diagram 2.

Diagram 2.
Cash-Out Merger*

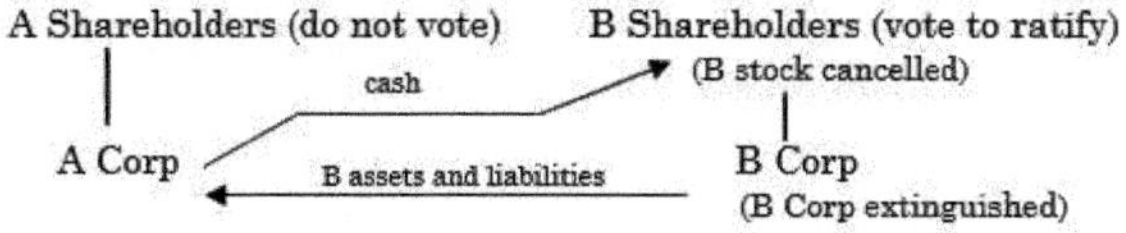

* This is a taxable transaction.

C. REQUIRED PROCEDURE FOR A STATUTORY MERGER

If both A Corp and B Corp are Delaware corporations, DGCL § 251 controls the acquisition. Section 251(a) authorizes both firms to engage in the transaction and § 251(b) requires that the board of directors of both firms pass a resolution approving an *Agreement of Merger*. The agreement contains the terms and conditions of the merger and states whether the certificate of incorporation (charter) of the survivor is amended. Thus, a merger provides an additional way to amend a corporate charter. Both constituent corporations, A Corp and B Corp, then must submit the agreement to a shareholder vote under § 251(c). A majority of *all the outstanding shares* entitled to vote must ratify the agreement. (MBCA § 11.04(e) reduces the voting requirement to a majority of those shares represented at the shareholders' meeting if a quorum exists, an easier standard to meet when compared to Delaware's.) The shareholders of neither constituent corporation can initiate the acquisition vote nor can they amend the agreement of merger; their vote is an up or down ratifying vote.

After the vote, the agreement (or a summary of the agreement entitled a *Certificate of Merger*) is filed with the Delaware Secretary of State to become effective on a date specified (within ninety days). On that date representatives of the constituent corporations meet and close the transaction.

The mechanics of the vote in statutory mergers deserves special mention. See also Chapter 4, § 1. In Delaware the default rule is that shares that do not have general voting rights (non-voting common shares and preferred shares with no voting rights unless there is a dividend arrearage) do not vote in major transactions. This seems harsh and the majority of other states do not follow Delaware's example. See MBCA § 11.04(f) (class voting on statutory mergers required in specified circumstances); *Shidler v. All Amer. Life & Fin. Corp.*, 298 N.W.2d 318 (Ia. 1980) (same as it relates to the Iowa corporate code). Yet it is important to note that preferred stock contracts in Delaware firms can and often do provide preferred stock shareholders with a class vote in acquisitions. The Delaware voting rights of preferred shareholders can be augmented in the preferred stock investment contract. Moreover, the minimum vote required in the Delaware statute is a majority of the outstanding shares, whether or not the shares are represented at the shareholder meeting. Since the turnout at shareholder meetings is often less than 75 percent of the outstanding voting shares, a successful vote on a merger can require an affirmative vote of well over a majority of those shares actually represented at the shareholder meeting (67 percent of the shares present if only 75 percent of the outstanding shares are represented, for example). Thus, the Delaware standard is harder to meet than one only requiring the affirmative vote of the holders of a majority of shares represented at a meeting at which a quorum exists.

There are four major exceptions to the voting procedures noted above. First, in DGCL § 251(f), the shareholders of the *surviving firm* in a statutory merger—A Corp in Diagram 1—do not have a right to vote if the rights, preferences and privileges of their shares survive the merger (their investment contract has not changed) and if their shares are not diluted by more than one-sixth. That is, the acquiring company cannot issue to new shareholders (B Corp shareholders in Diagram 1) an amount of shares that exceeds twenty percent of the number of voting shares of A Corp outstanding *before* the transaction. Viewed another way, the original A Corp shareholders must hold at least 83 percent of the A Corp voting shares (5/6ths) at the conclusion of the transaction. The legislature designed the exception to recognize that, when smaller firms merge with much larger firms, the transaction is more a purchase of the smaller firm than a traditional merger; thus, the larger firm's shareholders need not ratify the transaction. Some refer to this exception as the *small-scale merger exception* or the *20 percent rule*.

The second exception to the voting rules is for the statutory merger of a parent corporation and a subsidiary corporation when the parent holds 90 percent or more of the subsidiary's stock. Section 253 of the DGCL permits the merger of the subsidiary with and into the parent (an *upstream merger*) solely on a resolution of the parent's board of directors. The shareholders of neither the subsidiary nor the parent have a right to vote on the transaction. (MBCA § 11.04(h), by contrast, gives shareholders of the parent the right to vote if the parent issues stock in the parent to subsidiary shareholders that carries more than 20 percent of the outstanding voting power in the parent.) Many refer to this exception as the *parent-sub merger exception* or the *short-form merger exception*. If the subsidiary is the surviving corporation in the merger (a *downstream merger*), however, the shareholders of the parent corporation are entitled to vote. The MBCA has a similar requirement in § 11.04.

The third exception to the voting rules is the *medium-form merger exception* under DGCL § 251(h). This exception provides a cost-effective and time saving way to accomplish a second-step merger involving a publicly traded target corporation that follows a successful first-step tender offer for that target's shares. Under § 251(h), the need for target company shareholder approval is eliminated if the merger agreement between the parties contains an opt-in provision previously approved by the target's board of directors. Thus, § 251(h) can only be used for friendly (i.e., negotiated) deals. Also, use of § 251(h) is explicitly conditioned on the acquirer purchasing that number of shares in the first-step tender offer as is necessary to satisfy the transactional voting approval requirements under the DGCL and in the target corporation's certificate of incorporation (if any) *as if § 251(h) were not applicable*. Therefore, if the target's charter contains a super majority merger voting provision, or a separate class or series vote, the acquirer's first-step tender offer must satisfy those charter provisions before § 251(h) is available. The merger must be effected as soon as practicable following the consummation of the first-step tender offer, so that non-tendering shareholders will receive their merger consideration quickly—an important policy goal behind § 251(h). The MBCA followed Delaware's lead and now provides for a medium-form merger exception to shareholder voting in § 11.04(j).

The fourth exception to the voting rules is found in § 251(g) of the DGCL. It states that no shareholder voting is required in specified reorganizations of holding companies or in the specified creation of a holding company structure—the *holding company exception*. Google Inc., following § 251(g), implemented a holding company reorganization pursuant to an Agreement and Plan of Merger, dated as of October 2, 2015, among Google, Alphabet Inc. and Maple Technologies Inc. ("Merger Sub"). This resulted in Alphabet owning all of the outstanding capital stock of Google. Pursuant to the merger agreement, Merger Sub, a direct, wholly owned subsidiary of Alphabet and an indirect, wholly owned subsidiary of Google, merged with and into Google, with Google surviving as a direct, wholly owned subsidiary of Alphabet. Each share of each class of Google stock issued and outstanding immediately prior to the merger automatically converted into an equivalent corresponding share of Alphabet stock, having the same designations, rights, powers and preferences and the qualifications, limitations and restrictions as the corresponding share of Google stock being converted. Accordingly, upon consummation of the merger, Google's stockholders immediately prior to the consummation of the merger became stockholders of Alphabet. Alphabet, in turn, now owned Google and thus became Google's parent company.

§ 2. THE ASSET ACQUISITION

A. CASH-FOR-ASSETS ACQUISITION

Diagram 3 illustrates a *cash-for-assets acquisition*. In the first step of the transaction, A Corp pays B Corp cash consideration for B Corp's assets. A Corp may choose to assume some or even all of B Corp's liabilities as part of the transaction, but A Corp does not have to do so—it is the subject of negotiation between A Corp and B Corp. There is no change in the constitutional documents of A or B Corp, nor is there any change in the shares outstanding in either corporation. In the optional, but commonplace, second step of the transaction, B Corp dissolves, the B Corp charter is cancelled and B Corp shares are extinguished. After paying any residual liabilities not assumed by A Corp, the assets held by B Corp and the cash received in the transaction from A Corp are transferred to the B Corp shareholders in a liquidating distribution. The investment contract held by A Corp shareholders (the rights and privileges attached to the A Corp shares) and A Corp's constitutional document (its certificate of incorporation) are unchanged.

Diagram 3.
The Common Asset Acquisition: Cash-for-Assets with the Selling Corporation Dissolving*

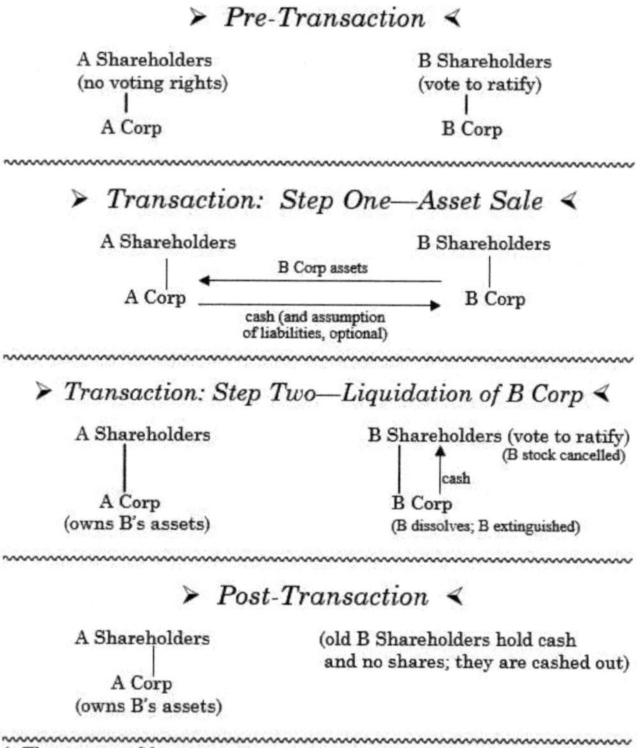

* This is a taxable transaction.

After an asset acquisition, B Corp must either reinvest the cash received in operating assets or dissolve and pass the cash in a liquidation distribution back to its shareholders. If B Corp invests the cash in assets generating passive income—income from the management efforts of others, such as stocks, bonds or rental property—the Internal Revenue Code deems B Corp a personal holding company, which has tax consequences that can be onerous. In addition, the acquisition cannot qualify for tax-free status. In most asset acquisitions then, B Corp dissolves after the acquisition.

After the transaction, old B Corp shareholders hold cash consideration (no shares) and A Corp holds title to B Corp's assets (and perhaps is obligated on some or even all of B Corp's pre-transaction liabilities). The *major differences* between Diagram 1, the stock swap merger, and Diagram 3 are: (a) who votes—A Corp shareholders do not vote in the asset acquisition, while B Corp shareholders vote on the sale of assets under DGCL § 271 and, if B Corp will be dissolved thereafter (typical), on the dissolution under DGCL § 275; (b) the post-transaction position of the old B Corp shareholders—in the merger the B Corp shareholders hold shares in the survivor, and in the asset acquisition the B Corp shareholders are cashed out; and (c) the location of B Corp's pre-transaction liabilities—in the merger A Corp assumes B Corp's liabilities by operation of law, and in an asset acquisition A Corp may choose not to assume B Corp's liabilities.

B. STOCK-FOR-ASSETS ACQUISITION

For a *stock-for-assets acquisition,* start with Diagram 3. Replace the cash consideration going to B

Corp with shares of A Corp common stock. Moreover, assume A Corp not only buys all of B Corp's assets but also assumes all of B Corp's liabilities. See Diagram 4 below. The end result is identical to the post-transaction position in Diagram 1. The shareholders of the constituent firms have pooled their ownership interests in a corporation (A Corp) that itself has the combined assets and liabilities of both firms. Delaware does not give the A Corp shareholders voting rights but the MBCA does if the voting power of their shares is diluted by more than one-sixth. MBCA §§ 6.21(f) & 11.04(h). Moreover, if A Corp is a New York Stock Exchange listed company, the Exchange's listing requirements also require that shareholders of A Corp vote on the acquisition if the shares A Corp issues exceed 20 percent of the voting shares it has outstanding prior to the stock-for-assets acquisition.

Diagram 4.
Stock-for-Assets Acquisition*

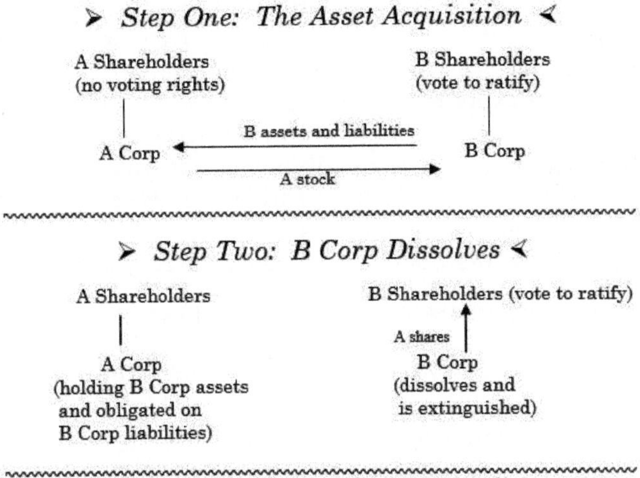

* This is a tax-free stock acquisition (a C reorganization).

If both A Corp and B Corp are Delaware corporations, the transaction is controlled by DGCL §§ 122 and 271. Section 122(4) is a general grant of power to Delaware corporations; the provision empowers A Corp to buy assets and B Corp to sell assets. Another general grant of power, § 122(13), authorizes A Corp to assume B Corp's liabilities. Section 271, however, is specific to asset acquisitions and conditions B Corp's general authority to sell all or substantially all of its assets on a ratifying shareholder vote. Under § 271, B Corp's board of directors, whenever it resolves to have the corporation sell "all or substantially all" of B Corp's assets, must submit a resolution to its shareholders and, subject to certain exceptions (e.g., a secured party's sale of company property or assets constituting collateral that is being effected under the terms of a mortgage or pledge agreement), the holders of a majority of the outstanding shares entitled to vote must ratify the transaction. B Corp's shareholders cannot initiate the transaction nor can they amend the acquisition agreement. A Corp shareholders are not entitled to vote on the transaction at all under Delaware law (but may be entitled to vote under stock exchange listing rules).

It is easy to determine whether a given company is selling "all" of its assets. All means *all.* The tougher question is whether it is selling "substantially all" of its assets. What constitutes "substantially all" under § 271 is colored by whether "the sale of assets [is] quantitatively vital to the operation of the corporation and is out of the ordinary and substantially affects the existence and purpose of the corporation." *Gimbel v. Signal Companies, Inc.,* 316 A.2d 599, 606 (Del. Ch. 1974). See also *Thorpe v. CERBCO, Inc.,* 676 A.2d 436 (Del. 1996) (sale of stock in subsidiary that constituted 68 percent of parent's assets and was parent's primary income-generating asset did require a shareholder vote).

MBCA § 12.02(a) replaces the "all or substantially all" standard with one that catches any "disposition [that] would leave the corporation without a significant continuing business activity." The section has a safe harbor. A significant business activity remains if the continuing business activity represents at least 25 percent of the total assets *and*

25 percent of either income (before income taxes) or revenues from pre-transaction operations.

If B Corp is to dissolve, a board resolution on dissolution must be submitted to B Corp shareholders under DGCL § 275 and then the holders of a majority of the outstanding shares entitled to vote must ratify the resolution. Often the vote on the asset sale and the vote on the dissolution are combined in one resolution. A certificate of dissolution is then sent to the Delaware Secretary of State. On the effective date of the dissolution, the corporation is dissolved and its stock extinguished. The corporation then has three years to wind up its affairs, paying its liabilities and passing back to shareholders any residual cash surplus.

§ 3. THE STOCK ACQUISITION

A. CASH-FOR-STOCK ACQUISITION

In a *cash-for-stock acquisition,* A Corp buys shares of B Corp stock directly from the hands of B Corp shareholders in exchange for cash. See Diagram 5 below.

After the transaction, A Corp owns the B Corp stock; thus, A Corp is now the *parent* corporation of a new *subsidiary* corporation, B Corp. Old B Corp shareholders have tendered and exchanged their shares for cash. There is no change in the certificates of incorporation (charters) of either A Corp or B Corp, nor is there any change in the investment contracts represented by an A Corp share or a B Corp share. Only the owner of the B Corp shares has changed. If

A Corp cannot convince all the B Corp shareholders to tender their shares for the cash consideration, then a minority block of B Corp stock remains outstanding. In that case, B Corp would not be a *wholly owned subsidiary* but rather a *partially owned subsidiary*.

Diagram 5.
The Basic Stock Acquisition: Cash-for-Stock*

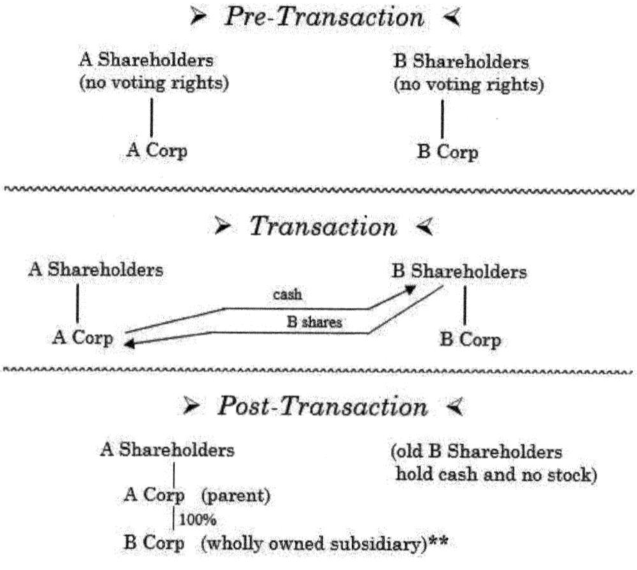

* This is a taxable transaction.

** This assumes *all* B Shareholders voluntarily took the cash in exchange for their shares.

B. STOCK-FOR-STOCK ACQUISITION

For a *stock-for-stock acquisition,* start with Diagram 5. Replace the cash consideration going to B Corp shareholders with shares of A Corp common stock. See Diagram 6. The end result is similar to the post-transaction position in Diagram 1, except that A Corp holds B Corp's assets and liabilities in a wholly owned subsidiary, a separate legal entity, rather than having combined the B Corp assets and liabilities with A Corp assets and liabilities in one legal entity. The advantage of the parent-subsidiary structure is that the creditors of B Corp, now a subsidiary, do not have a claim on A Corp assets, assets held by the new parent. If, in the future, A Corp wants a structure identical to the post-transaction structure in Diagram 1, it need only merge the wholly owned subsidiary with and into the parent with a simple board of directors' resolution under DGCL § 253 (a short-form merger).

Diagram 6.
Stock-for-Stock Acquisition*

➤ *Step One: The Stock Acquisition* ➤

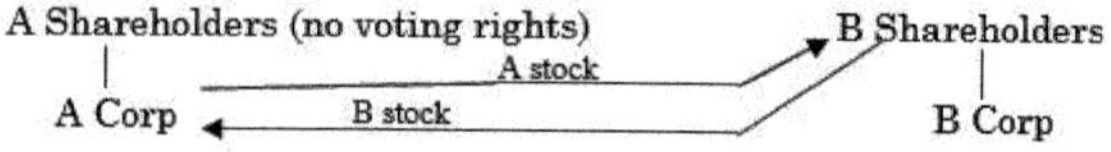

➤ *Post-Transaction* ➤

A Shareholders (plus old B Shareholders)
|
A Corp (parent)
|
B Corp (wholly owned subsidiary)**

* This is a tax-free stock acquisition (a B reorganization).
** This assumes that *all* B Shareholders tender their shares.

If both A Corp and B Corp are Delaware corporations, the authority for A Corp to purchase and hold the stock of another corporation is found in DGCL §§ 122(4) & (11) and 123 on general corporate powers. DGCL § 122(10) also empowers A Corp to manage the affairs of B Corp. Neither the shareholders of A Corp nor of B Corp have, under any provision of the DGCL, a right to vote on the stock acquisition. In theory, however, B Corp shareholders do not need the protection of a right to vote because each B Corp shareholder individually decides whether or not to accept the consideration offered by A Corp for his or her shares. The B Corp shareholders' right to refuse the offer is a substitute for their right to dissent in a vote.

In most states, the A Corp shareholders, shareholders in the purchaser, do not have the right to vote on the transaction nor to claim appraisal rights. The states that give shareholders in the purchaser voting rights in stock-for-stock acquisitions, based on the voting power of the stock issued as consideration, include California, New Jersey, Ohio and Rhode Island. See also MBCA §§ 6.21(f) & 11.04(h). If A Corp is a New York Stock Exchange listed company, the Exchange's listing requirements also require that shareholders of the purchaser vote on the acquisition if the shares A Corp issues exceed 20 percent of the voting shares it has outstanding prior to the stock-for-stock acquisition. NYSE Listed Co. Manual § 312.03(c). Other stock exchanges have similar rules.

There is a specialized section in the DGCL, however, § 203, that applies to stock acquisitions for publicly traded companies. Within the last 25 years, most states (at last count the number was over 40) have passed *anti-takeover statutes* that restrain stock acquisitions of publicly traded companies. Delaware's § 203 is such a statute. Most anti-takeover statutes give target shareholders voting rights, not on the stock acquisition itself but on the effect of the acquisition. If the target board disapproves of the stock acquisition, the shareholders may, for example, vote on whether the stock acquired by the purchaser retains voting rights or on whether the purchaser can, subsequent to a stock acquisition in which some shareholders do not sell into the offer, execute a second-step, cash-out statutory merger to gain 100 percent of the target stock. Delaware's section, known as a *business combination* or *freeze-out* statute, is of the latter ilk. Of course, by severely restricting the effect of an acquisition, the legislation in essence regulates the acquisition itself. Indeed, it would perhaps be more honest and understandable simply to condition stock acquisitions on a shareholder vote.

§ 4. THE STATUTORY SHARE EXCHANGE

The MBCA follows the basic organization in the DGCL with a minor addition. Section 11.03 provides a procedure for a *statutory share exchange* (often called a *compulsory share exchange*). In a statutory share exchange, one firm acquires all of the outstanding stock in a target firm through an affirmative shareholder vote of the target. It contrasts with a typical stock acquisition in which the purchaser makes offers to buy shares that each target shareholder may either accept or reject. Holders of a majority of the shares of the target must approve a statutory share exchange; holders of a majority of the shares of the purchaser need to approve the exchange only if target shareholders receive a substantial number of shares in the purchaser (usually an amount equal to 20 percent or more of the number of shares outstanding before the acquisition). A dissenting target shareholder may vote no, but if she loses the vote she must turn over her shares to the acquiring corporation; the exchange is *compulsory* on an affirmative majority shareholder vote. Over 20 states have adopted such a provision, yet few practitioners use the procedure. The light use of the procedure is due to its poor comparison with a *triangular statutory merger,* an acquisition structure we investigate below.

§ 5. SPECIAL APPLICATIONS OF THE BASIC TRANSACTIONAL FORMS

A. TWO-STEP STOCK ACQUISITIONS

Many stock acquisitions are *two-step acquisitions,* in which a first-step stock acquisition is followed by a *back-end* or *second-step merger.* In the second step, the purchaser *drops down* a wholly owned subsidiary (a process described below) and merges the subsidiary with the partially owned target. See Diagram 7. (The target is already partially owned due to the completion of the first-step stock acquisition.) This second-step merger is also known as a *squeeze-out* (or, less frequently, as a *freeze-out*).

Diagram 7.
Two-Step Acquisition: Stock Acquisition Followed by a Squeeze-Out Statutory Merger

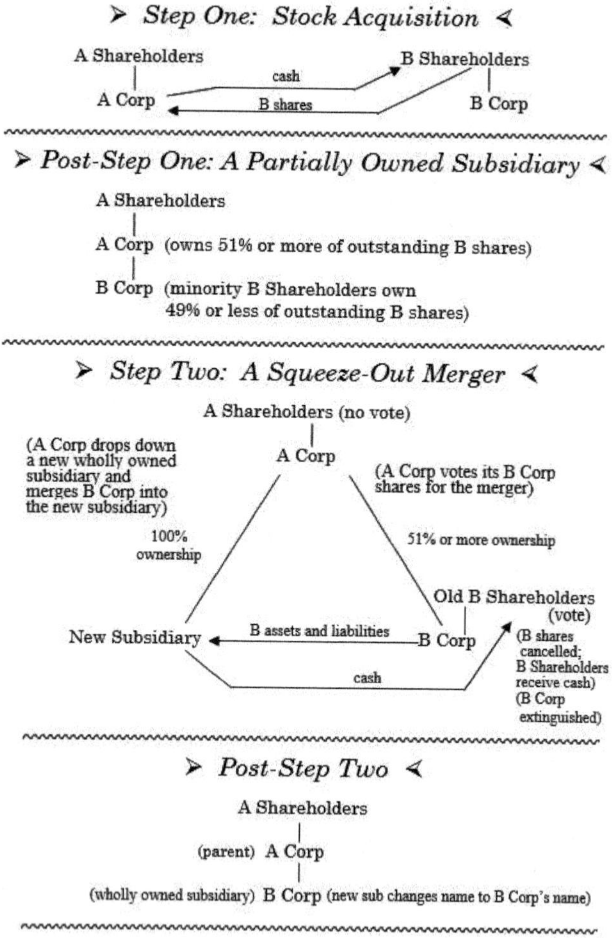

In a *drop-down* the purchaser itself acts as an incorporator for a new subsidiary corporation, usually a *shell* corporation, one that has no assets. The constituent parties to the back-end merger are the wholly owned shell subsidiary of the purchaser and the newly-acquired, partially owned subsidiary that was the target of the first-step stock acquisition. The firm gives the minority shareholders in the partially owned subsidiary cash or debt securities (debentures) in A Corp for their cancelled shares along with a kiss goodbye.

The purpose of such an acquisition is often speed—the purchaser can gain control of the target faster because it can close the first-step tender offer faster than it could close a single-step statutory merger or an asset sale. The second step, the *squeeze-out,* is necessary to convert a partially owned subsidiary into a wholly owned subsidiary (i.e., to eliminate the remaining minority shareholders).

If Delaware corporations are involved, shareholders of the parent corporation have no voting or appraisal rights in either the stock acquisition or the second-step merger. California and other states, however, give shareholders in the parent voting rights in the first or second step if the voting power of the shares they hold after the parent's issuance of shares in the transaction is five-sixths or less than what they had before the transaction. CCC §§ 1200(e) & 1201(b). See also MBCA §§ 6.21(f) & 11.04(h).

B. SINGLE-FIRM RECAPITALIZATIONS

In another, more notorious type of squeeze-out, a corporation with a minority block of shareholders undertakes a single-firm recapitalization through a statutory merger. The firm drops down a new wholly owned shell subsidiary and merges itself into the subsidiary. All of the stock in the corporation is cancelled. The majority shareholders in the original firm receive common stock in the surviving firm and the minority shareholders receive cash or debt securities. This same scheme can be used to replace outstanding shares of preferred stock with shares of common stock, thus eliminating the preferential rights of preferred shareholders in the process. See Diagram 8.

Diagram 8. Recapitalizations: A Statutory Merger as an Alternative to a Charter Amendment

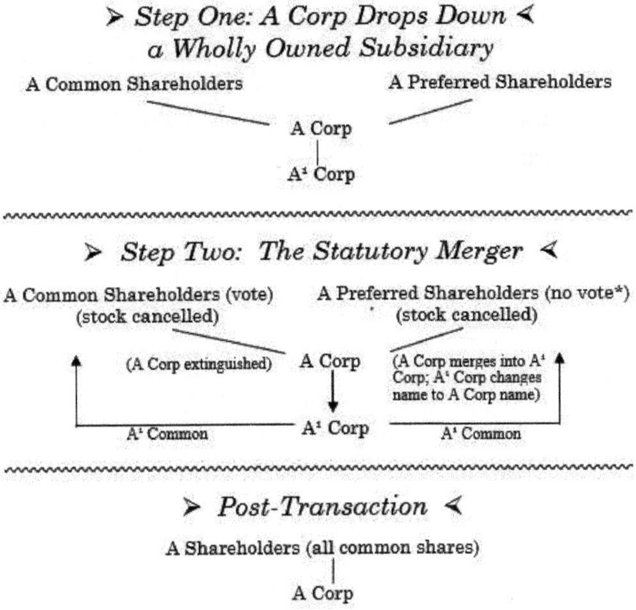

* In Delaware, the preferred shareholders do not vote on the merger unless their voting rights are expressly provided for in the certificate of incorporation. Under the MBCA, the preferred shareholders vote as a class. See MBCA § 11.04(f).

C. TRIANGULAR ACQUISITIONS

In triangular statutory mergers, the purchaser drops down a wholly owned subsidiary and the seller merges with the subsidiary. See Diagram 9. Since the subsidiary is a constituent party to the acquisition and the parent is not, and since by statute only the shareholders of a constituent party vote on statutory mergers, Delaware law provides that the shareholders of the parent do not vote on the acquisition. The only shareholder of the subsidiary is the parent itself and, in a triangular merger, the board of directors of the parent votes the stock in favor of the merger through a simple board resolution. Since triangular mergers limit the voting rights of purchaser shareholders and isolate the newly-absorbed seller liabilities in a subsidiary, free from the purchaser's assets, triangular mergers have become very popular. Again, the California general corporate code is not in accord, giving shareholders in the parent voting rights if the voting power of the parent shares they hold after the issuance of shares in the transaction is five-sixths or less than what they had before the transaction. CCC §§ 1200(e) & 1201(b). See also MBCA §§ 6.21(f) & 11.04(h) (vote required if issuance is for 20 percent or more of currently outstanding shares).

Triangular statutory mergers are known as *forward triangular mergers* when the target corporation merges with and into the shell subsidiary and *reverse triangular mergers* when the shell subsidiary merges with and into the target. A less popular triangular acquisition is the *triangular asset acquisition*. In a triangular asset acquisition, the purchaser drops down a shell subsidiary that purchases the assets of the target and the target dissolves.

Diagram 9.
Forward Triangular Merger*

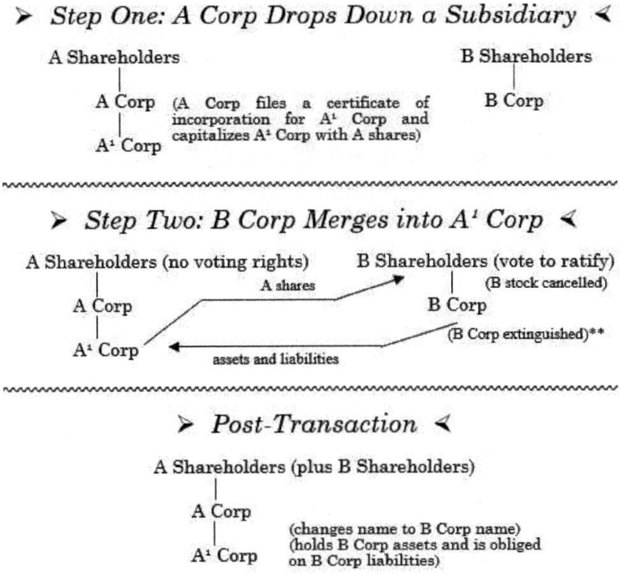

* This is a tax-free merger (an A(2)(D) reorganization). If B Shareholders receive cash for their shares instead of A Corp shares, it is a taxable exchange.

** It would be a reverse triangular merger if A¹ Corp merged with and into B Corp with B Corp surviving. In the exchange, B Shareholders all receive A shares (or cash) and A Corp, the shareholder of A¹ Corp, receives the only remaining B Corp shares.

D. LEVERAGED BUYOUT (LBO)

In a leveraged buyout, a group of investors, led by a leveraged buyout fund (usually a private limited partnership), creates an acquisition vehicle (a shell corporation) and funds the entity with some cash.

The acquisition vehicle then raises a substantial amount of additional cash by selling debt to banks and institutional investors. The vehicle uses its cash to purchase 50.1 percent of the outstanding voting shares of a publicly traded corporation (or enough to have *legal control* of corporate elections). The acquisition vehicle then merges with and into the target. The remaining voting shares of the target are exchanged for debt or non-voting preferred securities (the vehicle has exhausted its cash in the tender offer), and the owners of the acquisition vehicle take the only stock outstanding in the target. See Diagram 10.

The surviving target corporation assumes the debt of the acquisition vehicle in the second-step merger. The result transforms a publicly traded corporation into a privately held one with a significantly increased debt-to-equity ratio. The corporation has *gone dark;* it no longer needs to issue and file public periodic reports (annual and quarterly reports with the SEC). See *Pay 'N Pak Stores v. Court Square Capital LTD,* 141 F.3d 1178 (9th Cir. 1998). To pay back the new loans, the target will (1) sell new bonds (i.e., refinance), (2) reduce its expenses, and/or (3) sell off some of its assets or business divisions.

Diagram 10.
Leveraged Buyout (LBO)

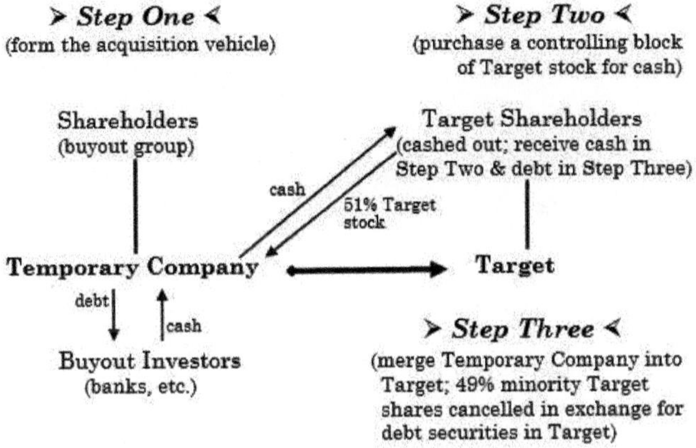

CHAPTER 2

THE ACQUISITION PROCESS AND ITS BASIC LEGAL DOCUMENTS

§ 1. THE CHRONOLOGY OF A TYPICAL NEGOTIATED ACQUISITION FOR A PRIVATELY HELD COMPANY

A privately held company is one that does not have public, periodic reporting requirements under the Securities Exchange Act of 1934 (hereafter SEA). SEA § 12(g)(1) & SEA Rule 12g–1. That is: (1) the company's shares are not traded on any national stock exchange, (2) the company has (a) 2,000 or fewer holders of record or 500 or fewer non-accredited holders of record and (b) $10 million or less in assets, and (3) the company has not made a registered public offering of securities under the Securities Act of 1933 (hereafter SA). SA § 5. Most privately held companies are much smaller than publicly held companies, although this is not always true (e.g., Meta (formerly Facebook) was already a multi-billion dollar company leading up to its 2012 initial public offering (IPO)).

Privately held companies commonly take the following path in their acquisition negotiations. The Chief Executive Officers (CEOs) of the two constituent corporations first meet and mutually agree on the potential success of further negotiations and on ballpark financial terms for a deal. The mutually agreed upon deal points generated by these preliminary negotiations are often embodied in a non-binding *Letter of Intent*. Most CEOs receive advice from their internal financial experts, usually the firm's Chief Financial Officer (CFO), and from outside investment bankers and accountants with whom they have had a prior long-standing relationship.

The preliminary agreement leads to the formal retention, by both constituent corporations, of a bevy of experts. The corporations hire lawyers to negotiate and draft the details of the acquisition documents and investment bankers and accountants to provide valuation estimates and other financial advice. The lead acquisition planner may come from any of the three professions—law, accounting or investment banking. The purchaser's lawyers and accountants perform a *due diligence* investigation of the seller. If the purchaser is using its stock as the consideration in the purchase, as in a stock swap for example, the seller may also perform a limited due diligence investigation of the purchaser. Indeed, in that situation the seller's former shareholders will become shareholders of the purchaser after the transaction closes.

In a due diligence investigation, lawyers and accountants pour over the official, internal books and records of the other party to the deal, verifying the price, checking the accuracy of factual representations, and looking for trouble spots. They are aided, in appropriate cases, by other experts, such as environmental engineers (a.k.a. "moon suiters") or real estate appraisers, who give assurance on matters of specific importance to the transaction at hand.

Once the CEOs agree on a final price and on a final draft of the acquisition agreement, they present the agreement to their respective boards of directors. If the deal is structured as a statutory merger under state corporate codes, the agreement is entitled an *Agreement of Merger*. If the deal is structured as a stock purchase, the agreement is entitled a *Stock Purchase Agreement*. If the deal is structured as an asset acquisition, the agreement is entitled an *Asset Purchase Agreement*.

The time between the negotiation of the preliminary agreement and the date of board approval varies considerably and may be from two weeks to three months. The boards of directors ask questions, make comments, deliberate and, if all goes well, vote their approval of the acquisition agreement. In this regard, new § 147 of the DGCL provides that whenever the DGCL requires board approval of a document (including merger and acquisition agreements), that document can be approved in "final form or in substantially final form." A document will be deemed to be in "substantially final form" under § 147 if all of the material terms are either set forth in the document or are determinable through other information or materials presented to or known by the board of directors.

Experts continue their due diligence investigations after board approvals and up until the time of the closing, verifying that the closing conditions in the agreement are satisfied. If a closing condition running in favor of a particular party is neither satisfied in general nor waived by that party, then that party has a walk-right (i.e., the right to walk away from the deal).

If shareholders of one or both of the constituent corporations must vote to ratify the agreement, lawyers prepare shareholder meeting notices and disclosure documents. The company formally calls a special shareholder meeting to approve the deal or notifies shareholders that the acquisition will be on the agenda at the firm's annual meeting, depending on timing. The time between the board vote and the shareholder meetings is at least 30 days and often up to three months, determined by the notice requirement in state corporate codes. If the parties need the approval of a government agency (the Federal Communications Commission for media mergers or the Comptroller of the Currency for bank mergers, for example), the time period is lengthened considerably. If things go according to plan, the shareholders of one or both of the constituent corporations approve the acquisition by the requisite majority specified in the applicable state corporate codes (usually the affirmative vote of the holders of a majority of the outstanding voting shares).

Twenty to thirty days after the shareholder vote, lawyers and CEOs meet to close the transaction. At the closing, once the parties are assured that the conditions in the acquisition agreement are satisfied, the parties exchange the deal consideration—cash-for-stock, cash-for-assets, or stock-for-stock and so on. In statutory mergers, the parties file the Agreement of Merger (or a short form Certificate of

Merger) with an appropriate state official (usually the Secretary of State) that, among other things, eliminates at least one of the constituent corporations and names the surviving corporation. In an asset acquisition, the selling corporation typically files Articles of Dissolution with the Secretary of State, dissolving the selling corporation and distributing the deal proceeds to its shareholders in the form of a liquidating dividend.

§ 2. PRICING ISSUES IN STOCK-FOR-STOCK ACQUISITIONS

Most all negotiated acquisitions have substantial time delays between the signing of the acquisition agreement and the closing. Some acquisition techniques, such as cash tender offers, minimize the time delay; others, such as stock swap mergers, may have delays of over six months to a year. Whenever there is such a delay, pricing issues become more complex, as one party or the other will absorb the consequences of the value of the seller changing during the delay.

In stock swaps there is the added concern over changes in the value of the stock of the purchaser. In stock swaps, the purchaser exchanges its shares for the shares in the hands of the seller's shareholders. To establish a price, the two parties must come to an agreement on the relative value of the two companies. After the parties negotiate an agreement on price and establish an exchange ratio for the stock of the two parties (e.g., 1.2 shares of purchaser's stock for each share of seller's stock), the value of one or both of the parties may change dramatically between the signing of the agreement and the time of the closing. Market-wide trends, such as a substantial decline in the financial markets, industry-specific market trends and company-specific performance may all affect the value of either or both of the constituents' stock. If the changes occur before any ratifying shareholder votes, the shareholders may reject the agreement. One can easily point to spectacular failures of large combinations to illustrate the problem (the collapse of the 1998 Tellabs/Ciena and United HealthCare/Humana mergers, for example).

Moreover, if the purchaser is publicly traded, the market may judge the exchange ratio harshly. More and more frequently purchasers in a stock swap merger are witnessing a fall in their stock price within minutes of the announcement of the transaction. The fall in stock price is due to the market's judgment that the purchaser will be overpaying, thus diluting the value of its own stock, or that the purchaser will not be able to manage the new assets well. If the price fall in the purchaser stock is substantial, the shareholders of the seller who are to receive purchaser stock may balk. The seller may pressure the purchaser to offer additional consideration on the threat of abandoning the transaction, exacerbating the diluting effect of the deal on the purchaser's shareholders.

If the firms use a *fixed exchange ratio,* that is, a stock exchange ratio that is set when the board votes on the agreement of merger and does not change through the closing (e.g., 1.2 to 1 (1.2 shares of purchaser's stock for each share of seller's stock)), the seller's shareholders bear both general market risk and the specific risk associated with the value of the purchaser's stock price. A decline in the relative market value of the purchaser decreases the value the seller's shareholders receive at the closing. The seller's shareholders may refuse to ratify the proposal if the price change precedes their shareholder meeting. The purchaser, by contrast, enjoys the certainty of the fixed exchange ratio, primarily the effect of the deal on future earnings per share (either accretive (good) or dilutive (bad)). The downside risk for the purchaser is that a flagging exchange value may encourage third parties to make higher, competing offers to the seller and steal the deal at the eleventh hour.

Thus, most sellers ask for downside price protection. A purchaser's traditional rebuttal is that a fixed exchange ratio reflects the inherent relationship between the constituent companies' fundamental values at the time the price is set and that this relationship should not be affected by market volatility not attributable solely to a deterioration in the quality of the purchaser's securities. If the price decline is due to industry-wide or market-wide phenomena, the seller will have experienced a comparable price decline in its stock as well and the parties should consider the economic relationship between the parties to be unchanged. Most sellers argue in response that the firms may have differing sensitivities to even market-wide price shocks.

A seller with negotiating leverage may argue, therefore, for either a *walk-away* or a *floating exchange ratio* with a *price collar*. Both devices depend on an easily ascertainable stock price for the purchaser, which usually means that the purchaser must be a publicly traded company.

A walk-away is an express condition in the acquisition agreement that gives the seller the option to walk away from the acquisition if the market value of the purchaser's stock falls below a specified price level. For example, a fixed exchange ratio walk-away would permit the seller to terminate the agreement if, at the time of closing, the purchaser's stock has decreased by 10 percent, a *single trigger*. Some walk-away clauses have a *double trigger*—the seller may terminate the agreement if either the stock value decreases by a specified percentage or more or if the purchaser's stock price decreases by a specified percentage or more relative to a defined peer group of stocks in pre-selected companies.

A floating exchange ratio is a promise to fix the cash value offered to selling shareholders at closing (e.g., $100 per seller share). It is, therefore, a promise by the purchaser to tender at closing the number of shares that equals the fixed value (e.g., $100 divided by the current market price of one purchaser share). Most floating ratios base the value due on an average market price for the purchaser's stock during a period, usually 10 to 30 trading days, prior to the closing or prior to the date on which the seller's shareholders will vote to approve the transaction. Under a floating exchange ratio, the purchaser bears the market risk of a decline in the price of its stock. It will have to issue more shares to each seller shareholder on any price decline.

There are two problems with a floating exchange ratio. First, the rate must be carefully calculated so it will not terminate a desirable acquisition solely due to *temporary* market fluctuations (the Brazilian *real* may be devalued and jolt the market for a short time, for example). The second problem is that a floating exchange ratio exposes purchaser shareholders to the possibility of massive dilution in the value and voting power of their shares, the potential dilution being limited only by the amount by which the stock price is likely to decline.

To protect against extreme dilution, acquisition agreements with floating exchange ratios often place a cap on the maximum number of shares the purchaser will issue in the exchange. Sellers will, in turn, insist on a cap on the minimum number of shares to be delivered. The upper and lower limits, known as a *price collar*, provide upper and lower market price limits to the transaction. Sellers may want to supplement a collar with a walk-away, if a price decline in the purchaser's stock causes the exchange ratio to hit the high end of the collar. Purchasers, in response, may want to reserve contractually the right to waive the upper collar, issuing additional shares to make the seller's shareholders whole, so as to void the seller's walk-away right and preserve the deal (a *fill-or-kill option*).

In the absence of a price collar on a floating exchange ratio, the purchaser will often demand a walk-away right based on a maximum number of shares that it is willing to issue in the transaction. Sellers agreeing to such a walk-away may negotiate for the right to waive the requirement for additional shares under the floating exchange ratio and hold the purchaser to closing the transaction based on the original price, a *reverse fill-or-kill option*.

A common alternative to the floating exchange ratio coupled with a price collar is a fixed exchange ratio that is adjusted only if the value of the purchaser's stock falls by (or increases by) more than a fixed percentage (e.g., plus or minus 10 percent). The adjustment can be automatic or discretionary with the purchaser, a fill-or-kill option. If automatic, the adjustment is usually capped with upper and lower limits on the number of shares the purchaser will have to deliver.

In any corporate acquisition, at the center of the negotiation is the question of value, how much is the acquisition target worth as it stands alone and how much its value will increase when combined with the purchaser (the *synergy* gains). Valuation is a very inexact inquiry, with capable people showing substantial disagreements over values assigned to the same assets. The juxtaposition of the two valuation issues is most clearly seen if the target's stock is publicly traded. If the stock has a sufficient float and the company has made adequate public disclosure, the market price of the stock multiplied by the number of outstanding shares (which equals *total market capitalization*) is the starting point for the valuation of the business. But a purchaser of the entire publicly traded company will typically pay a sizeable premium over the market price of the stock (often averaging around 30 percent)—a *control premium*. The size of the premium is determined predominately by what the purchaser believes it can do with the target company assets that the target company itself is not currently doing.

Valuation is more difficult in those transactions in which the target is privately held and there is not a reliable market price for the target stock. The general "rule of thumb" method of valuation, which clients will use as a starting point for more detailed analysis, is often based on *multiples*. The purchaser is principally interested in the income stream that a given target business will produce. Valuation is done by multiplying the target's historical earnings by an appropriate number (the *multiple*) that reflects the target's earnings, growth and business risks. This method assumes that the historical figures on the target's income statement are, at some level, predictive of future performance.

The earnings figure on the income statement used for the valuation may be (1) after taxes (net earnings with tax payments subtracted), (2) before taxes (net earnings before the tax payments have been subtracted), (3) before interest and taxes (*EBIT*), or (4) before interest, taxes, depreciation and amortization (*EBITDA*). Of the four historical earnings calculations, multiples on EBITDA are the most commonly and widely used in informal discussions. EBITDA more accurately reflects the actual *cash flows* of the target.

The EBIDTA multiple used in any given valuation varies widely with the target's industry, the size of the business, the general market and economic conditions and factors intrinsic to the target's operations. The higher the multiple the more aggressive (i.e., higher) the valuation, usually based on anticipated high target growth; the lower the multiple the more conservative (i.e., lower) the valuation, usually based on predictions of flat target growth. Multiples currently collect on an average of eleven or twelve to EBIDTA for firms in mature, traditional industries.

More sophisticated valuations, prepared by experts such as investment bankers when deal discussions are serious, use a *discounted cash flow* (*DCF*) analysis. Experts predict the future net cash flow of the target (i.e., estimated cash flowing into the business *less* estimated cash flowing out of the business) and discount the future estimated amounts to present value, using a discount rate that reflects the time value of money, the risk of currency inflation, and the risk of volatility in the projections. They will also prepare a more detailed comparables analysis, based on various selected financial fundamentals. Finally, they will research comparable transactions to see at what prices comparable companies have been sold in other acquisitions.

§ 3. BASIC ACQUISITION DOCUMENTS

Most acquisitions of privately held companies follow a predictable trail in the execution of the legal documents. The documents also have a predictable structure. There may be substantial variety in the detail of the documents, however.

In the preliminary negotiations one often sees a Letter of Intent, a Confidentiality Agreement and, if one of the parties is publicly traded, a public announcement. Lawyers undertaking a legal audit, also known as a legal due diligence investigation, will use an Acquisition Review Check List to prepare both for signing the acquisition agreement and the closing. The essential terms of the deal are contained in an acquisition agreement that looks to an exchange of consideration on the pre-arranged closing date.

A. THE CONFIDENTIALITY AGREEMENT

The Confidentiality Agreement (or Non-Disclosure Agreement (NDA)), if used, may be the first document the parties sign in an acquisition negotiation. A good one defines categories of confidential information very broadly and obligates the purchaser to keep information received from the seller in strict confidence. The agreement often limits who in the employ of the purchaser may have access to the information, specifies the location of documents containing the proprietary information, and includes relevant notice requirements. A seller should not give a prospective purchaser sensitive business information until the purchaser has signed a Confidentiality Agreement.

Sometimes the Confidentiality Agreement is consolidated into the Letter of Intent, but many lawyers believe this is a mistake. The seller intends the Confidentiality Agreement to be an enforceable contract whether or not the parties ever execute a Letter of Intent and, if executed, whether or not the Letter of Intent is legally binding. When the parties sign a definitive acquisition agreement, language in that agreement usually replaces and supersedes the obligations of any outstanding, earlier Confidentiality Agreement.

B. THE LETTER OF INTENT (LOI)

A purchaser and a seller often enter into a Letter of Intent at the conclusion of a successful initial phase of negotiations. The letter, usually prepared by counsel to the purchaser, identifies the structure of the contemplated transaction and summarizes its basic terms, including terms of payment and the principal conditions to the closing. These conditions may include, for example, approvals by government agencies and consents by third parties, financing arrangements by the purchaser, and achievement of stated net earnings by the target. The purchaser and seller anticipate that a definitive written acquisition agreement will follow.

The parties to most Letters of Intent do not view the letter as establishing binding contractual rights on the deal itself; it is a moral obligation to close the deal on the stipulated terms. At the option of the parties, Letters of Intent can be binding contracts with open-ended terms—the strongest contract is an agreement on essential terms with other terms implicitly agreed to ("*gap-filled*") as whatever is reasonable, based on custom and practice. E.g., *Iteck Corp. v. Chicago Aerial Ind., Inc.*, 248 A.2d 625 (Del. 1968). The weakest contract is an agreement to bargain in good faith towards a deal. E.g., *Teachers Ins. & Annuity Assoc. v. Tribune Co.*, 670 F. Supp. 491 (N.Y. 1987). Courts are left to determine whether Letters of Intent are legally binding contracts when the parties are not explicit on their legal effect. The cases are fact-specific as judges and juries seek to discern the parties' objective intent; there is much room in such a trial for effective advocacy. See, e.g., *R.G. Group, Inc. v. Horn & Hardart Co.*, 751 F.2d 69 (2d Cir. 1984). Good lawyers include explicit language on the legally binding effect of the letter that leaves no room for doubt.

Clients like Letters of Intent, while their lawyers often do not. Both the purchaser and seller to an acquisition prefer a preliminary commitment from the other before they incur the substantial costs of negotiating a definitive agreement and performing or allowing to be performed a due diligence review of the seller. Both parties can see if there are deal-breaking terms and conditions. The letter also helps the purchaser in lining up financing and establishes a clear trigger for compliance with regulatory filings (e.g., antitrust filings under the HSR Act) and for public announcements.

Lawyers worry that courts will use the letter to give a disgruntled party relief if an anticipated deal does not close. Letters of Intent also affect bargaining leverage. Sellers push purchasers into settling key terms in some detail before purchasers have access to a seller's records and information. Once agreed, the party asking for changes from the terms in the Letter of Intent, usually the purchaser, has the burden of justification when the seller exclaims, "I thought we had a deal!" Once the parties sign a Letter of Intent, however, the bargaining advantage may be with the purchaser, as the letter creates an expectation of an acquisition on the part of third parties—investors, customers and vendors—that may pressure seller managers to close a deal and accede to a purchaser's additional demands. In any event, a purchaser often wants a "no-shop" commitment from the seller and maximum flexibility to change the terms once it learns more about the seller through due diligence; a seller, by contrast, wants a clear understanding on the price and other key parts of the acquisition agreement, including understandings on employment agreements for retaining desired personnel.

C. THE ACQUISITION AGREEMENT

Most acquisition agreements for privately held companies follow a basic structure. Section 1 is a glossary of *defined terms*. Section 2 contains the details of the *basic exchange*—the stock or assets to be acquired, the consideration to be paid and the timetable for the closing. Usually, Sections 3 and 4 contain the *representations and warranties* of the seller and purchaser, respectively. Following the reps and warranties are two sections on contractual *covenants* (a.k.a. promises)—Section 5 containing covenants of the seller and Section 6 containing covenants of the purchaser. The next two sections—Sections 7 (for the purchaser) and 8 (for the seller)—contain *conditions precedent* to the obligations of both parties to execute the exchange at the closing. The next section usually outlines the circumstances in which each party may terminate the deal (Section 9 on *termination*). This section is followed by a section on *indemnification* (Section 10) specifying remedies for each party's breach of the agreement. A final section (Section 11) contains *miscellaneous provisions*.

The major difference between a stock purchase acquisition of a privately held company and an asset acquisition is in the length of Section 2 on the identification of the basic exchange. When the purchaser is buying assets, the assets must be identified in Section 2 and its accompanying schedules. Moreover, when the purchaser is assuming liabilities in an asset deal, the liabilities assumed must be carefully specified. In many asset acquisitions, the purchaser agrees to assume those liabilities ordinary and necessary to the daily operations of the business purchased but does not assume extraordinary or contingent liabilities.

The representations (reps) in Sections 3 and 4 are statements of past or existing facts about the seller or purchaser made by the seller or purchaser, as the case may be, and running in favor of the other party. *Intentional* misrepresentations (a.k.a. "lies" or "fraud") are actionable in tort, and under the right circumstances a plaintiff could even sue for punitive damages. To take the intent element off the table, purchasers require sellers (and vice versa) to *warrant* or *guarantee* that their representations are, indeed, true. Thus, by making a representation also a warranty (hence, "reps and warranties"), the sellers and purchasers guarantee that their representations are true. Intent is no longer important.

The seller's reps are detailed descriptions about the business being acquired and are much more detailed than the purchaser's. The seller's common reps include not only matters routine to all businesses (a representation that the entity is in "good standing" legally, for example) but also extensive provisions on such matters as environmental claims, employee benefits, intellectual property and products liability claims, each of which could result in significant liabilities of the purchaser after closing. The purchaser's reps deal mainly with a purchaser's ability and authority to enter into the acquisition and, where the purchaser needs to secure financing for the deal, the purchaser's ability to obtain it.

Because sellers hate giving money back to purchasers when they breach their reps and warranties, they seek to water them down through the use of *knowledge qualifiers* and *materiality qualifiers*. Both mechanisms shift the risk of future problems back onto purchasers. In the case of a knowledge qualifier, a seller will seek to insert "to the best of its knowledge" or "to its knowledge" in front of a given rep and warranty (e.g., "to the Seller's knowledge, the Seller's business complies with all applicable environmental laws"). Doing so reintroduces the element of *intent* back into the rep and warranty—something the warranty aspect was designed to eliminate. To help offset this, a purchaser, in turn, will attempt to add the gloss "after due inquiry" to the seller's knowledge clause: "To the Seller's knowledge *after due inquiry* . . . ." In the case of a materiality qualifier, a seller will seek to push *nonmaterial* problems relating to a given rep and warranty onto the purchaser (e.g., "the seller's business complies in all material respects with all applicable environmental laws").

Many of the representations refer to a Disclosure Letter (or Schedule) that supplements the acquisition agreement. This letter has sections for lists of items that correspond with specified representations. Sometimes the lists give full descriptions—laundry lists. For example, a part of the Disclosure Letter will contain a list of all real property, leaseholds or other interests owned by the seller and a corresponding representation affirming that the list in the Disclosure Letter is complete and accurate and that seller owns, with good and marketable title, all property it purports to own. Other parts of the Disclosure Letter may contain exceptions to a blanket statement in the representations—an exceptions list. For example, a representation will state that there are no contracts with relatives of board members *other than* those listed in the Disclosure Letter and the letter will list a contract between the seller and a mother-in-law.

Some parties append schedules to an acquisition agreement, one schedule per representation section, rather than use a Disclosure Letter; however, the purpose and effect is the same.

The conditions precedent to the obligations of the purchaser and seller in Sections 7 and 8 specify what must be true for the parties to be bound at the closing to execute the basic exchange (cash-for-stock, cash-for-assets, and so on). These provisions detail what each party can expect from the other at the closing. One of the important conditions is a *bring-down* clause in which the seller reaffirms all of its representations as accurate as of the closing date (i.e., the seller "brings down" the reps from the signing date to the closing date). Thus, each representation operates (often subject to a materiality qualifier) as a closing condition. Other conditions include the performance of each of the covenants, such as obtaining all necessary governmental consents and opinions of counsel, and the presentation of the required supplementary documents (an escrow agreement, an employment agreement, a release and an estoppel certificate, for example). In the acquisition of a publicly traded company, the conditions may include *comfort letters* from accountants on tax and accounting matters and *fairness opinions* from independent investment bankers on the reasonableness of the price from a financial point of view.

If a condition is not satisfied, a party to whom the condition runs may elect not to close the deal: a *walk-away right*. Note the difference between conditions and covenants. A breach of a covenant (a promise) gives remedies under the indemnification section; the failure of a condition justifies a refusal to close. An agreement states explicitly that accuracy of most of the reps and warranties at both the time of the signing of the agreement and the closing and the satisfaction of most covenants covering obligations due at closing are closing conditions. There are often conditions in addition to those relating to covenants or reps and warranties, however.

Sellers will negotiate for a materiality qualification on many of the conditions. Sellers want purchasers' walk rights contingent on only non-trivial failures of conditions; that is, the purchaser can refuse to close only if there are *material* inaccuracies in the representations. Similarly, most indemnification sections—providing for damages if one party breaches the contract—provide sellers with a *basket* amount (a minimum amount that damages must exceed before the seller owes anything). This deductible recognizes that representations on an ongoing business are unlikely to be perfectly accurate and that the parties do not want disputes over insignificant amounts.

A substantial majority of the indemnification provisions place limits on the right of the purchaser to pursue remedies other than those specified in the language of the provision. A majority of the sections also cap the indemnification obligation at 30 to 50 percent of the purchase price. Many sections include not only general language to the effect that the seller will indemnify the purchaser for breaches, but also language specific to indemnification for tax problems and for environmental claims.

A purchaser intends the indemnification section to specify and add to otherwise available remedies and to provide that the remedies *survive* the closing. A seller negotiates for an exclusive declaration of remedies and an *as-is* sale—no survival of the remedies after the closing. The survival right is particularly important in light of the intensive legal audit undertaken by the purchaser's representatives. The purchaser may not have discovered a major problem with the seller's business and after closing will want to sue the seller for a false representation. The purchaser's remedies must survive the closing and a court must hold that the purchaser was not at fault somehow for not finding the defect in its acquisition review of the seller's business (that the purchaser did not somehow assume the risk or the like).

Online HealthNow, Inc. v. CIP OCL Investments, LLC, 2021 WL 3557857 (Del. Ch.), dealt with the efficacy of a survival clause. After the closing, the purchaser alleged that several representations and warranties within the stock purchase agreement (SPA) were knowingly false when made in order to fraudulently induce the purchaser into executing the SPA and consummating its acquisition of the target. The Delaware Chancery Court noted that to state a claim for fraudulent inducement, "a plaintiff must well plead (1) a false statement or misrepresentation; (2) that the defendant knew was false or made with reckless indifference to the truth; (3) the statement induced the plaintiff to enter the agreement; (4) the plaintiff's reliance was reasonable; and (5) the plaintiff was injured as a result." In their defense, the defendants argued, among other things, that the survival clause in the SPA expressly provided that the seller's reps and warranties terminate upon closing. Therefore, any claim (including a fraud claim) arising from those reps and warranties was extinguished when the deal closed.

The court, however, disagreed with the defendants' argument. While noting that a survival clause prevents a post-closing claim for breach of a warranty that did not survive the closing, the court held that the seller cannot invoke a clause in a contract allegedly procured by fraud to eviscerate a claim that the contract itself is an instrument of fraud.

The final section of miscellaneous provisions contains those boilerplate provisions taught in first-year contracts courses as necessary. Most of the provisions aid courts in interpreting the basic contract: There are provisions on integration (remember the parol evidence rule?), waiver, severability, section headings, form of notices, time is of the essence, choice of governing law and venue, and so on. There are also a few provisions that add material terms to the deal—the provision on successors and assigns, who pays the deal's expenses, and who may make public announcements about the transaction.

D. DOCUMENTS THAT SUPPLEMENT THE ACQUISITION AGREEMENT

The Employment or Non-Competition Agreement. If the purchaser wants the services of one or more of the key employees of the seller, the purchaser may demand an *employment agreement* that binds the employee to stay with the business after the acquisition. The employment agreement will often contain a non-competition clause (a *non-compete*), discouraging a retained individual from leaving the purchaser's employment after the acquisition. If, however, the purchaser is not retaining seller employees who have had access to sensitive business information, the purchaser may demand a *non-competition agreement* to stop employees of the seller from exploiting information by competing with the business once the purchaser takes over. This can be accomplished by a restrictive covenant in the acquisition agreement or by means of a separate agreement.

As a general matter, courts do not like non-competes as they potentially prevent a person from earning a living in the field of her choice. Thus, courts will enforce them only if they are reasonable in geographic scope and duration and are necessary to protect clear business interests in trade secrets and goodwill. E.g., *Intertek Testing Services NA, Inc. v. Eastman,* 2023 WL 2544236 (Del. Ch.) (Delaware law); *Wilson v. Electro Marine Systems, Inc.,* 915 F.2d 1110 (7th Cir. 1990) (New York and Illinois law).

Moreover, on April 23, 2024, the Federal Trade Commission approved a highly controversial ban on non-competes covering U.S. workers. As a matter of policy, the FTC had concluded that non-competes unlawfully stifle competition and depress wages for U.S. workers, and that banning them would encourage competition, innovation and increased wages. The ban prohibits an employer from entering into, or attempting to enter into, a non-compete clause with a "worker" (including, e.g., employees and independent contractors) or representing that a worker is subject to a non-compete clause. Importantly, the ban *does not apply* to non-competes entered into by a person in connection with a bona fide sale of a business entity. See 16 C.F.R. § 910.3(a).

The FTC's ban, which was scheduled to become effective on September 24, 2024, was subjected to litigation almost immediately. On July 3, 2024, in *Ryan LLC v. Federal Trade Comm'n,* 2024 WL 3297524 (N.D. Tex.), the District Court for the Northern District of Texas determined that the plaintiffs' challenge to the ban was likely to succeed on the merits. Therefore, the court issued a preliminary injunction preventing the ban from going into effect as scheduled. Importantly, the court limited the preliminary injunctive relief solely to the plaintiffs because of ambiguity over the appropriate circumstances in which a federal court may issue a nationwide injunction. See also *Properties of the Villages, Inc. v. Federal Trade Comm'n,* 2024 WL 3870380 (M.D. Fla.) (entering a limited injunction prohibiting the enforcement of the FTC's ban against the plaintiffs); but see *ATS Tree Services, LLC v.*

Federal Trade Comm'n, 2024 WL 3511630 (E.D. Pa.) (denying plaintiff's request to preliminarily enjoin the FTC's ban). Subsequent to these decisions, the U.S. Supreme Court severely limited the availability of universal (nationwide) injunctions. See *Trump v. Casa, Inc.*, 606 U.S. 831 (2025).

An asset purchaser needs to ensure that all existing non-competition agreements and confidentiality agreements with seller employees are assigned to it, regardless of whether those employees are being retained by the purchaser. Otherwise, in the future those employees may compete against the purchaser or freely exploit seller trade secrets and other valuable seller information now being used by the purchaser. *Chemetall GMBH v. ZR Energy, Inc.*, 320 F.3d 714 (7th Cir. 2003).

The Release. In an acquisition the principal shareholders (and perhaps other agents, employees and officers of the seller) deliver a *release* at the closing. The release usually covers all claims which the releasing parties had, or arising from any matter that existed, as of the closing date against the purchaser and the seller. Without such a release, imagine what might happen. If a purchaser could assert claims against individual shareholders of the seller, then those shareholders might assert that the claims relate to actions taken by them as officers and directors of the seller. They could then present a claim for indemnification against the successor of the seller, the purchaser. The release provides a clean break from the prior owners.

The Non-Negotiable Promissory Note. If the purchaser delivers a promissory note to the seller at the closing as part of the exchange, the note will contain standard terms, e.g., the interest rate, the amortization schedule, the manner of payment, events of default, and remedies. The seller wants the promissory note to be negotiable (i.e., transferable), while the purchaser wants the promissory note to be non-negotiable. If the note is non-negotiable, the seller cannot pass it on to a holder in due course (free from purchaser claims under the acquisition agreement). Moreover, a non-negotiable note is subject to the purchaser's set-off rights for any claims the purchaser may have against the seller for breach of the acquisition agreement. See *D'Oench, Duhme & Co. v. FDIC*, 315 U.S. 447 (1947) (set-off rights not effective against holders in due course). As such, the note secures, in a fashion, the obligations of the agreement. Other issues to be resolved include whether the note is secured, the availability of a guarantor, and the priority of the purchaser's obligation relative to the purchaser's other debts. Potential collateral could include the stock or assets received by the purchaser in the acquisition. In a stock acquisition, if the note is secured by the assets of the seller, the transaction generates fraudulent transfer (conveyance) risks.

Documents on Performance Guarantees—an Escrow Agreement. The *escrow agreement* provides for an escrow of some of the payment funds to satisfy claims the purchaser may have or develop under the acquisition agreement for matters such as the seller's breach of a representation. Sellers often ask that access to the escrowed funds be the purchaser's exclusive post-closing remedy, thus effectively capping the purchaser's damages (if any) at the amount escrowed. Most escrow agreements provide for an institutional escrow agent that dispenses the funds under the terms specified. If the purchaser makes no claims against the funds, they revert to the seller after a specified period of time (typically after one year).

Earn out Agreement. Earn outs, whether in a separate agreement or contained within the main acquisition agreement, can bridge the pricing gap between a seller and a purchaser. The purchaser pays the seller a base price at the closing. If, however, the purchased business performs in the future up to the seller's rosy expectations for that business, then the purchaser owes the seller additional money. If the business does not, then the seller's sole consideration is the base price. Earn outs can also help a cash-strapped purchaser finance an acquisition, as additional earn out payments to the seller (if earned) will not have to be made until points in the future. Earn outs create contractual problems, however, as the purchaser—now exclusively in control of the acquired business—can take steps to avoid earn out payments, including the diversion of funds or mischaracterization of accounts.

What obligations does a purchaser owe the seller in an earn out situation? In *O'Tool v. Genmar Holdings, Inc.*, 387 F.3d 1188 (10th Cir. 2004), the purchase agreement between the purchaser and seller contained an earn out provision. After the closing, the purchaser reorganized the purchased business and integrated it into the purchaser's existing operations. The seller successfully argued that the reorganization diminished the profits earned by the purchased business while also benefitting the purchaser's other pre-existing divisions. The seller sued the purchaser for breach of an "implied" covenant of good faith. The Tenth Circuit affirmed the District Court's refusal to grant the purchaser's "judgment as a matter of law" (JMOL) and its jury instructions.

As a result of *O'Tool,* it is clear that a purchaser of assets subject to an earn out provision must segment those assets from the purchaser's pre-existing operations until the earn out expires. Importantly, the purchaser does not owe the seller any fiduciary obligations with respect to the way in which it actually operates the purchased assets going forward, unless the purchaser expressly agrees to accept those obligations. E.g., *Richmond v. Peters,* 173 F.3d 429 (6th Cir. 1996). Indeed, even though the seller is in a position very similar to a shareholder of the purchaser (who also takes a part of the profits), the seller is *not* a shareholder of the purchaser—the purchaser has fiduciary duties only to its *actual* shareholders.

In their acquisition agreements, life science companies often utilize a type of earn out pegged to future drug developments. For example, in September 2018, Alexion Pharmaceuticals acquired Syntimmune, Inc. for $400 million upfront and up to $800 million in contingent milestone payments tied to the development and commercialization of ALXN1830, a monoclonal antibody designed to treat certain autoimmune diseases. The merger agreement required Alexion to use "commercially reasonable efforts" ("CRE") for seven years to develop and commercialize ALXN1830. The merger agreement defined "CRE" by reference to what a comparable biopharmaceutical company would do when developing a similar product under similar circumstances, considering factors such as safety, efficacy, order of entry, and likelihood of regulatory approval.

In April 2020, Alexion decided to move funding away from ALXN1830, citing COVID-19-related pressures and a focus on more advanced "priority" programs. In July 2021, Alexion itself was acquired by AstraZeneca. After a full portfolio review of Alexion's drug programs, AstraZeneca deprioritized the indications for which ALXN1830 had previously been under development in favor of two new indications: thyroid eye disease ("TED") and chronic antibody mediated rejection ("cAMR"). However, when interim Phase 1 clinical trial data proved to be uninspiring, Alexion paused dosing in its clinical trial. Later, when the probability of ALXN1830's success in treating TED and cAMR dropped off, Alexion terminated the ALXN1830 program altogether.

On behalf of Syntimmune's former stockholders, Shareholder Representative Services LLC ("SRS") brought suit against Alexion in the Delaware Chancery Court. After a trial on the merits, the court issued two post-trial rulings. In the first ruling (*Shareholder Representative Serv. LLC v. Alexion Pharma., Inc.*, 2024 WL 4052343 (Del. Ch.)), the court found that Alexion had breached its obligations to use CRE. The court highlighted that the definition of CRE in the merger agreement was an objective, outward-facing definition. Indeed, rather than being pegged to the acquiring company's internal business imperatives, the definition was based on the conduct expected of a reasonable biopharmaceutical company under similar circumstances. According to the court, Alexion was guided by its internal priorities, corporate goals and subjective state of mind. Alexion's decisions were driven by unique rationales that would not lead typical biopharmaceutical companies to take similar measures.

In its second post-trial ruling (*Shareholder Representative Serv. LLC v. Alexion Pharma., Inc.*, 2025 WL 1661215 (Del. Ch.)), the court awarded approximately $181 million in expectation damages to SRS on behalf of Syntimmune's former stockholders, plus pre- and post-judgment interest bringing the total damage award to approximately $220 million.

In determining the appropriate measure of expectation damages, the court followed *Fortis Advisors LLC v. Johnson & Johnson,* 2024 WL 4048060 (Del. Ch.), which held that damages should be the expected value of the earn out payments at the time of breach. Therefore, the court started with the amounts of the milestone payments for each of the merger agreement's un-reached milestones, then probability-adjusted those amounts based on each milestone's likelihood of achievement. In doing so, the court rejected Alexion's argument that SRS was required to establish that Alexion "was more likely than not to achieve a given milestone to establish proximate cause," because the injury was the "loss of expected value associated with milestone payments." Thus, as long as any particular milestone had a nonzero chance of being achieved, Alexion's breach—which brought each probability to zero—caused injury in the amount by which the expected value of the milestone payment was reduced. The court did discount the expected milestone payments to present value using the dates when the milestones were projected to be achieved, thus leading to the $181 million damage award.

E. DUE DILIGENCE DOCUMENTS

The purchaser's attorneys use an acquisition review checklist to do a thorough legal audit of the seller's business. Many lawyers refer to the audit as *legal due diligence,* a reference from the due diligence investigation conducted by an underwriter's counsel in a public offering of securities. The audit precedes the signing of a final acquisition agreement to help the purchaser accurately price the seller's business and continues after the signing in preparation for the closing to give the purchaser, at the time of closing, a high level of confidence in the accuracy and completeness of the seller's representations and warranties in the acquisition agreement. The acquisition review begins with an *engagement letter* from the purchaser to its lawyers, specific to the transaction. The lawyers then send a *document request* to the lawyers for the seller asking for copies of documents needed to answer questions on the checklist. The purchaser's lawyers then prepare a *work program,* with deadlines, and prepare answers to the questions on a comprehensive checklist. Not surprisingly, parties today use digital or virtual data rooms (VDRs), and thus actual paper copies of documents rarely change hands.

§ 4. THE CONTRACT FOR AN ACQUISITION OF A PUBLICLY TRADED COMPANY

An acquisition contract for a publicly traded company is typically shorter than one for a privately held company. The document has very limited seller reps and warranties and no post-closing indemnification rights against the seller's public shareholders.

The purchaser of a publicly traded company has the comfort of having access to substantial public information about the seller (all subject to the powerful antifraud provisions of the federal securities acts) and hence does not need a comprehensive set of reps and warranties. The seller will commonly represent that it has made all required filings with the SEC and that the filings comply with the federal securities acts in all material respects. Occasionally, the purchaser will also ask the seller to represent separately that the financial statements in the annual and quarterly reports have been prepared in accordance with GAAP (Generally Accepted Accounting Principles), fairly present the financial condition of the seller, or are correct and complete.

In the acquisition of a publicly traded company, the consideration will be disbursed to a diffuse group of seller shareholders either on or immediately after the acquisition. Post-closing relief from those shareholders often is not practicable. As a result, the acquisition agreement usually does not give the purchaser indemnification rights against the seller's shareholders. Thus, seller representations and warranties mainly serve a due diligence function and, if they are not materially correct as of the closing date, provide the purchaser with a walk right. The only indemnification section is one that protects the officers and directors of the seller from liability for claims arising from the transaction.

CHAPTER 3

LITIGATION ON ACQUISITION CONTRACTS

§ 1. ONE OF THE PARTIES REFUSES TO CLOSE

After the parties to an acquisition have executed an acquisition contract, one of the parties may terminate the deal and refuse to close. Most corporate codes provide that an acquisition agreement may provide expressly that a board of directors retains the power unilaterally to abandon a merger before the merger's effective date (usually the closing date) even after any ratifying shareholder vote. E.g., DGCL § 251(d) (mergers and consolidations), § 271(b) (asset sales). The MBCA has an opt-out provision (agreements may be abandoned unless they otherwise provide), in contrast to the opt-in provision in the Delaware code, and also states that an abandonment is subject to the contractual rights of the other party. MBCA § 11.08(a).

Rather than abandon a deal, some boards prefer to let their shareholders vote a deal down when circumstances surrounding the deal sour. In 1998 the Delaware legislature amended DGCL § 251, governing mergers, to require that the board of directors declare the advisability of a merger agreement before submitting it to the shareholders. The section was also amended to provide that a merger agreement may require that it be submitted to the shareholders even if the board, subsequent to its initial approval thereof, determines that the agreement is no longer advisable and recommends that the shareholders reject it.

A. THE SELLER REFUSES TO CLOSE

The reference in the MBCA to the contractual rights of a frustrated party in an abandoned acquisition agreement raises the question of whether a seller's board can bind itself contractually not to abandon an acquisition and to use its best efforts to obtain an affirmative shareholder vote. If so, the purchaser can successfully sue the seller for contract damages even though the seller's board has exercised its expressly reserved right to abandon an acquisition agreement. In *Allegheny Energy, Inc. v. DQE, Inc.*, 171 F.3d 153 (3d Cir. 1999), for example, the Third Circuit was willing to levy more than damages; the court held that it would specifically enforce an acquisition agreement when the contract language in a stock swap merger conditioned termination on a material breach of the agreement that could not be cured.

A Second Bidder Offers More Value. The most difficult case for the selling board occurs when a second bidder offering more value appears after the board has signed an acquisition agreement with an initial bidder but before the closing of that deal. If the selling board has signed an acquisition agreement containing a best efforts to close clause, what is the import of the clause?

A best efforts to close clause can be very strict (the board must recommend the deal to shareholders even if a higher offer has been made and may not negotiate or enter into competing contracts with other bidders) or have some leeway (the board must recommend the deal to shareholders if there are no higher offers and the board can neither solicit other offers nor give confidential information to other potential bidders). Most clauses are of the latter ilk and are called *no-shop* clauses. The obligation of a board to be candid with its shareholders means that a strict clause could produce the odd result of a board telling their shareholders of a higher offer and then recommending they accept a lower offer.

At issue is the power of the seller to enter into such contractual provisions. The Ninth Circuit has held that the selling board has such power. *Jewel Cos., Inc. v. PayLess Drug Stores Northwest, Inc.*, 741 F.2d 1555 (9th Cir. 1984). But the Delaware courts view the stronger versions of such a clause (prohibiting the seller from considering competing offers, for example) as an inherent breach of the selling board's fiduciary duty. See *Omnicare, Inc. v. NCS Health Care, Inc.*, 818 A.2d 914 (Del. 2003).

Many acquisition agreements moot the *Jewel* case problem by including an express *fiduciary out* clause. The provision protects the directors of a target company from having to choose between violating their fiduciary obligation to shareholders and violating a purchase agreement. Under the language of a fiduciary out provision, the directors are excused from any action that would constitute a violation of their fiduciary duty. For example, such a clause would allow a target board to negotiate with a third party despite a no-shop clause or waive the requirement that a board recommend a deal to its shareholders.

Suits Against the Second Bidder. If a court finds that a second bidder induces a seller to breach a valid and enforceable contract with an initial bidder, the second bidder may be liable to the frustrated first bidder for tort damages. See *Jewel,* supra. One of the largest jury verdicts ever awarded, $10.53 billion, came in such a case. *Texaco, Inc. v. Pennzoil Co.,* 729 S.W.2d 768 (Tex. Ct. App. 1988).

In *NACCO Indus., Inc. v. Applica Inc.,* 997 A.2d 1 (Del. Ch. 2009), NAACO/Hamilton Beach had entered into a merger agreement with a target (Applica). The agreement contained a "no shop" clause, whereby the target could not initiate negotiations with any third party. However, the target could respond to an unsolicited offer from a third party if the target's board determined in good faith that negotiations would reasonably lead to a deal that was "superior" to the one with NAACO/ Hamilton Beach. Another provision in the merger agreement required the target to "promptly notify" NAACO/Hamilton Beach of the arrival of any third party and the status of any negotiations.

A third party did arrive on the scene (Harbinger/ Salton) and submitted a topping bid, thus turning NAACO/Hamilton Beach into a jilted suitor. The jilted suitor then brought a series of claims against the winning bidder and the target, including breach of contract, common law fraud, and tortious interference with contract. In denying the defendants' motion to dismiss, the court held that the jilted suitor had stated valid claims. In particular, the court found that the jilted suitor's allegations readily supported a claim that the target did not comply in a commercially reasonable fashion with the "no shop" and "prompt notification" provisions in its merger agreement with the jilted suitor.

Termination Fees. When the purchaser has leverage in an acquisition negotiation, it will often insist on including termination fees in the acquisition agreement. A common example is found in the facts of *Brazen v. Bell Atlantic Corp.*, 695 A.2d 43 (Del. 1997). The parties to a stock swap merger agreement agreed that a party would pay the other $200 million if the party's board terminated the agreement or the party's shareholders refused to ratify the agreement because there was a competing offer for that party. If the competing offer resulted in an acquisition within 18 months of the merger agreement, the terminating party would owe an additional $350 million. A shareholder sued based on coercion, arguing that the shareholders' failure to vote "yes" on the merger could result in their company having $550 million less in its bank account! The Delaware Supreme Court, however, rejected that argument and upheld the clause. In doing so, the court used the liquidated damages test from contract law: The damages have to be uncertain and the amount agreed upon has to be reasonable and not punitive. The result was not surprising. The Delaware courts routinely uphold termination fees that are less than four percent of deal value, which the termination fee in *Brazen* was.

B. THE PURCHASER REFUSES TO CLOSE

If the purchaser refuses to tender consideration at the closing (perhaps it has buyer's remorse), the seller may have a cause of action for breach. Such cases are rare, but they do exist. In an asset acquisition the answer is straight-forward: The seller itself sues for traditional contract damages. In aborted stock acquisitions of privately held firms, the seller's shareholders, who would have received the consideration directly from the purchaser, are typically signatory parties to the acquisition contract and are therefore the primary plaintiffs on the contract. The seller, through its agents, is also often a signatory to the contract in a stock acquisition and can sue for reliance losses. In aborted tender offers for publicly traded corporations, tendering shareholders can sue under a contract theory (in addition to claims based on violations of the federal securities acts) if the bidder refuses to close when all the tender offer conditions have been met. See, e.g., *In re Gulf Oil/Cities Service Tender Offer Litig.*, 725 F.Supp. 712 (S.D.N.Y. 1989).

In statutory mergers, the seller's shareholders would have received the consideration from the purchaser but they are often not included on the acquisition contract. The seller's shareholders must sue on some form of third party beneficiary theory; the seller can sue for reliance damages. In some contracts there is boilerplate language stating that the contract confers no rights on third parties to sue on the contract. E.g., *Consolidated Edison, Inc. v. Northeast Utilities*, 426 F.3d 524 (2d Cir. 2005) (discussed more fully in Chapter 3, § 1.C below). In such cases, if a seller cannot sue on its shareholders' behalf, the clause limits the damages to the seller's reliance expenditures. At least one court has held that under such language the firm cannot sue on behalf of its shareholders. See *In re Gulf Oil,* supra. In the *Cities Service* case, for example, the seller recovered greenmail payments spent to clear out a competing bidder and attorney fees spent on the failed deal. *Cities Service Co. v. Gulf Oil Corp.,* 980 P.2d 116 (Okla. 1999).

When purchasers seek to exit deals, they sometimes point to their contractual right to walk away if the seller experiences a "material adverse effect or change." Such was the case in *Akorn, Inc. v. Fresenius Kabi AG,* 2018 WL 4719347, *aff'd,* 198 A.3d 724 (Del. 2018) (TABLE). Fresenius Kabi AG agreed to acquire Akorn, Inc. by means of a merger. In the merger agreement, Akorn made extensive representations about its compliance with applicable regulatory requirements. Fresenius' obligation to close was conditioned on three things. First, Akorn's representations must have been true and correct both at signing and at closing, except where the failure to be true and correct would not reasonably be expected to have a contractually defined "Material Adverse Effect" (MAE). Second, Akorn must have complied in all material respects with its obligations under the agreement. Third, Akorn must not have suffered an MAE between signing and closing.

Shortly after the parties signed the merger agreement, Akorn's business performance fell off a cliff, delivering results that fell materially below Akorn's prior-year performance on a year-over-year basis. The dismal results continued, leading Fresenius' management team to become concerned that Akorn had suffered an MAE. Moreover, Fresenius received two letters from an anonymous whistleblower who made disturbing allegations about Akorn's product development process failing to comply with regulatory requirements. The letters called into question whether Akorn's representations in the merger agreement regarding regulatory compliance were accurate and whether Akorn had been operating in the ordinary course of business.

Soon thereafter, Fresenius gave notice that it was terminating the merger agreement. Fresenius asserted that Akorn's representations regarding regulatory compliance were so incorrect that the deviation would reasonably be expected to result in an MAE. Fresenius also cited the section in the merger agreement that conditioned Fresenius' obligation to close on Akorn not having suffered an MAE generally.

Akorn, in turn, sued in the Delaware Chancery Court seeking a declaration that Fresenius' attempt to terminate the merger agreement was invalid and a decree of specific performance compelling Fresenius to close. Given that the Delaware Chancery Court had previously held that a breach of an acquisition agreement by a purchaser justifies a decree of specific performance forcing the purchaser to close (see *In re IBP, Inc. Shareholders Litig.*, 789

A.2d 14 (Del. Ch. 2001)), Akorn's request for specific performance was to be expected.

According to the court, for the purpose of determining whether an MAE has occurred, the important consideration is whether there has been an adverse change in the seller's business that is consequential to the seller's *long-term earnings power* over a commercially reasonable period (measured in years rather than months). The court added that a purchaser faces a heavy burden when it attempts to invoke an MAE clause in order to avoid its obligation to close. A short-term hiccup in the seller's earnings should not suffice; rather an adverse change should be material when viewed from the longer-term perspective of a reasonable acquirer. While evidence of a significant decline in earnings by the seller during the period after signing but before closing is *not irrelevant,* for such a decline to constitute an MAE, poor earnings results must be expected to persist significantly into the future.

Based on the facts, the court sided with the purchaser, Fresenius. The court highlighted that a sustained decline in Akorn's business performance that was durationally significant and which would be material to a reasonable purchaser had occurred, thus causing an MAE in general. Additionally, the court noted that Akorn's regulatory representations in the merger agreement were untrue, the deviation from the representations could not be timely cured, and the degree of deviation would reasonably be expected to result in an MAE. Thus, Fresenius could not be forced to close and was legally entitled to terminate its agreement with Akorn.

Not surprisingly, the COVID-19 pandemic gave rise to a number of cases in which the purchaser sought to escape its agreement to acquire the seller given the uncertainty caused by the pandemic. Such was the case in *AB Stable VIII LLC v. MAPS Hotels and Resorts One LLC,* 268 A.3d 198 (Del. 2021). The purchaser (MAPS Hotel and Resorts One LLC) had agreed to purchase fifteen hotel properties from the seller (AB Stable VIII LLC) for $5.8 billion. Before a closing could occur, the COVID-19 pandemic began in earnest and inflicted heavy damage on the hospitality industry. In response to the pandemic—and without securing the purchaser's consent—the seller made drastic changes to its hotel operations. Thereafter, the purchaser called off the deal, relying on the seller's failure to comply with the "ordinary course" covenant in the sale agreement.

The seller sued in the Delaware Chancery Court to require the purchaser to complete the transaction. However, the court sided with the purchaser, noting that the seller had violated the ordinary course covenant by failing to operate in the ordinary course of its business. After all, it had closed hotels, laid off or furloughed thousands of employees, and implemented other drastic changes to its business—all without the purchaser's consent which was required under the agreement. While the seller ultimately did seek the purchaser's approval to make changes, the seller waited two weeks after it had begun to make changes and, when the purchaser requested additional information from the seller about the changes being made, the seller never responded to the request.

On appeal, the seller argued that it satisfied the ordinary course covenant because the covenant did not preclude it from taking reasonable, industry-standard steps in response to the pandemic. Moreover, the seller argued that its breach of the notice requirement in the ordinary course covenant was immaterial, because the purchaser's denial of any request the seller could have made would have been unreasonable given that the purchaser itself was taking the same drastic actions at its own properties in response to the pandemic.

The purchaser countered by highlighting that the changes the seller made to its hotels were far from ordinary or routine. Indeed, among other changes the seller had closed two of its fifteen hotels entirely and severely limited operations at the other thirteen. Those changes, according to the purchaser, were a drastic departure from the past practices of the seller's hotel operations, thereby breaching the ordinary course covenant. According to the purchaser, the ordinary course covenant's plain language required the seller to continue normal and routine operations—as measured by its past practice without regard to the pandemic—or to give notice to the purchaser so the purchaser could decide whether to consent to any deviations from past practice.

The Delaware Supreme Court sided with the purchaser and affirmed the lower court's judgment. It noted that the seller had agreed to a covenant that required it to operate its hotels in the ordinary course of business consistent with past practice. While the seller might have been within its rights to respond to the regular ups and downs of the hotel business, the court highlighted the lower court's factual findings that the seller took drastic actions that were not consistent with its own past responses. While the seller's actions might have been reasonable in response to a world-wide pandemic, they were inconsistent with past practice and far from ordinary. Moreover, the seller could have timely sought the purchaser's approval before making drastic changes to its hotel operations, approval which could not be unreasonably withheld. However, the seller failed to do so in a timely manner and, when it ultimately did so, it refused to respond to the purchaser's legitimate request for more information. As a result, the seller breached the agreement's ordinary course covenant which, in turn, excused the purchaser from closing.

C. THIRD PARTY BENEFICIARIES

Shareholders and employees of the target who are not parties to an acquisition agreement sometimes try to sue the purchaser if the deal closes and things do not go according to plan. They have also sued when deals have *failed* to close. For example, in *Consolidated Edison, Inc. v. Northeast Utilities,* 426 F.3d 524 (2d Cir. 2005), Northeast Utilities, the purchaser, balked at closing a deal to purchase Consolidated Edison, the seller, when the latter's stock price declined prior to closing. NU claimed that Con Ed had suffered a *material adverse change* in its business, thus giving NU the right to walk. However,

Con Ed claimed that its stock price had slid because of a sinking stock market. The court addressed whether shareholders of Con Ed could sue as third party beneficiaries, claiming as damages the $1.2 billion control premium the deal offered. While the court believed that shareholders of Con Ed would become third party beneficiaries at the effective time of the merger, that time never arrived as NU had walked. Before that time, the merger agreement effectively limited third party rights through a boilerplate "no-third-party-beneficiaries" provision.

In response to *Consolidated Edison,* M&A practitioners representing sellers began inserting provisions into their agreements that addressed the recovery of lost premiums. Three variations of these so-called "*Con Ed* provisions" have proliferated. The first expressly provides stockholders with third-party beneficiary status. The second turns the target into an agent of the stockholders, thus allowing the target to recover damages on their behalf. The third focuses on the definition of damages resulting from a purchaser's wrongful breach. That definition specifically includes lost premiums in an attempt to allow the target itself to recover those premiums.

In 2024, the Delaware General Assembly amended DGCL § 261 to address *Consolidated Edison.* The amendment clarifies that a merger agreement may specify "penalties or consequences" for noncompliance that occurs *prior* to the effective time of the merger. This includes a "reverse termination fee" requiring a would-be acquirer in a failed transaction to pay the target an amount based on the stockholders' loss of the transaction premium. Moreover, the merger agreement may expressly authorize the target itself to retain the stockholders' lost premium payments without any obligation to distribute them to the stockholders. Thus, the amendment to DGCL § 261 removes any ambiguity about the validity of *Con Ed* provisions under Delaware law.

D. "SANDBAGGING"

Is it fair for a purchaser to learn of an operational problem at the seller's business during due diligence, then, without disclosing its discovery to the seller, insist that the seller represent in the merger agreement that the problem does not exist, and then, post-closing, sue the seller for indemnification due to the seller's breach of that representation? Doing so is known as "*sandbagging*" in the context of an M&A transaction. The ability to sandbag encourages a purchaser to be silent at the closing, purposefully misleading the seller on the purchaser's due diligence findings, rather than negotiate the conflict. It encourages litigation as the purchaser's incentive to settle is significantly reduced post-closing. The purchaser, with the deal no longer at risk, has an inexpensive lottery ticket for litigation.

In *Eagle Force Holdings, LLC v. Campbell,* 187 A.3d 1209 (Del. 2018), the Delaware Supreme Court, in dicta, addressed sandbagging. In this case, the purchaser received pre-signing (as opposed to post-signing but pre-closing) knowledge of a representation and warranty breach by the seller, but nonetheless proceeded with the closing and then sought indemnification from the seller for the breach post-closing. In a footnote, the majority opinion acknowledged the debate over whether sandbagging is permitted under Delaware law. However, the majority sidestepped the defendant seller's argument that the plaintiff purchaser's *reliance* was required in such situations, stating that the court "[had] not yet resolved this interesting question." The majority added:

> [W]e observe that a majority of states have followed the New York Court of Appeals' decision in *CBS Inc. v. Ziff-Davis Publishing Co.,* 75 N.Y.2d 496, 554 N.Y.S.2d 449, 553 N.E.2d 997 (1990), which holds that traditional reliance is not required to recover for breach of an express warranty: the only "reliance" required is that the express warranty is part of the bargain between the parties. *Id.,* 554 N.Y.S.2d 449, 553 N.E.2d at 1001 ("This view of 'reliance' . . . reflects the prevailing perception of an action for breach of express warranty as one that is no longer grounded in tort, but essentially in contract.") . . . We need not decide this interesting issue because such claims are not before the court.

In his partial dissent, however, Chief Justice Strine took a more direct approach: "[T]o the extent [plaintiff] is seeking damages because [defendant] supposedly made promises that were false, there is doubt that he can then turn around and sue because what he knew to be false remained so. Venerable

Delaware law casts doubt on [plaintiff's] ability to do so . . . ."

Given the ambiguity that exists under Delaware law, many purchasers are adding pro-sandbagging provisions to their agreements. Such a provision explicitly allows a purchaser to close and then sue for breach despite the purchaser's previous knowledge of a breach. This obviates any need for the purchaser to prove "reliance" on the representation and warranty in question. Whether a pro-sandbagging provision is legal depends on the jurisdiction in which litigation over it is brought. Compare *Hendricks v. Callahan*, 972 F.2d 190 (8th Cir. 1992) (pro-sandbagging provisions are not enforceable), with *CBS v. Ziff-Davis Publishing Co.*, 553 N.E.2d 997, 1002 (N.Y. 1990) (such provisions are enforceable).

In response, many sellers are insisting on adding anti-sandbagging provisions to their agreements. If such a provision were to be added to the agreement, a purchaser would have to reveal its discoveries before or at the closing and renegotiate the price to reflect the discovery, waive the problem or walk away from the deal. Alternatively, a seller may also ask the purchaser to execute at closing a release on known but undisclosed defects. If the purchaser refuses to sign the release, it shows its hand, prompting a renegotiation of the price.

§ 2. NASTY POST-CLOSING SURPRISES

A. THE PURCHASER DISCOVERS IT HAS OVERPAID

There are numerous cases involving claims by a purchaser, who has taken control of a seller after closing on an acquisition, that the seller is not what it was represented to be. In other words, the purchaser overpaid for the seller and the overpayment was due to the seller's breach of its reps and warranties under the acquisition agreement. Many cases revolve around the accuracy of the seller's financial statements. See, e.g., *Medcom Holdings Co. v. Baxter Travenol Labs, Inc.*, 106 F.3d 1388 (7th Cir. 1997) (balance sheet overstated asset values). The U.S. Supreme Court decision in *Landreth Timber Co. v. Landreth,* 471 U.S. 681 (1985), made all stock acquisitions subject to the general antifraud prohibition of SEA Rule 10b–5. Rule 10b–5 has become an attractive alternative to breach of contract claims for frustrated purchasers. Sellers, attempting to limit such claims, ask purchasers to sign "no-reliance" clauses. The federal circuit courts have split on the effect of such clauses. E.g., *AES Corp. v. Dow Chem. Co.*, 325 F.3d 174 (3d Cir. 2003).

B. THE SELLER OR THE SELLING SHAREHOLDERS DISCOVER THEY WERE UNDERPAID

Courts usually do not listen to a seller board's claim that it sold too dearly. E.g., *Ontario Teachers'*

Pension Plan Board v. IG Holdings Inc., 2000 WL 1234592 (S.D.N.Y.) (pension plan sold stock into a tender offer and later discovered the sale was below market value).

PART II

LEGAL RULES AFFECTING THE CHOICE OF ACQUISITION FORM

CHAPTER 4

SHAREHOLDER VOTING AND APPRAISAL RIGHTS

As was noted throughout Chapter 1, state corporate codes allocate shareholder voting and appraisal rights in acquisitions depending on whether the acquisition is a statutory merger, a sale of all or substantially all the assets, or a stock acquisition. Since a desired end result can often be achieved through more than one transactional form, lawyers have structured transactions to minimize the costs of shareholder voting and appraisal requirements. Their efforts have two parts. First, lawyers pick a state of incorporation, usually Delaware, which gives them planning flexibility. A firm then changes its place of incorporation through a merger or a charter amendment. Second, lawyers choose among the state's statutory sections to minimize shareholder voting and appraisal rights.

§ 1. STATE STATUTORY LAW ON SHAREHOLDER VOTING

A. ACQUISITIONS USING STOCK

When the purchaser is paying for the target with shares of voting common stock of the purchaser (or securities convertible into common shares), shareholder voting rights are the most robust. The general rule in the state statutes is that the shareholders of both constituent firms have voting rights. But five important exceptions result in the general rule usually applying only in large, stock swap statutory mergers.

The first two exceptions are found in most states' corporate codes and the last three are found in Delaware's code.

Exception One. If the amount of common stock in the purchaser used in the acquisition is less than 20 percent of its outstanding shares pre-transaction, the purchaser shareholders do not vote. E.g., DGCL § 251(f) (statutory mergers; all common included in the calculation); MBCA §§ 6.21(f) & 11.04(h) (all acquisitions; only voting common included in the calculation); CCC §§ 1200(e) & 1201(b) (a five-sixths rule for all acquisitions; only voting common included in the calculation).

Exception Two. In stock-for-stock acquisitions, the target firm shareholders do not vote. The target shareholder's individual decision on whether or not to tender their shares supplants their need for a collective vote.

Exceptions three through five are found in the Delaware code and those states that follow Delaware's example. California, Ohio and the states that adopted the 1999 revisions to the ABA's Model Business Corporation Act do not have these exceptions.

Exception Three. If the purchaser in an asset acquisition is a Delaware corporation (or incorporated in a state that follows Delaware's statute), the purchaser shareholders do not vote. But see MBCA § 6.21(f) (purchaser shareholders vote if their share ownership is significantly diluted by the transaction); CCC §§ 181(c), 1200(c) & 1201(a) (same).

Exception Four. If the purchaser in a triangular merger is a Delaware corporation (or incorporated in a state that follows Delaware's statute), the purchaser shareholders do not vote. In such triangular mergers, the shareholders in the target firm vote but the shareholders in the parent company do not. (The parent board of directors holds and votes the shares of the subsidiary used as an acquisition vehicle in the merger.) But see MBCA § 6.21(f) (purchaser shareholders vote if their share ownership is significantly diluted by the transaction); CCC §§ 1200(e) & 1201(a) (same).

Exception Five. If the purchaser in a stock acquisition is a Delaware corporation (or incorporated in a state that follows Delaware's statute), the shareholders in the purchaser, as well as those in the target firm, do not have voting rights. But see MBCA § 6.21(f) (purchaser shareholders vote if their share ownership is significantly diluted by the transaction); CCC §§ 181(b), 1200(b) & 1201(a) (same).

B. ACQUISITIONS FOR CASH OR CASH EQUIVALENTS

When the purchaser is paying cash or cash equivalents (non-voting, non-convertible stock or non-convertible debt) for the target, shareholders have more limited voting rights. In general, the shareholders of the purchaser do not vote. In

Delaware the cash equivalents category does not include non-voting common stock but does include non-voting preferred stock. DGCL § 251(f).

In cash-for-asset acquisitions, the shareholders in the target vote if the asset sale constitutes all or substantially all of the target's assets, but the shareholders in the purchaser do not. DGCL § 271; MBCA § 12.01(a) (but no target shareholder vote required when sale of all or substantially all of the assets is in the "usual and regular course of business"). In cash mergers, the shareholders of the target vote, but those in the purchasing corporation do not, if and only if the target merges into the purchaser and there is no change to the rights and privileges of the shares held by the shareholders of the purchaser. DGCL § 251(f); MBCA § 11.04(h). In cash-for-stock acquisitions, the shareholders of neither constituent corporation have voting rights.

C. "REVERSE ACQUISITIONS": ALLOCATING THE VOTE IN DELAWARE CORPORATIONS

The differences in voting rights among the various types of acquisitions empower lawyers not only to minimize voting rights but also to allocate the voting rights among the constituent parties. The choice of a cash-for-assets acquisition, for example, eliminates the voting rights of the shareholders of the purchaser. By doing a *reverse acquisition,* that is, having the actual target firm technically purchase the assets of the actual purchaser (the little fish swallows the big fish), planners can allocate the voting rights to shareholders in the purchaser and eliminate the shareholder voting rights in the target. In Diagram 4 in Chapter 1, § 2.B, assume that A Corp is the target and B Corp is the purchaser. In the stock-for-assets reverse acquisition, the A Corp stock transferred to B Corp constitutes over 51 percent of the A Corp voting stock outstanding after the acquisition. Planners thus transfer control of A Corp to B Corp and then dissolve B Corp, distributing the controlling block of A Corp voting stock through to the original B Corp shareholders. Under Delaware statutes, the shareholders of B Corp vote and the shareholders of A Corp do not even though A Corp is buying B Corp. Under California statutes and the Model Business Corporation Act, however, A Corp shareholders in a reverse asset acquisition do have the right to vote. MBCA § 6.21(f); CCC §§ 181(c), 1200(c) & 1201(a).

D. VOTE BUYING: LEGAL OR ILLEGAL?

Whenever a shareholder vote is required on an acquisition, various parties may seek to influence the outcome of that vote through so-called "vote buying." Delaware case law makes it clear that some vote buying is perfectly legal, but other vote buying—particularly by management—is not.

According to the Delaware Chancery Court in *Schreiber v. Carney*, 447 A.2d 17 (Del. Ch. 1982), vote buying is *illegal per se* if "the object or purpose [of the vote buying] is to defraud or in some way disenfranchise the other stockholders." The court also noted that, even absent these deleterious purposes, vote buying is so easily susceptible of abuse it must be viewed as a voidable transaction subject to a test for *intrinsic fairness.*

At first blush, the court's application of the intrinsic fairness test seems difficult to reconcile with the Delaware General Assembly's explicit validation of shareholder voting agreements in DGCL § 218(c). Significantly, however, in *Schreiber* it was management of the defendant corporation that was buying votes in favor of a corporate reorganization. Shareholders, on the one hand, are free to do whatever they want with their votes, including selling them to the highest bidder. Management, on the other hand, may not use corporate assets to buy votes in a hotly contested proxy contest about an extraordinary transaction that would significantly transform the corporation, unless it can be demonstrated, as it was in *Schreiber,* that management's vote buying activity does not have a deleterious effect on the corporate franchise. Indeed, the board of the defendant corporation in *Schreiber* had bought votes to eliminate a minority hold out position in a deal favored by a majority of the shareholders. Moreover, management's vote-buying was ratified through an independent and fully informed vote of the disinterested shareholders.

In *Hewlett v. Hewlett-Packard Co.,* 2002 WL 549137 (Del. Ch.), Walter Hewlett, a dissenting member of the board of directors of the purchaser, Hewlett-Packard, mounted a proxy contest to defeat a proposed merger between HP and Compaq Computer. He lost a very close vote. He then sued, arguing that HP had illegally bought votes sufficient to ratify the deal. Specifically, he alleged HP management had induced Deutsche Bank—a holder of at least 25 million shares of HP stock—to switch 17 million of its "no" votes to "yes" votes at the eleventh hour. He further alleged that Deutsche Bank switched its votes as a result of a combination of inducement and coercion, orchestrated by HP's management, and not for reasons relating to the merits of the transaction.

The Chancery Court denied HP's motion to dismiss the case. However, after a trial was held, the court found in favor of HP. The court concluded that the plaintiff had failed to prove that HP management improperly enticed or coerced Deutsche Bank into voting in favor of the merger. But the case was not over. The lawsuit attracted the attention of federal officials, including those at the SEC. They investigated the vote buying allegations and ultimately forced the investment advisory unit of Deutsche Bank to pay a $750,000 settlement for failing to disclose a conflict of interest as required when it voted its clients' proxies. Apparently, most of Deutsche Bank's 25 million shares of HP stock were beneficially owned by *clients* of Deutsche Bank, and not by Deutsche Bank itself.

§ 2. STATE STATUTORY LAW ON SHAREHOLDER APPRAISAL RIGHTS FOR DISSENTING SHAREHOLDERS

Shareholders who have the right to vote on acquisitions or recapitalizations often (but not always) have, by state statute, *dissenters' rights.*

Dissenters' rights are also known as *appraisal rights* or *buy out rights*. All states give shareholders who dissent to certain types of acquisitions a right to petition a state court for the fair cash value of their shares, payable to them by the surviving or purchasing firm. In essence, the codes provide a mandatory, contingent put option to all common shareholders, triggered by certain acquisitions and with an exercise price set at fair value as determined by the court. Appraisal rights give dissenting shareholders the ability to break free of the decision made by the majority.

If a substantial minority block of shareholders demands cash in these proceedings, known as appraisal proceedings, and the constituent firms in a stock swap acquisition are cash poor, the mere notice by the dissenting shareholders that they might assert their appraisal rights can terminate the acquisition. Many acquisition agreements in stock swap deals expressly condition closing on the absence of even a small percentage (three percent or more) of shareholders claiming dissenters' rights. Moreover, in all types of acquisitions it can be very embarrassing to a board of directors if a state judge gives a dissenting shareholder more money than the board negotiated for shareholders that supported the acquisition. If this happens, shareholders that voted for the transaction may turn around and sue the board for a breach of its fiduciary duty.

There are six central issues to the basic definition of an appraisal remedy: First, what kinds of transactions trigger the right? Second, how are the rights perfected procedurally by dissenting shareholders? Third, how do courts determine the fair value of the shares? Fourth, do dissenting shareholders receive interest on the amount determined to be fair value? Fifth, what are the steps that states have taken to prevent shareholders from "gaming" the system through appraisal arbitrage? And sixth, is the right the exclusive remedy for dissenting shareholders?

A. THE SCOPE OF THE APPRAISAL REMEDY

Under the Delaware corporate code, the general rule is that dissenting shareholders in statutory mergers and consolidations, including short-form mergers under DGCL § 253 in which the minority shareholders do not even have a right to vote, have appraisal rights. DGCL § 262. In short-form mergers a partially owned subsidiary merges with and into its parent, but the merger is dependent on the parent owning at least 90 percent of the subsidiary's stock at the time of the merger.

Importantly, DGCL § 262 is limited in two significant ways when compared to similar provisions in other state corporate codes. First, the Delaware provision applies only to mergers and consolidations; it neither applies to asset sales under § 271 nor to amendments to the certificate of incorporation under § 242. By contrast, most states provide appraisal rights to the shareholders of the seller in an asset sale and almost half the states give appraisal rights to dissenting shareholders when certain amendments to the certificate of incorporation are approved.

The few other states that do give full voting rights have a much more limited exception than does Delaware. The New York Business Corporation Law and the Model Business Corporation Act give appraisal rights to shareholders of corporations selling substantially all their assets for stock in the purchasing corporation but not to shareholders of corporations selling substantially all their assets for cash if the seller dissolves within a year of the sale. NYBCL § 910(a)(1)(B); MBCA § 13.02(a)(3). California provides appraisal rights to seller shareholders in stock-for-assets acquisitions but not cash-for-assets acquisitions, regardless of whether the seller dissolves. CCC § 1300 (omitting reference to § 1001 transactions). The drafters argue that appraisal rights ought to apply only when shareholders receiving stock are forced to become shareholders in a different corporation.

Second, the Delaware provision has an exception for securities of publicly traded corporations, the *market-out exception.* DGCL § 262(b). Shareholders of a seller that is publicly traded who receive stock in a buying firm surviving a statutory merger do not have appraisal rights. Shareholders in a purchaser that is publicly traded, who vote on a stock swap statutory merger in which the purchaser survives, and whose shares do not change, do not have appraisal rights. Moreover, while not initially subject to the market-out exception, medium-form mergers under DGCL § 251(h) are now subject to that exception.

Most other states more closely link voting rights and appraisal rights in acquisitions. Some states grant appraisal rights even when shareholders have no voting rights. Michigan and South Carolina, for example, grant dissenters' rights to shareholders of a corporation after an acquisition of a controlling block of the shares.

As noted above, appraisal rights are controversial. The 1984 version of the ABA Revised Model Business Corporation Act contains a chapter on appraisal rights that is one of the most liberal grants of appraisal rights in the history of state corporate codes. In a complete reversal of approach, the Committee on Corporate Laws recommended in 1999 that states adopt a new chapter that substantially reduces the scope of the chapter that had been in place since 1984. Some states may choose to keep the 1984 version; others may adopt the 1999 model. The 1999 version competes with Delaware for the title of most conservative state provision. The 2016 version of the MBCA continues to reflect this reduced scope.

The 2016 version of the MBCA de-links shareholder voting and appraisal rights in several important contexts and, thereby, eliminates appraisal rights in several instances in which they would have been available under the 1984 provisions. First, shareholders entitled to vote on an acquisition are not entitled to appraisal rights if the transaction would not alter the terms of the securities they hold. Shareholders of the surviving corporation in a merger, for example, even if voting on the acquisition (because the firm issues a new block of stock that exceeds 20 percent of the stock currently outstanding), do not have appraisal rights if their shares remain outstanding after the merger and the rights and privileges of their shares remain the same. MBCA § 13.02(a)(1). Second, the 2016 version eliminates appraisal rights on amendments to the articles of incorporation unless the amendment effects a reverse stock split. MBCA § 13.02(a)(4). Third, the 2016 version includes a market-out exception that was not in the 1984 provisions. MBCA § 13.02(b)(1)(ii). The market-out exception is both narrower and broader than the Delaware exception. The market-out exception does not apply in conflict-of-interest transactions. A conflict of interest exists when the senior managers or the controlling shareholders have interests in both parties in an acquisition. The market-out exemption is not lost, however, if senior management receives specified financial benefits from employment, consulting, or severance contracts as a result of the transaction. MBCA § 13.02(b)(4). Interestingly, however, the MBCA market-out exception applies to all cash exchanges for publicly traded stock while the Delaware provision does not. MBCA § 13.02(b)(3). Fourth, a corporation may amend its certificate of incorporation to eliminate appraisal rights for preferred shareholders (with a delayed effective date of one year). MBCA § 13.02(c). Lastly, the 2016 version limits appraisal rights in some asset sales constituting all or substantially all of the seller's assets; if a seller liquidates within a year of the transaction and the shareholders receive cash, seller shareholders do not have appraisal rights despite being entitled to vote on the asset sale in the first place. MBCA § 13.02(a)(3).

B. CONTRACTUAL MODIFICATION OF APPRAISAL RIGHTS

The Delaware courts have long held that preferred shareholders can contractually waive or modify their rights to appraisal *ex ante,* so long as the waiver or modification is clear. See *Halpin v. Riverstone Nat'l, Inc.,* 2015 WL 854724, at *1 (Del. Ch.); *In re Appraisal of Metromedia Int'l Group, Inc.,* 971 A.2d 893, 901–03 (Del. Ch. 2009). If no such waiver or modification exists, then preferred shareholders have the same appraisal rights as common shareholders in the event of a merger. See *In re Appraisal of Goodcents Holdings, Inc.,* 2017 WL 2463665, at *3 (Del. Ch.). In practice, a contractual waiver or modification of appraisal rights for preferred stock is commonplace.

The MBCA has included a contractual waiver for preferred shareholders in its appraisal section, so long as preferred shareholders have the right to vote separately as a group on the transaction in question. If the waiver is added through a charter amendment, the waiver is required to have a one year delayed effective date. MBCA § 13.02(c).

What about common stockholders? Can they contractually waive their appraisal rights? In *Manti Holdings, LLC v. Authentix Acquisition Company, Inc.,* 261 A.3d 1199 (Del. 2021), the Delaware

Supreme Court affirmed the Chancery Court's holding that a corporation may enforce an advance waiver of appraisal rights against its own common stockholders. In *Manti Holdings,* the lower court held that former stockholders of Authentix Acquisition, through their execution of a 2008 stockholders' agreement, had waived their statutory appraisal rights in connection with a sale of the company by merger.

The Delaware Supreme Court agreed with the lower court's ruling. In doing so, the Delaware Supreme Court recognized that there are certain fundamental features of a corporation that are essential to the corporation's identity and cannot be waived. According to the court, however, the right to seek judicial appraisal is not one of them. The court held that the petitioners had waived their appraisal rights under the terms of the stockholders' agreement, and the DGCL did not bar enforcement of that waiver. According to the court, the petitioners were sophisticated investors, represented by counsel, that agreed to a clear waiver of their appraisal rights in exchange for valuable consideration. Moreover, the court held that the surviving corporation in the merger was an "intended beneficiary" of the stockholders' agreement, and thus had standing to enforce its provisions against the petitioners.

C. APPRAISAL PROCEDURES

The appraisal procedures in the MBCA are significantly different from the procedures in Delaware's corporate code. The Model Act seeks to readjust the balance between the corporation and the dissenting shareholders in favor of shareholders. The principal changes are aimed, first, at eliminating much of the delay in getting funds into the hands of dissenting shareholders; second, at forcing corporations to take more initiative in settling the claims; and, third, at shifting more of the expenses of the procedure to the corporation.

Under Delaware law, a corporation contemplating a transaction that gives rise to shareholder appraisal rights must notify shareholders of these rights 20 days before the corporation submits the transaction to shareholders for approval. Each dissenting shareholder planning on demanding appraisal rights must so notify the corporation before the vote on the transaction. If other shareholders ratify the transaction, the corporation must notify dissenting shareholders (i.e., those who gave proper notice), within 10 days of the transaction's effective date, that appraisal rights are available. The shareholder must then, within 20 days of the second notice, make a demand on the corporation for an appraisal of her shares. If the shareholder is dissatisfied with the corporation's response, she must, within 120 days of the transaction's effective date, file a petition in the Court of Chancery demanding a determination of the fair value of her stock. A trial on the petition can take *several years*. As a result of this lengthy process, the dissatisfied shareholder may not receive money for her shares for quite some time. The procedure also requires a dissenting shareholder to make three timely written demands of different formats to perfect the right.

The MBCA, by contrast, stresses the importance of getting some cash value in the dissenting shareholders' hands quickly and requires fewer shareholder demands. Under Chapter 13 of the MBCA, corporations, in their notice of a shareholder meeting, must inform shareholders of their appraisal rights. Dissenting shareholders must give the corporation a written notice before the pivotal shareholder meeting of their intent to demand appraisal. Once the transaction is approved, the corporation must, within 10 days, notify the dissenting shareholders of the maturation of their appraisal rights and send them a specified form. If the dissenting shareholder returns the form within 40 days and demands payment, the corporation must pay that shareholder, within 30 days, cash equal to the *corporation's* estimated fair value for the shares. If the dissenting shareholder is dissatisfied with the amount, she may, within 30 days of payment, inform the corporation of her *own* estimate. If the corporation fails to settle the discrepancy, the corporation must commence a proceeding within 60 days of the shareholder's demand to determine the fair value of the shares. If the corporation fails to settle or sue, it must pay the shareholder her demand. The effect of the Model Act's procedure is to place some cash in the hands of dissenters soon after the meeting and to place the obligation to petition a court on the corporation rather than the dissenting shareholder. As seen in Chapter 4, § 2.E, Delaware now allows corporations to make prepayments to shareholders seeking appraisal in order to tap down the practice of interest rate arbitrage. DGCL § 262(h).

DGCL § 262(j) does not provide for the shifting of dissenting shareholders' attorney and expert witness fees and expenses to the corporation. However, upon a motion from a dissenting shareholder, the Delaware Chancery Court may order all or a portion of that shareholder's expenses, including reasonable attorney's fees and the fees and expenses of experts, to be charged pro rata against the value of all the shares that sought appraisal. Shareholders in Delaware, therefore, ought not to sue unless they can cover the potential expenses of attorneys and experts that can run into six figures. Departing from the DGCL's approach, the MBCA shifts attorney's fees and expert witness fees to the corporation except in situations where shareholders have acted "arbitrarily, vexatiously, or not in good faith" with respect to their appraisal rights. MBCA § 13.31(a).

D. CASE LAW ON FAIR VALUE IN APPRAISAL PROCEEDINGS

The valuation process in appraisal proceedings has two separate components. First, judges, usually listening to widely different views from competing financial experts, must value the shares at issue. In *Weinberger v. UOP, Inc.*, 457 A.2d 701 (Del. 1983), the Delaware Supreme Court held that this included "proof of value by any techniques or methods which are generally considered acceptable in the financial community and otherwise admissible in court." The valuation is of the company as a whole and not the individual shares. Because the valuation of an entire corporation will include an intrinsic *control premium* (an amount in excess of the trading price of stock that reflects the value of controlling the corporation) that exists independently of any given deal, a dissenting shareholder will naturally receive her pro rata share of that premium. Expert witnesses calculate value, and then a percentage of the valuation amount is awarded to the dissenting shareholders according to the percentage of their equity interest.

Courts refuse to include a minority discount when valuing a minority block of shares. By contrast, a purchaser in an arm's-length sale will apply a minority discount when purchasing a minority block of stock, because those shares do not carry any significant indicia of control. Thus, a controlling block will command a higher price than a non-controlling block in the open market. However, shareholders seeking appraisal never desired to part with their shares in the first place—they are *unwilling* sellers. They wished to continue with their investment but are being forced out through a merger. Hence, courts refuse to apply a minority discount in an appraisal context. See *Cavalier Oil Corp. v. Harnett,* 564 A.2d 1137 (Del. 1989).

In *M.G. Bancorporation, Inc. v. Le Beau,* 737 A.2d 513 (Del. 1999), the Delaware Supreme Court reviewed a number of different valuation methods proffered by the financial experts of the respective parties. The case itself revolved around a short-form merger conducted pursuant to DGCL § 253. Southwest Bancorp owned over 91 percent of the stock of M.G. Bancorporation (MGB). MGB itself was a holding company. Its primary assets were stock in two subsidiaries, both of which were banks.

In order to rid itself of the minority shareholders of MGB, Southwest merged MGB with and into itself pursuant to § 253. Southwest paid the minority shareholders $41 per share as merger consideration. Pursuant to DGCL § 262(b), the minority shareholders were entitled to appraisal rights, and some of them perfected them. At issue, therefore, was the "fair value" of the shares held by the dissenting shareholders. After a trial featuring extensive testimony from the experts for both sides, the Delaware Chancery Court determined that the shares were worth $85 per share, a dramatically different number from the $41 per share that MGB had offered in the merger.

The valuation methods proffered by the experts fell into four main categories. The first category included comparable valuations. This involved determining MGB's value based on the values of other comparable companies that had recently been sold. The second category included valuations based on book value. Book value is a balance sheet-based valuation method that is calculated by subtracting a company's total liabilities from its total assets. The third category included valuations based on earnings. This involved looking at earnings multiples and price-to-earnings (P/E) ratios to determine value. The final category included valuations based on discounted net cash flow (DCF).

In *LeBeau,* the Delaware Supreme Court made it clear that the lower court is not bound to accept a particular expert's valuation or methodology *in toto*. Rather, the court can make its own independent calculation by either adapting or blending the factual assumptions of the parties' experts. The ultimate selection of a valuation framework is within the court's discretion. Indeed, definitively adopting the valuation of one expert as part of an "either/or" approach is at variance with the court's statutory obligation to engage in an independent valuation exercise.

Furthermore, the Delaware Supreme Court underscored that the lower court's valuation will be accorded a high level of deference. In the absence of legal error, the standard of judicial review is "abuse of discretion." The lower court will be found to have abused its discretion when either its factual findings do not have support in the record or its valuation is not the result of an orderly and logical deductive process.

The second component of the valuation process relates to acquisition gains. To wit, if the appraisal statute is not specific on the matter, judges must address the bottomless policy question of whether dissenting shareholders should participate in the gains from the acquisition itself and, if so, how to measure those gains. Should shareholders receive the value of their shares before the announcement of the merger affects share price or should shareholders claim a portion of the gains generated by the merger itself? Sometimes the question is put in terms of whether the shareholders should receive a part of the "control premium" in acquisitions that involve a change in control. Occasionally the question is explicitly resolved by state statute. More often the matter is left to the judiciary.

The Delaware statute directs the courts to

> . . . determine the fair value of the shares exclusive of any element of value arising from the accomplishment or expectation of the merger or consolidation, together with interest, if any, to be paid upon the amount determined to be the fair value. In determining such fair value, the Court shall take into account all relevant factors. . . .

DGCL § 262(h). In *Weinberger,* the Delaware Supreme Court held that "[o]nly the speculative elements of value that may arise from the 'accomplishment or expectation' of the merger are excluded." Elements of future value, including the nature of the enterprise, which are known or susceptible of proof as of the date of the merger and not the product of speculation, may be considered.

In *Le Beau,* the Delaware Supreme Court clarified its holding in *Weinberger.* It first stated that the underlying assumption in an appraisal valuation is that the dissenting shareholders would be willing to maintain their investment position had the merger not occurred. It then added that the corporation must be valued as a going-concern based upon its *operative reality* as of the time of the merger.

Cede & Co. v. Technicolor, Inc., 684 A.2d 289 (Del. 1996), elaborated on what operative reality means. The case involved a two-step acquisition of Technicolor by Ronald Perelman's MacAndrews & Forbes Holdings, Inc. (MAF). Step one consisted of a friendly tender offer in which MAF ultimately purchased 82.19% of Technicolor's stock for $23 per share in cash. Step two consisted of Macanfor Corp., a newly-formed, wholly-owned subsidiary of MAF, merging with and into Technicolor (a reverse triangular merger). Technicolor's remaining shareholders were squeezed out through the merger and received $23 in cash as merger consideration.

Prior to the deal, Technicolor's business strategy had been driven by a plan championed by its Chair, Morton Kamerman. This strategy—the Kamerman Plan—remained in effect until step one of MAF's takeover was completed. Ronald Perelman had developed a strategy for Technicolor (the Perelman Plan) that called for Technicolor to sell off many of its businesses while focusing on only two. After step one of MAF's takeover was completed, but *before* the second step merger was consummated, Perelman had Technicolor begin implementing his strategic plan.

Cinerama, a beneficial owner of Technicolor stock, sought appraisal rights in the Delaware Chancery Court. It argued that Technicolor should be valued as it existed on the date of the merger. This would mean that Technicolor would be valued based on the implementation of the Perelman Plan rather than the Kamerman Plan. Technicolor, in turn, argued that it should be valued as if the strategies of the Kamerman Plan remained in place.

The Delaware Supreme Court agreed with Cinerama. It noted that in a two-step acquisition, the purchaser typically takes control of the target upon the completion of the first step tender offer. Accordingly, the purchaser is in a position to implement its plans for the target immediately—even before the second step merger is consummated. This, in fact, is exactly what Perelman had done. To the extent value has been added to the target following a change in majority control, that value accrues to the benefit of all shareholders of the target—majority as well as minority—and must be included in the appraisal process on the date of the merger.

Other states have attempted to resolve the issue relating to acquisition gains by establishing a valuation date. States that do not want to include acquisition value in the appraisal award require that a court value the corporation on the eve of the shareholder vote and that the valuation exclude any premium for the deal itself. NJBCA § 14A:11–3; OGCL § 1701.85(C). By contrast, a few states expressly include acquisition value in the statutory language. New York is an example of a state legislature that bit the bullet on valuing the potential of the transaction itself. NYBCL § 623(h)(4). The MBCA is moving towards the New York position.

In the 1984 version of the MBCA, fair value is determined "immediately before the effectuation of the corporate action to which the dissenter objects, excluding any appreciation or depreciation in anticipation of the corporate action *unless exclusion would be inequitable.*" MBCA § 13.01(3) (1984) (italics added). The 2016 version of the section omits the final "excluding" clause of the 1984 version and invites the court to use "customary and current valuation concepts and techniques generally employed for similar businesses in the context of the transaction requiring appraisal." MBCA § 13.01 (definition of "fair value"). The Official Comment to the 2016 version notes that the omission "permits consideration of changes in market price of the corporation's shares in anticipation of the transaction, to the extent the changes are relevant." The Comment draws a distinction, however, between general market value and value attributable to the unique plans of the purchaser. The former is includable in the award, while the latter is not. The drafters, in essence, respect the claim of a dissenting shareholder that the firm could be sold for a higher price to someone else but do not respect the claim that the managers could have negotiated for a higher price from the actual purchaser.

In Delaware, acquisition-specific elements of value are not to be included, but adjustments to counter built-in minority discounts are, although the position is not free from confusion. See *MPM Enterprises v. Gilbert,* 731 A.2d 790 (Del. 1999). The Delaware Supreme Court seems to want to award dissenting shareholders a portion of an intrinsic control premium that exists independently of any given deal.

The Delaware Chancery Court appears increasingly willing to rely on the merger price itself as a proxy for "fair value," at least when *unaffiliated* mergers are involved. This willingness is illustrated in *In re Appraisal of PetSmart, Inc.*, 2017 WL 2303599 (Del. Ch.). According to the court, the sale process that PetSmart followed in selling itself involved "a robust pre-signing auction among informed, motivated bidders." Indeed, the deal price was "forged in the crucible of objective market reality." Given that the PetSmart financial projections available to conduct a discounted cash flow valuation "were, at best, fanciful," the court relied on the merger price. This was true even though only financial bidders ultimately submitted bids and the most likely strategic bidder (PetSmart's main competitor) was not contacted at all (although the PetSmart board had a reasonable basis for excluding it).

The Delaware Chancery Court, however, has also espoused reasons to be wary of using deal price as a proxy for fair value. According to the court in *In re Appraisal of Dell Inc.*, 2016 WL 3186538 (Del. Ch.), these reasons include, among others:

- Shifting the determination of fair value to the deal parties by embracing deal price as fair value *inappropriately shifts* the responsibility to determine fair value to the parties from the courts.

- The time delay between signing and closing a deal could lead the deal price (determined at signing) to be inaccurate as of the closing date.

- The market for entire companies is "chunky" and thus less efficient than the market for individual shares.
- Deal price often includes synergies (the split of joint gains), and synergies are to be excluded in determining fair value under § 262.
- Management buyouts (like the one involved in *Dell*) are rife with conflicts of interest, and thus deal prices in MBOs must be closely scrutinized.

Despite the leanings of the Delaware Chancery Court, the Delaware Supreme Court has refused to create a legal presumption that deal price is the best evidence of fair value. *DFC Global Corp. v. Muirfield Value Partners, L.P.*, 172 A.3d 346 (Del. 2017). In *DFC Global,* the Delaware Supreme Court "decline[d] to engage in that act of creation" because it "has no basis in the statutory text, which gives the Court of Chancery in the first instance the discretion to 'determine the fair value of the shares' by taking into account 'all relevant factors.' " Noting that the "language [in DGCL § 262(h)] is broad," the court would continue to apply it *as is* "until the General Assembly wishes to narrow the prism through which the Court of Chancery looks at appraisal value in specific classes of mergers[.]"

Nevertheless, in a later decision the Delaware Supreme Court highlighted that when a public company with a deep trading market is sold at a substantial premium to the preannouncement price, after a process in which interested purchasers all had a fair and viable opportunity to bid, the deal price is a strong indicator of fair value, as a matter of economic reality and theory. *Verition Partners Master Fund Ltd. v. Aruba Networks, Inc.*, 210 A.3d 128 (Del. 2019).

Importantly, however, the deal price typically includes some value relating to synergies stemming from the accomplishment of the merger. This stems from the fact that target fiduciaries bargain for a premium that includes a share of the anticipated synergies. But including synergistic value in an appraisal award is taboo under DGCL § 262(h). Therefore, appraisal cases post-*DFC* and *Dell* refer to "*deal price minus synergies*" as a potential indicator of fair value rather than just "deal price." See, e.g., *BCIM Strategic Value Master Fund, LP v. HFF, Inc.*, 2022 WL 304840 (Del. Ch.); *In re Appraisal of Regal Entertainment Group,* 2021 WL 1916364 (Del. Ch.). According to the Delaware Supreme Court, deal value minus synergies "should be given considerable weight by the Court of Chancery absent deficiencies in the deal process." *Aruba Networks, supra,* at 137.

When would it be appropriate for the Delaware Chancery Court to equate "deal price minus synergies" with "fair value" when determining an appraisal award? Subsequent court decisions make it clear that deal price warrants deference in a court's determination of fair value *only when* the deal process, deal protections and informational disparities among potential purchasers are not preclusive to the emergence of other bidders. In other words, transactions must be "*Dell* compliant." A *Dell* compliant transaction is one where "(i) information was sufficiently disseminated to potential bidders, so that (ii) an informed sale could take place, (iii) without undue impediments imposed by the deal structure itself." *In re Appraisal of AOL Inc.,* 2018 WL 1037450, at *8 (Del. Ch.). In other words, it is a transaction where "the deal process developed fair *market* value." Id. (emphasis in original).

E. AWARDING INTEREST

Dissenting shareholders of Delaware corporations are entitled to receive interest on the amount the Delaware Chancery Court determines to be fair value. DGCL § 262(h) provides:

> Unless the Court in its discretion determines otherwise for good cause, interest from the effective date of the merger through the date of payment of the judgment shall be compounded quarterly and shall accrue at 5% over the Federal Reserve discount rate (including any surcharge) as established from time to time during the period between the effective date of the merger and the date of payment of the judgment.

This rate is referred to as the "legal" or "statutory" rate of interest in Delaware.

The Chancery Court has little discretion to adopt a different rate, unless doing so is necessary to avoid an inequitable result. E.g., *Merion Capital, L.P. v. 3M Cogent, Inc.,* 2013 WL 3793896 (Del. Ch.). For example, one of the parties to the proceeding may have engaged in an improper delay (in order to increase the number of days it will receive interest) or made a bad faith assertion of a valuation claim (in order to increase the principal on which interest is calculated). See id.

F. DISCOURAGING APPRAISAL ARBITRAGE

Appraisal arbitrage is an investment strategy employed by hedge funds and other shareholder activists. They purchase shares in a target after the record date for a merger involving that target and pursue the appraisal remedy as their investment strategy. The arbitrageurs prefer shares of targets where a large number of "no" votes to the merger is likely. The arbitrageur can earn a return based on (a) any positive difference between the appraised value of their shares (as determined by the court) and the value offered by the acquirer and (b) interest on the appraised value accruing from the date of the merger until the date the judgment is paid (which could be several years). As seen earlier, Delaware is particularly generous when it comes to awarding interest, as its statutory rate of interest is *5 percent above* the Federal Reserve's discount rate! DGCL § 262(h). Thus, with respect to the interest component of appraisal arbitrage, many arbitrageurs seek to earn interest on their invested money at an interest rate significantly higher than prevailing market interest rates (a strategy known as *interest rate arbitrage*) by pursuing appraisal rights.

In 2016, the Delaware legislature attacked appraisal arbitrage by amending DGCL § 262 in two ways. First, subsection (h) of § 262 was modified in an attempt to tap down interest rate arbitrage. That subsection now allows a surviving corporation to pay an amount in cash to dissenting shareholders *prior* to the entry of judgment in an appraisal proceeding. The stated purpose is to halt interest from accruing on the prepayment amount, and thus reduce the attractiveness of interest rate arbitrage. Indeed, if the surviving corporation makes a prepayment, interest will only accrue on (a) the difference, if any, between the prepayment amount and the fair value of the shares as determined by the Chancery Court and (b) interest already accrued at the time the surviving corporation makes the prepayment, unless accrued interest up to that point is also paid at that time. Dissenting shareholders need not refund any overpayment made by a surviving corporation unless they have agreed to a "clawback" provision in the prepayment agreement. See *In re Appraisal of Panera Bread Co.*, 2020 WL 506684, at *43 (Del. Ch.).

Second, subsection (g) of § 262 was modified by adding a *de minimis exception* to appraisal rights. With respect to a constituent corporation to a merger or consolidation with shares listed on a national securities exchange, the Chancery Court *must dismiss* all appraisal proceedings as to all shareholders of shares of that corporation *unless* (1) the total number of shares entitled to appraisal exceeds 1 percent of the outstanding shares of the class or series eligible for appraisal, (2) the value of the consideration provided in the merger or consolidation for such total number of shares exceeds $1 million, or (3) the merger was approved pursuant to the short-form merger provision of DGCL § 253 or 267.

G. EXCLUSIVITY OF THE APPRAISAL REMEDY

State courts have also struggled with the relationship of the special appraisal remedy procedure to litigation based on allegations of breaches of fiduciary duty. Companies want the appraisal remedy to be the exclusive remedy for shareholders complaining about mergers or other covered transactions. Shareholder plaintiffs would prefer to add appraisal proceedings to their pre-existing arsenal of remedies for attacking mergers—breach of fiduciary duty, securities violations and fraud. Neither side has gotten its way. Delaware courts allow shareholders to file additional requests for relief if they uncover evidence in the course of discovery of the pending appraisal case to support claims beyond those of garden-variety fiduciary breaches. *Cede & Co. v. Technicolor, Inc.*, 542 A.2d 1182 (Del. 1988). See also *Weinberger v. UOP, Inc.*, 457 A.2d 701, 714 (Del. 1983) (appraisal remedy not adequate "where fraud, misrepresentation, self-dealing, deliberate waste of corporate assets, or gross or palpable overreaching are involved"). The remedy in the general proceedings attacking a merger is limited, however, to injunctive relief and rescissory damages, damages that put the shareholders in the same financial position they would have occupied had the transaction not taken place.

Since *Technicolor,* the consolidated breach of fiduciary duty action and appraisal proceeding has been a fixture of Delaware law. The breach of fiduciary duty claim seeks an equitable remedy that requires a finding of wrongdoing. The appraisal proceeding seeks a statutory determination of fair value that does not require a finding of wrongdoing. In *Technicolor,* the Delaware Supreme Court stated that when presented with such a case, the court should address the breach of fiduciary duty action first, because a finding of liability and the resultant remedy could potentially moot the appraisal proceeding.

The MBCA limits a dissenting shareholder to its appraisal remedy except in certain limited instances, including where: (1) the transaction was not properly authorized or approved; (2) approval was obtained through fraudulent means; and (3) the transaction is an interested transaction and the conflict of interest has not been properly cleansed. MBCA § 13.40(b).

§ 3. STATE CASE LAW ON ACQUISITION FORM

A. THE DE FACTO MERGER DOCTRINE

The advantage of a stock-for-assets acquisition or a stock-for-stock acquisition over a stock swap statutory merger is that, in all but a few states, the shareholders in the purchaser do not have the right to vote on the transaction nor the right to an appraisal of their shares. The states that give voting rights to purchaser shareholders, based on the voting power of the stock issued for use as consideration, are, as noted above, California, New Jersey, Ohio, and Rhode Island. See MBCA § 6.21(f). Purchaser shareholders who are angry at not having voting and appraisal rights in such transactions have taken the matter to court, asking judges to reclassify stock-for-asset transactions or stock-for-stock acquisitions as *de facto* (in reality) statutory mergers. Shareholders in these proceedings ask, in essence, judges to reclassify a given acquisition as a statutory merger and, in so doing, give shareholders their voting and appraisal rights under a state's statutory merger section. With infrequent and largely discredited exceptions, the shareholders have lost. See *Heilbrunn v. Sun Chem. Corp.*, 150 A.2d 755 (Del. 1959).

As noted previously, shareholders in Delaware corporations also do not have appraisal rights if their corporation is the target in an asset acquisition. Shareholders in such acquisitions have complained, arguing that they have been deprived of their appraisal rights through pure transaction form manipulation. The Delaware Supreme Court rejected their *de facto* merger arguments in *Hariton v. Arco Electronic,* 188 A.2d 123 (Del. 1963):

> We now hold that the reorganization here accomplished through § 271 and a mandatory plan of dissolution and distribution is legal. This is so because the sale-of-assets statute and the merger statute are independent of each other. They are, so to speak, of equal dignity, and the framers of a reorganization plan may resort to

either type of corporate mechanics to achieve the desired end.

Courts have also applied the "equal dignity" rule to reject the voting claims of shareholders of the *parent* in a triangular acquisition (see Diagram 9 in Chapter 1, § 5.C), *Equity Group Holdings v. DMG, Inc.*, 576 F. Supp. 1197 (S.D. Fla. 1983), and to reject the voting claims of shareholders of the purchaser in a stock acquisition (see Diagram 7, Step One, in Chapter 1, § 5.A). *Irving Bank Corp. v. Bank of New York Co., Inc.*, 530 N.Y.S.2d 757 (N.Y. Sup. Ct. 1988).

There have been a few courts—a very few—that have found for the plaintiff shareholders under a de facto merger theory. E.g., *Rath v. Rath Packing Co.*, 136 N.W.2d 410 (Iowa 1965); *Farris v. Glen Alden Corp.*, 143 A.2d 25 (Pa. 1958); *Applestein v. United Board & Carton Corp.*, 159 A.2d 146 (N.J. Sup. Ct. 1960). The Iowa and Pennsylvania legislatures subsequently repudiated *Rath* and *Farris* in amendments to the states' corporate codes. *Applestein* is the lone example of a successful and unrepudiated application of the de facto merger doctrine to shareholder voting claims. See NJBCA § 14A:10–12 (codifying the case). In Chapter 5, § 2, we will see that the de facto merger doctrine has considerably more life when target firm *creditors* are the plaintiffs.

The failure of the de facto merger arguments should not be a source of concern. Shareholders can enjoy voting rights in triangular acquisitions or asset acquisitions by negotiating for express provisions in a corporation's certificate of incorporation (or by reducing the price they are willing to pay for stock without those rights). *Pasternak v. Glazer,* 1996 WL 549960 (Del. Ch.) (certificate of incorporation protects the voting rights of the shareholders of the purchasing corporation in a triangular acquisition).

B. SQUEEZE-OUTS OF MINORITY SHAREHOLDERS

In a *cash-out transaction,* the purchaser does not want the shareholders of the seller to end up holding voting common stock in the purchaser. The purchaser wants to pay cash for the seller's assets or, if cash is not available, to pay the seller's shareholders in non-voting investments in the purchaser—debentures (debt) or non-voting preferred or common stock (equity). The traditional methods are found in Diagram 3 (Chapter 1, § 2.A), the cash-for-assets acquisition, and Diagram 5 (Chapter 1, § 3.A), the cash-for-stock acquisition.

A cash-out is also possible using a statutory merger procedure. For a *cash-out statutory merger,* start with Diagram 1 (Chapter 1, § 1.A) and replace the A Corp shares going to the B Corp shareholders with cash. See Diagram 2 (Chapter 1, § 1.B). The end result is identical to the post-transaction position in Diagram 3 (Chapter 1, § 2.A), the cash-for-assets transaction (where the purchaser also assumes all of the seller's liabilities).

Planners use cash merger transactions to eliminate minority shareholders. The minority block is often a group of residual shareholders that did not tender their shares in a first step stock acquisition (see Diagram 7, Step One, in Chapter 1, § 5.A). The transactions are known as *squeeze-outs* (or, less frequently, as *freeze-outs*). In a typical squeeze-out, a corporation holding shares in a partially owned subsidiary drops down a new wholly owned shell subsidiary and merges the partially owned sub with and into the wholly owned sub (see Diagram 7, Step Two, in Chapter 1, § 5.A). The firm gives the minority shareholders in the partially owned subsidiary cash or debt securities (debentures) for their cancelled shares (and a kiss goodbye).

In another type of squeeze-out, a corporation with a minority block of shareholders drops down a new wholly owned shell subsidiary and merges itself into that subsidiary (see Diagram 8 in Chapter 1, § 5.B). All the stock in the corporation is cancelled. The majority shareholders in the original firm receive stock in the surviving firm and the minority shareholders receive cash or debt securities (and a kiss goodbye).

Minority shareholders, who are expelled against their wishes in both types of squeeze-outs, claim foul. For a short time, the Delaware Supreme Court asked corporations to prove a *legitimate business purpose* for cash-out mergers. *Singer v. Magnavox Co.,* 380 A.2d 969 (Del. 1977). The court later overturned the decision, finding it unworkable, and held that merger provisions in corporate codes do authorize such transactions, subject to shareholder claims for fraud or other forms of overreaching. E.g., *Weinberger v. UOP, Inc.,* 457 A.2d 701 (Del. 1983) (a cash-out merger between a parent and its partially owned subsidiary). *Singer* may still be followed in other jurisdictions, however. E.g., *Coggins v. New England Patriots Football Club,* 492 N.E.2d 1112 (Mass. 1986).

A related problem occurs when a firm uses a squeeze-out merger to eliminate its preferred shareholders. In cash-out merger transactions, preferred shareholders who receive cash for their shares have been surprised by the ease with which firms avoid dividend or liquidation preferences or redemption rights attached to their shares. The corporation drops down a wholly owned subsidiary and merges into the subsidiary, exchanging the stock of the subsidiary for the outstanding stock of the corporation. Preferred shares are exchanged for cash, debt or common shares. Dividend arrearages (if any) and liquidation preferences are gone for good.

The preferred shareholders, who hold non-voting stock, can lose their shares without a right to vote on the cash-out merger. The class voting provisions of DGCL § 242 on statutory recapitalizations (amendments to the certificate of incorporation require a majority vote of all affected classes of stock) and the absence of class voting provisions in DGCL § 251 on statutory mergers cause lawyers to use statutory mergers to avoid class voting. Preferred shareholders who do not have class voting rights in the merger have asked judges to block such acquisitions. The courts have refused to do so. See *Federal United Corp. v. Havender,* 11 A.2d 331 (Del. 1940). Courts have also refused to construe the general privileges on preferred shares as having been triggered by a squeeze-out merger. See *Rauch v. RCA Corp.*, 861 F.2d 29 (2d Cir. 1988) (preferred shareholders lost claim for redemption price); *Rothschild Int'l Corp. v. Liggett Group,* 474 A.2d 133 (Del. 1984) (preferred shareholders lost claim for liquidation preference).

Preferred shareholders who wish to protect the special privileges of their shares in cash-out mergers can do so with express language in their investment contracts, embodied in their firm's certificate of incorporation. E.g., *Elliott Assoc., L.P. v. Avatex Corp.,* 715 A.2d 843 (Del. 1998).

§ 4. STOCK EXCHANGE LISTING RULES ON SHAREHOLDER VOTING

A. INTRODUCTION TO STOCK EXCHANGE LISTING REQUIREMENTS

Our stock markets consist of purchasers and sellers of securities trading at mutually agreeable prices. Markets that are deep (have many participants), liquid (have substantial trading volume at any one time), efficient (trading expenses are minimized) and honest (free of manipulation and fraud) are a national treasure. A healthy secondary trading market means firms can raise money to capitalize their businesses at lower cost. Stock prices act as guideposts to optimal allocations of capital and other investment. Small investors participate in the trading. The markets also provide employment for banks, institutional investors, broker-dealers, accountants, and lawyers—professionals that service the trading markets.

For the past several decades our stock markets have consisted of two national exchanges: the New York Stock Exchange (NYSE), which is nicknamed the "Big Board," and the much smaller NYSE American (formerly the American Stock Exchange); six regional stock exchanges (Boston, Cincinnati, Midwest (Chicago), Pacific (Los Angeles and San Francisco), Philadelphia (Philadelphia and Miami), and Spokane (local mining and Canadian issues, non-reporting trades); and our over-the-counter, broker-dealer market (Nasdaq is its largest, automated component). Options on stock are also traded on these exchanges and also on two other exchanges, the Chicago Board Options Exchange (CBOE) and the Nasdaq International Securities Exchange (ISE).

Under the SEA, exchanges must register with the Securities and Exchange Commission (SEC). The SEC has oversight responsibility for exchange rules and proceedings. The SEA classifies stock exchanges as "Self-Regulatory Organizations" (SROs). They have their own operating rules and structure, and they control their membership with admission and disciplinary rules. Congress has granted the SEC power to oversee SRO operations, to approve all SRO rules and regulations, and, in a rarely-used power, to write SRO rules itself.

Each exchange has listing requirements for firms whose securities are traded on the exchange. Companies agree to meet those requirements in a *listing contract* signed with the exchange. An exchange may impose penalties for violations of a listing contract that include suspension of trading in a corporation's stock and, in extreme cases, delisting of the firm's securities.

An exchange designs listing requirements to attract stock trading volume to the exchange's members: Firms that meet an exchange's listing requirements are, in theory, more attractive to traders in the market than firms that do not. In signing a listing contract, firms promise, among other things, to maintain a minimum float in their securities (i.e., a sufficient number of shares available for trading purposes), to respect conditions on corporate actions that affect outstanding securities, and to be candid and truthful about firm affairs.

Exchanges have strong incentives to provide rules and enforcement mechanisms that increase investors' returns, and thereby increase investors' demand for listed securities. An exchange has an incentive to create listing rules that are neither too harsh nor too lenient. If the exchange listing requirements are too harsh, firms may view listing as imposing too many costs for the benefit of a listing and choose to list on a different, competing exchange. There will be too few securities to trade. If the listing requirements are too lenient, too many firms may engage in acts that defraud or otherwise disadvantage investors, and these traders will not have confidence in the *bona fides* of the firms listed. In an important sense, the listing requirements and how and whether they are enforced are an important part of the public image of any exchange.

B. THE NYSE LISTING REQUIREMENTS ON SHAREHOLDER VOTING IN ACQUISITIONS

The NYSE Listed Company Manual has an important shareholder voting requirement that affects acquisitions of firms whose securities are listed on the exchange. The requirement applies as *an addition* to the shareholder voting requirements mandated by state statutory law.

Listed firms must agree to obtain shareholder approval prior to the issuance of common stock in any transaction, if either (a) the common stock has or will have upon issuance voting power equal to or in excess of 20 percent of the voting power outstanding before the issuance of such stock or (b) if the number of shares of common stock to be issued is or will be equal to or in excess of 20 percent of the number of shares of common stock outstanding before the issuance of the stock. NYSE Listed Co. Manual § 312.03(c)(1) & (2). The National Association of Securities Dealers Automated Quotations System (Nasdaq) has a similar rule. Nasdaq Marketplace Rule 5635. Note that technically the exchange does not require the vote, but rather requires that a firm's certificate of incorporation, written to comply with exchange listing requirements, compels the vote.

The voting majority required in the NYSE Listed Company Manual is different than the voting majority required by most state corporate codes. The NYSE Manual requires only a majority vote of all shares represented or present at the shareholder meeting; that is, votes cast "for" must exceed votes cast "against" plus abstentions. NYSE Listed Co. Manual § 312.07. While the NYSE takes quorum into consideration (no legally binding action can be taken at a shareholder meeting unless a quorum of shares is represented in person or by proxy), its Manual does not provide for a separate quorum requirement. Instead, the NYSE leaves the quorum requirement to state corporate codes to avoid confusion. Most state corporate codes on acquisitions, if applicable, require, by contrast, a majority vote of all *outstanding* shares entitled to vote without regard to quorum. See, e.g., DGCL § 251(c). Thus, while the NYSE takes the concept of quorum into consideration, state corporate codes often do not.

The NYSE also has a special shareholder voting rule for acquisitions in which a senior officer of the acquirer has a substantial stake in the target company, *conflict-of-interest acquisitions*. Acquirer shareholder approval is necessary prior to the issuance of common stock, or of securities convertible into or exercisable for common stock, where such securities are issued as consideration in a transaction or series of related transactions in which a director, officer or substantial security holder of the acquirer has a five percent or greater interest (or such persons collectively have a ten percent or greater interest), directly or indirectly, in the target company or assets to be acquired or in the consideration to be paid in the transaction or series of related transactions and the present or potential issuance of common stock, or securities convertible into common stock, could result in an issuance that exceeds either five percent of the number of shares of common stock or five percent of the voting power outstanding before the issuance. NYSE Listed Co. Manual § 312.03(b)(ii). Nasdaq requires a vote in conflict-of-interest acquisitions if the consideration offered represents five percent or more of the outstanding shares of the purchaser in either number or voting power. NASD Marketplace Rule 5635(a)(2).

CHAPTER 5
SUCCESSORSHIP ISSUES

Successorship in acquisitions is the somewhat awkward reference to a body of issues on the location of constituent party assets and liabilities once an acquisition has closed. Successorship issues usually (but not always) turn on the form of the transaction under state corporate codes.

State corporate law codes provide that, when two firms merge, the surviving firm (or the new firm) succeeds to the assets and liabilities of the merged firm or firms automatically, as a matter of law. DGCL § 259; MBCA § 11.07(a)(3). Documents of title in the name of the seller are, without need of a formal re-registration (although it may be good practice to do so), considered to be owned by the surviving firm. All creditors of the seller can sue the survivor on their obligations.

The survivor in a merger, of course, retains its own, pre-acquisition assets and liabilities. The survivor has not changed its formal identity. A similar rule applies to *both* sides of a stock acquisition. When a firm is acquired through the acquisition of its stock, the firm automatically retains all prior assets and liabilities because the corporation continues its prior independent legal existence. The purchaser retains its own assets and liabilities because it has not changed its formal identity either.

In contrast, when a purchaser acquires some or all of the assets of the seller, the general rule is that the purchaser does not assume any liabilities, except those specifically identified as assumed in the asset acquisition agreement. Courts, however, will force purchasers to pay un-assumed seller liabilities when the courts decide that equity requires it.

§ 1. ASSIGNMENTS OF LICENSES, LEASEHOLDS AND OTHER VALUABLE CONTRACT RIGHTS

If the target in an acquisition has valuable contract rights, at issue is whether the contracts will transfer to the purchaser through the acquisition. Some of the contracts are silent on the matter, some have general *anti-assignment clauses* and others have clauses specific to acquisitions, so-called *change in control* clauses. Change in control clauses present the easiest case; the terms of the clause control the effect of an acquisition on the contract rights and obligations. Most change in control clauses stop all transfers of the contract rights in all forms of acquisitions unless a party on the other side of the contract gives prior written consent to the transfer. The more difficult cases are presented by contracts that are either silent or only have general anti-assignment clauses.

A. ASSET ACQUISITIONS

In asset acquisitions each asset is individually transferred by agreement from the target to the purchaser. One of the disadvantages of an asset acquisition is that the lawyers must transfer individually title to each asset—re-deed land, re-title vehicles and so on—and each contract right. Contract rights held by the seller that are silent on assignment do not transfer without the consent of an opposite party if the contracts are *personal* (contracts for personal services, for example); contracts that are not personal (leases) transfer without the consent of an opposite party. Contracts that are not personal (leases) with general anti-assignment (or anti-transfer) clauses also do not transfer without the consent of an opposite party.

Problems can and do arise with asset acquisitions. In *Chemetall GMBH v. ZR Energy, Inc.,* 320 F.3d 714 (7th Cir. 2003), Chemetall acquired Morton International's zirconium powder business by means of an asset purchase. Joseph Fraval, a 20-year employee of Morton, left Morton three years after the acquisition. He then formed a competing company, Zr Energy, Inc., with another former Morton employee. Chemetall sued Fraval for breaching his Employee Trade Secret Agreement with Morton. That agreement prohibited Fraval from using or disclosing information regarding "improvements, inventions, or know-how relating to" Morton's business. The agreement was to be effective during and after Fraval's employment and was to "inure to the benefit of [Morton's] successors and assigns." However, the Asset Purchase Agreement between Chemetall and Morton did not *explicitly* assign Fraval's agreement to Chemetall—that is, the agreement was not included in the "purchased assets," as such term was defined in the Asset Purchase Agreement. Nevertheless, the District Court found enough "intent" in other provisions of the Asset Purchase Agreement to conclude that the parties meant to include Fraval's agreement as a transferred asset.

The Seventh Circuit affirmed, and the lawyers who drafted the Asset Purchase Agreement breathed a huge sigh of relief!

Debt security holders can also throw a wrench into a company's plan to sell significant assets. Debt security holders are contract claimants on the company's assets, and their contract is typically called a *trust indenture.* The trust indenture sets out the rights of debt security holders with respect to security over the assets of the company (i.e., collateral), defines any restrictions on the company's operations and financing activities, assigns the relative ranking of the indebtedness, and grants the rights and remedies that are available to the debt security holders if the trust indenture covenants are violated.

One boiler plate covenant—a *successor obligor clause*—affects acquisitions in particular. The clause requires an acceptable survivor (the purchaser in an asset acquisition or the survivor to a merger) to assume the debt securities of the seller. The theory is that the debt should follow the assets that generate the cash flow needed to pay down the debt. A default on a successor obligor clause may result in the debt securities being accelerated—that is, the outstanding principal and interest on the debt securities become *immediately due and payable.*

Sharon Steel Corp. v. Chase Manhattan Bank, 691 F.2d 1039 (2d Cir. 1982), presents the challenging situation where a seller with debt securities outstanding sells off assets in a *piecemeal fashion.* That is, it sells substantial assets (but not substantially all of its assets) to one purchaser and then, later on, literally sells all of its remaining assets to a different purchaser. Which sale, if any, triggered the successor obligor clause? Which purchaser is required to assume the debt securities of the seller?

In *Sharon Steel,* the second purchaser argued that it literally bought all of the seller's remaining assets and thus triggered the successor obligor clause. However, the debt security holders clearly desired that the first purchaser assume their obligations, because they brought suit through their indenture trustee. They claimed that the successor obligor clause was breached when the second purchaser attempted to assume their debt.

In resolving the case, the Second Circuit highlighted that a successor obligor clause benefits both borrowers and lenders. The clause enables the former to sell entire businesses and liquidate, to consolidate or merge with another corporation, or to liquidate their operating assets and enter a new field free of the public debt. However, the clause also ensures that lenders are assured a degree of continuity of assets. Finding that the seller and the second purchaser had attempted to manipulate the successor obligor clause to the seller's favor, the court found that the seller had breached the clause. The court held that boilerplate successor obligor clauses do not permit assignment of the public debt to another party in the course of a liquidation unless "all or substantially all" of the assets of the company *at the time the plan of liquidation is determined upon* are transferred to a single purchaser. This, of course, was not done in this case.

B. STATUTORY MERGERS

All state codes have specific statutes on the effect of a statutory merger on the preexisting rights and obligations of the constituent parties. DGCL §§ 259 & 261. As a general matter, the statutes contain language directing that all rights and obligations of the constituent parties pass to the surviving entity in a statutory merger as a matter of law. Courts have held that the merger statutes override most contracts that are implicitly or expressly non-assignable or non-transferable. The courts do so by holding that a merger transaction "vests" rights in the survivor and is not a technical "assignment" or "transfer." In other words, if a target firm holds non-assignable contracts, it can merge into a purchaser and the purchaser can claim rights under the contracts. For example, an expressly non-assignable lease will transfer in a statutory acquisition. E.g., *Dodier Realty & Inv. Co. v. St. Louis Nat'l Baseball Club,* 238 S.W.2d 321 (Mo. 1951).

There is a significant exception, however. The Sixth Circuit has held that, because patent rights are creatures of federal and not state law, federal law on patent licenses overrides the effect-of-merger provisions in state corporate codes. *PPG Indus., Inc. v. Guardian Indus. Corp.,* 597 F.2d 1090 (6th Cir. 1979). Patent licenses do not transfer as a matter of law in mergers. Since patent licenses are "personal," only those licenses with express provisions permitting assignment or transfer will transfer in statutory mergers. There is some question, however, whether the case turned on the specific language of a state corporate code provision, language that has since been changed. E.g., *TXO Prod. Co. v. M.D. Mark., Inc.*, 999 S.W.2d 137 (Tex. Ct. App. 1999).

C. STOCK ACQUISITIONS

Stock acquisitions—transferring control of a corporation through the transfer of its stock—do not affect contracts of the corporation unless a contract is explicit on the matter. Contracts that are silent or have general anti-assignment clauses remain in force through the acquisition. Courts have held that general anti-assignment clauses only stop legal assignments or transfers of the contract itself and that there has been no such transfer or assignment in a stock acquisition. Only the investment contracts represented by the stock have been transferred. E.g., *Branmar Theatre Co. v. Branmar*, 264 A.2d 526 (Del. 1970). Only contracts that have change in control clauses that protect specifically against stock ownership changes apply to stock acquisitions.

§ 2. STATE LAW ON SUCCESSOR LIABILITY

In statutory mergers the liabilities of the disappearing corporation reattach to ("vest in") the survivor by operation of law. In stock acquisitions, the liabilities of the target remain with the target; only ownership of the target changes.

In asset acquisitions, the problem cases occur when a purchaser elects *not* to assume the liabilities of the seller in the acquisition. The seller accepts compensation for its assets and applies the compensation against its liabilities when it dissolves. Some creditors may not get paid before dissolution or may have claims that arise after dissolution. The most sympathetic claimants are those *long-tail* or *contingent* claimants whose injuries do not occur until long after the acquisition and the dissolution of the seller; products liability claimants are a high profile subgroup.

Dissatisfaction with any remedies such creditors may have against the seller's shareholders (who are difficult to find) has led frustrated creditors to make claims against the *purchaser* of the assets under the doctrine of *successor liability*. The creditors argue that the decoupling of the seller's assets and liabilities was inequitable. After all, it is the collection of assets—operating as a business—that generates the cash necessary to pay down liabilities.

The general rule on successor liability in asset acquisitions has long been subject to a common law, four-part traditional test. In the mid-1970s, several new tests emerged in the case law. Some of the new tests are in state law—the most important are in California and Michigan (each state has a follower or two)—and some are in federal law developed by federal courts struggling to apply open-ended federal statutes. States fall into two camps on successor liability. The larger camp, represented by Illinois, follows the traditional rule with the four exceptions. The smaller camp, represented by California,

Michigan and New Jersey, takes a more aggressive stance in favor of the creditors.

The traditional state law test for successor liability in asset acquisitions is that the purchasing corporation assumes the seller's liabilities when: (1) it expressly agrees to assume them in the contract; (2) the asset sale amounts to a *de facto merger;* (3) the purchaser is a *mere continuation* of the seller; or (4) the sale is for the fraudulent purpose of escaping liability for the seller's obligations. E.g., *Cargo Parter AG v. Albatrans, Inc.,* 352 F.3d 41 (2d Cir. 2003); *Ruiz v. Blentech Corp.,* 89 F.3d 320 (7th Cir. 1996).

In most states, the de facto merger exception and the mere continuity exception operate in much the same fashion. The owners of the seller must take stock in (i.e., become owners of) the surviving firm. In the mere continuity exception, the owners of the seller are the only owners of the purchaser; in the de facto merger exception, the owners of the seller join the prior owners of the purchaser. In both exceptions, the purchaser must continue the essential operating business of the seller in much the same form. Finally, the seller must dissolve or otherwise become a shell (have no assets).

Michigan has expanded and renamed the de facto merger exception. Its *continuity-of-enterprise* exception relaxes the requirement that the seller owners take stock in the purchaser. *Turner v. Bituminous Casualty Co.,* 244 N.W.2d 873 (Mich. 1976). California adopts a fifth test, the *products line* exception. *Ray v. Alad Corp.,* 560 P.2d 3 (Cal. 1977). See also *Ramirez v. Amsted Indus., Inc.,* 431 A.2d

811 (N.J. 1981). The California products line exception provides that a corporation that purchases a manufacturing business and continues to produce the seller's line of products assumes strict liability in tort for defects in units of the same product line *previously manufactured and distributed* by the seller (despite the fact that the purchaser *did not actually make* the particular products in question). The exception applies in cases involving tort claims where: (1) the plaintiff lacks an adequate remedy against the seller/manufacturer; (2) the purchaser knows about product risks associated with the line of products that it continues to produce; and (3) the seller transfers goodwill associated with the product line to the purchaser.

Wary purchasers use a combination of strategies to minimize nasty surprises from unpriced, unwittingly absorbed liabilities from asset acquisitions. First, purchasers conduct a thorough due diligence investigation of the seller's business, liabilities and insurance before the closing. Second, purchasers insist on several specialized provisions in the acquisition agreement. The purchaser agrees to assume only specifically identified liabilities and secures a comprehensive and thorough set of specific representations and warranties from the seller warranting that there are no other outstanding problems that could lead to additional liabilities. There are, among others, specific reps and warranties on litigation, labor disputes, products liability and environmental claims. The reps and warranties are backed by an indemnification clause from the seller and, if possible, from the seller's shareholders. The seller may secure the indemnification obligation by funding an escrow account or by providing a bond or some other form of purchaser insurance. Third, the purchaser may use a triangular acquisition to place the new assets in a wholly owned subsidiary. Fourth, to the extent possible in light of business imperatives, the purchaser may minimize the appearance of business continuity, avoiding factors that might lead a court to impose successor liability. And fifth, the purchaser may require the seller to maintain its separate corporate existence and its own liability insurance for a specific period of time following the sale (this is not practical in a tax-free reorganization).

§ 3. FEDERAL LAW ON SUCCESSOR LIABILITY

In 1973, the U.S. Supreme Court fashioned a special rule of successor liability for unfair labor practice claims brought under the National Labor Relations Act (NLRA). *Golden State Bottling Co. v. NLRB,* 414 U.S. 168 (1973). If a new employer has acquired substantial assets of its predecessor and continued without interruption or substantial change the predecessor's business operations, those employees who have been retained and who have claims against the predecessor can reassert their old claims against the new employer. The successor must have notice (actual or constructive) of the old claims, however.

The federal circuit and district courts have began using this *notice test* whenever federal labor statutes created the liability in issue. The courts have applied the notice test in finding successor liability in employment discrimination cases—see, e.g., *Rojas v. TK Comm., Inc.*, 87 F.3d 745 (5th Cir. 1996) (Title VII); *EEOC v. Vucitech,* 842 F.2d 936 (7th Cir. 1988) (same)—and in cases on liability for pension obligations (delinquent pension contributions, termination liability and multi-employer withdrawal liability). E.g., *Chicago Truck Drivers, Helpers & Warehouse Workers Union Pension Fund v. Tasemkin,* 59 F.3d 48 (7th Cir. 1995); *Stotter Div. of Graduate Plastic Co. v. District 65, United Auto Workers,* 991 F.2d 997 (2d Cir. 1993); *Brend v. Sames Corp.,* 2002 WL 1488877 (N.D. Ill.). See also *Steinbach v. Hubbard,* 51 F.3d 843 (9th Cir. 1995) (a claim for minimum wage under the Fair Labor Standards Act).

There is a split in the federal circuit courts, however, on whether there is a federal common law of successor liability under federal environmental statutes, such as CERCLA (the Superfund Act). Two Circuit Courts, the Sixth and the Ninth Circuits, say no, state law should apply. *Atchison, Topeka & Santa Fe Ry. Co. v. Brown & Bryant,* 132 F.3d 1295 (9th Cir. 1997); *Anspec Co. v. Johnson Controls, Inc.,* 922 F.2d 1240 (6th Cir. 1991). The Seventh Circuit has applied the *Golden State Bottling Co.* notice test. *North Shore Gas Co. v. Salomon,* 152 F.3d 642 (7th Cir. 1998). See also *Smith Land & Improvement Corp. v. Celotex Corp.,* 851 F.2d 86 (3d Cir. 1988). The smart money is on the application of state law, given the U.S. Supreme Court's clear hostility towards the development of a federal common law as expressed in *U.S. v. Bestfoods,* 524 U.S. 51 (1998). E.g., *New York v. Nat'l Serv. Indus., Inc.,* 460 F.3d 201 (2d Cir. 2006).

The federal courts applying a federal law on successor liability in environmental cases are also split on whether they should stay with the traditional common law test for successor liability or if they should follow the more liberal substantial continuity rule. The substantial continuity rule relaxes the mere continuity plank of the common law test that requires that the ownership and business of the successor be identical to the ownership and business of the predecessor.

§ 4. THE SPECIAL CASE OF COLLECTIVE BARGAINING AGREEMENTS

The U.S. Supreme Court has decided a series of cases on the duty of a purchasing corporation to the employees of the selling corporation when those employees are unionized and have a current collective bargaining agreement in place with the selling corporation. A collective bargaining agreement is a contract between workers and an employer. Parties litigate claims arising out of a collective bargaining agreement under § 301 of the NLRA. Most collective bargaining agreements, but not all, have arbitration clauses creating a duty to arbitrate grievances.

Successors have been held bound by a duty to arbitrate under a predecessor's collective bargaining agreement if the agreement had not expired at the time of the acquisition and there is a substantial continuity of identity in the business enterprise before and after the acquisition. *John Wiley & Sons, Inc. v. Livingston,* 376 U.S. 543 (1964). In applying the standard, the court looks to whether the purchaser has continued the operations of the seller and has hired a significant percentage of the seller's employees. See *Howard Johnson Co. v. Detroit Local Joint Executive Bd.,* 417 U.S. 249 (1974).

The U.S. Supreme Court has also held that a purchasing corporation has a lesser duty, the duty to bargain with the labor union of the selling corporation, so long as the purchasing corporation is in fact a successor of the selling corporation and the majority of its employees were employed by its predecessor. *Fall River Dyeing & Finishing v. NLRB,* 482 U.S. 27 (1987). Imposing a duty to bargain on a successor employer is not as severe as imposing the old collective bargaining terms, including a duty to arbitrate, on a successor employer. *NLRB v. Burns Int'l Sec. Serv., Inc.,* 406 U.S. 272 (1972). A purchasing corporation under a duty to bargain is not bound to observe the substantive terms of the collective bargaining contract the union had negotiated with the selling corporation. The factual distinction between cases that require a successor's duty to arbitrate as opposed to the lesser duty to bargain is less than clear in the case law.

Imposing a duty to bargain on a successor is significant for various reasons. It recognizes a bargaining relationship between an employer and a union and an agency relationship between a union and a group of employees. Without it, a union has to engage in an organizing drive, which is typically very costly and has an uncertain outcome. When the duty to bargain applies, the employer must bargain with the union over mandatory topics, risking an economic strike if a contract cannot be signed. Under the NLRA it is an unfair labor practice for an employer or a union to refuse to bargain collectively, and the employer must meet at reasonable times and confer in good faith with respect to wages, hours, and other terms and conditions of employment. While the parties have an obligation to meet and confer in good faith, that obligation does not compel either party to agree to a proposal or require the making of a concession. Moreover, the new employer may be unable to institute changes unilaterally in mandatory topics without first bargaining to impasse. Finally, the duty to bargain forces the parties to disclose information in certain defined contexts. When, for example, an employer claims that it is financially unable to meet the union's demands, it must corroborate such claims on request.

The courts have made it clear that an asset purchaser cannot avoid a duty to bargain, or in an appropriate case a duty to arbitrate, by discriminating against employees of the seller because of their union status. For example, a new employer may not discover from the old employer the union sympathies of its employees and refuse to hire those identified as sympathetic. The cases suggest that, if a new employer maintains the old operations intact, hiring new, inexperienced, non-union employees in preference to experienced, union employees, judges will presume anti-union animus on the part of the new employer. By contrast, if the purchaser changes operations substantially so that experience in the old operation would be of little value in the new operation, no such inference is warranted.

§ 5. LIABILITY AVOIDANCE SCAMS AND COUNTERACTING LEGAL RULES

If only a portion of a firm's assets are being transferred, if a firm is being liquidated after a business failure, or if the seller values some significant assets or liabilities more highly than the purchaser does, the parties typically will choose to structure the transaction as a sale of assets, rather than as a merger, and identify specifically which assets and liabilities are transferred. Alternatively, in a case in which the purchaser wants only some of the seller's assets, prior to the sale the seller could push down (transfer) the desired assets into a new, wholly-owned subsidiary and then use a statutory merger or stock sale to effectively sell the desired assets to the purchaser.

In an asset acquisition, so long as the purchaser pays fair market value for the assets it buys and the seller applies the consideration received in the acquisition to the debts of the business, creditors of the seller are made better off by a rule that permits the parties to allocate assets and liabilities to the highest valuing user. Indeed, an asset acquisition may actually maximize the value available to seller creditors. If, by contrast, the seller in the acquisition uses the transaction as a vehicle to avoid applying the money received to the debts of the business and instead distributes the consideration received to its shareholders, then creditors are worse off.

Opportunistic sellers have used three strategies to hurt creditors. All three involve an asset sale. In each, those who control the seller after the asset acquisition, a non-operating company holding passive assets (cash or stock in the purchaser) and still on the hook for all long-tail liabilities, attempt to distribute the assets to themselves and other shareholders ahead of the creditors.

The first strategy calls for the control group to liquidate and dissolve the seller, passing the sale proceeds out in liquidation proceeds. The dissolution provisions of state corporate codes regulate such distributions. The second strategy requires the control group to cause the seller to declare either a one-time, extraordinary dividend or share redemption using the sale proceeds as the dividend or the repurchase payment. The *legal capital* statutes in state corporate codes and state statutes on *fraudulent conveyances* apply to limit the distributions.

And a third strategy (the mafia version) requires the control group to cause the seller to enter into a variety of sweetheart deals with the controlling shareholders, milking the assets over time. Controlling shareholders can distribute corporate assets as excessive salary payments, through sales of the assets for less-than-fair-market value, through loans to shareholders at less-than-market interest rates, through guarantees of shareholder debt, through pledges to shareholders on loans from shareholders to the firm in which the firm defaults on the underlying debt and the assets are forfeited to the shareholders, and so on. Doctrines on breach of fiduciary duty, statutes on conflict-of-interest, and state statutes on fraudulent conveyances apply to this strategy.

In both the second and third strategies, after the shareholders milk the seller of all its assets, the seller becomes a shell company, the shareholders then often stop the payment of the seller's annual state franchise fees, and the state dissolves the shell "administratively," as a matter of law, for non-payment.

The success of the three strategies depends in part on the deficiencies in the countervailing law and in serendipity. If the claimants sit on their rights, then they lose them. *State bulk sales laws,* still in place in a dwindling number of states, force sellers in asset sales to notify all claimants of an asset sale to put them on notice of their potential vulnerability.

The doctrine of successor liability in asset sales that holds the *purchaser* liable for the debts of the seller is a doctrine that reflects our dissatisfaction with (and ignorance of, perhaps) these other legal protections.

A. DISSOLUTION PROCEDURES IN STATE CORPORATE CODES

All state corporation codes provide for the dissolution of corporations. Under the traditional approach, state codes have permitted corporations to dissolve and pay out any surplus to shareholders after paying off all *known* creditors. After dissolution, the corporation winds up its affairs, paying off its creditors and distributing any surplus to shareholders. Most traditional corporate law statutes bar claims of creditors who come forward after the statutorily mandated notice and claims period. As to known creditors, this system is satisfactory; if the asset seller receives fair value for the assets, existing creditors of the seller are no worse off and, when the seller dissolves, have an opportunity to present their claims for payment ahead of any distributions to shareholders.

But this statutory structure provides an opportunity for asset purchasers and sellers to share the gains of avoiding the claims of *unknown* future tort and environmental creditors—the *long-tail* or *contingent* claimants. Only limited protection of such claims is available under traditional statutes. E.g., MBCA § 14.07(c) (1979). The 1979 MBCA provision authorized suits against a dissolved corporation for two years after dissolution. Some state courts held that the provision barred claims that arose after the two-year period; other courts held the statute did not provide a statute of limitations but only affected a claimant's ability to sue a firm as opposed to its shareholders. Regardless, whether the claimants sue the firm or its shareholders, the claimants must eventually pursue the dissolved firm shareholders individually and then only to the extent of their personal distribution (or a pro rata share of the claim if less). The old shareholders can be hard to trace.

In recognition of the problems with the 1979 provision, the MBCA has gone through four major revisions: 1984, 1999, 2010 and 2016. The 1984 version, followed in several states, extends the claim period to five years from the traditional two- or three-year period on the assumption that most of the long-tail claims would arise during that period. MBCA § 14.07(c) (1984). At the same time the 1984 revision clarified that the section had the effect of a statute of limitations on long-term claims and not just a statement on the capacity of a dissolved firm to be sued. MBCA § 14.07(d) (1984). When not barred, claims may be enforced against the dissolved corporation to the extent of undistributed assets and against shareholders to the extent of the shareholders' pro rata share of the obligation or the value of the assets distributed to them in liquidation, whichever is less. The 2000 MBCA amendments reduced the five-year period to three years. The 2016 MBCA retains the three-year period.

Delaware has recently taken an innovative approach. Like the traditional approach, the DGCL requires that a dissolving corporation make provision to pay all contingent, conditional, or immature contractual claims known to the corporation—the traditional rule. DGCL §§ 280–282. Section 281(b) also requires, however, that a dissolving corporation formulate a plan of distribution that provides for claims "that have not been made known to the corporation or that have not arisen but that, based on facts known to the corporation or successor entity, are likely to arise or to become known to the corporation or successor entity within 10 years after the date of dissolution." If the amount provided is insufficient, claimants may pursue shareholders for amounts received in the liquidating distribution or their pro rata share of the claim, whichever is less, subject to the statute of limitations on the claim itself. DGCL § 282(a). But directors of a dissolved corporation are not liable personally if such a plan of distribution was formulated properly and the amounts set aside were reasonable at the time the plan was made. DGCL § 281(c).

For shareholders in dissolving Delaware corporations who want to cut off long-tail claims, a safe harbor procedure is available. A dissolving corporation may petition the Court of Chancery to determine the amount and form of security that is

> reasonably likely to be sufficient to provide compensation for claims that have not been made known to the corporation or that have not risen but that, based on facts known to the corporation or successor entity, are likely to arise or to become known to the corporation or successor entity within 5 years after the date of dissolution or such longer period of time as the Court of Chancery may determine not to exceed 10 years after the date of dissolution.

DGCL § 280(c)(3). See *In re RegO Co.*, 623 A.2d 92 (Del. Ch. 1992) (holding that assets held in trust for benefit of known and likely creditors were insufficient). The court may appoint a guardian *ad litem* to represent the long-tail claimants. DGCL § 280(c)(3). On compliance with the court decree, shareholders are not liable for any claims begun after the three-year winding-up period established by § 278 (see DGCL § 282(b)), and directors are not personally liable to any claimants. DGCL § 282(c).

The MBCA now follows Delaware's lead. MBCA § 14.08(a), similar in effect to the Delaware provision, creates a court proceeding that gives directors and shareholders a safe harbor in providing for contingent claims that are not barred by publication. The dissolving firm provides security for claims that are reasonably estimated to arise after the effective date of dissolution.

B. LEGAL CAPITAL OR INSOLVENCY STATUTES

Limitations on dividends and redemptions are found in the statutes of all corporate codes. The statutes are in a state of evolution; a few states (including Delaware) have the old statutes (*legal* or *stated capital statutes*) with shares of stock with par values, while most other states have provisions (*insolvency statutes*) that do not depend on the stated capital concept. Section 6.40(c) of the MBCA, a modern statute, provides that no distribution may be made to shareholders if, after giving it effect, (1) the corporation would not be able to pay its debts as they become due in the usual course of business (the *equity insolvency test*); or (2) the corporation's total assets would be less than the sum of its total liabilities plus the amount that would be needed, if the corporation were to be dissolved at the time of the distribution, to satisfy the preferential rights upon dissolution of shareholders whose preferential rights are superior to those receiving the distribution (the *balance sheet test*). Any director that votes for or assents to a distribution made in violation of § 6.40(c) is personally liable to the corporation for the amount of the distribution deemed illegal. MBCA § 8.32(a). Any proceeding against a director must be brought within two years of the illegal distribution. MBCA § 8.32(c)(1). A director found liable can assert contribution rights against other directors and against any shareholder who received part of an illegal distribution for the amount received if the shareholder knew the distribution was illegal when made. MBCA § 8.32(b).

C. FRAUDULENT CONVEYANCE STATUTES

Fraudulent conveyance laws are aimed at protecting creditors' right to execute judgments on assets of debtors in the event of a default. If a debtor has transferred property to frustrate collection efforts by creditors, creditors may sue under state law to set aside any improper transfer and obtain a lien on the transferred property to the full extent of their claims. Similarly, trustees in bankruptcy (or debtors in possession) are empowered under federal bankruptcy law to recover for the benefit of creditors the value of any property improperly removed from the bankrupt debtor's estate. Fraudulent conveyance provisions are found in § 548 of the Bankruptcy Code and in state acts. State provisions are typically modeled on the Uniform Fraudulent Conveyance Act (1918) (UFCA), the Uniform Fraudulent Transfer Act (1984) (UFTA), or the newer Uniform Voidable Transactions Act (2014) (UVTA) (adopted by 26 states as of 2025, including New York and California). A trustee in bankruptcy is also empowered to invoke state fraudulent conveyance law to invalidate pre-bankruptcy transfers. Bankruptcy Code § 544(b).

The UVTA and the insolvency statutes in state corporate codes (such as § 6.40(c) of the MBCA noted above) overlap, but the UVTA is broader in scope. The MBCA applies only to distributions by a corporation to its shareholders "in respect of any of its shares." UVTA § 4(a) applies to any transfer of property by any debtor to anybody and for any purpose whenever there is *actual* or *constructive* intent to defraud creditors.

Thus, the UVTA, like the UFTA and UFCA before it, catches transfers that show an "actual intent to hinder, delay or defraud creditors" (the *actual intent test*). UVTA § 4(a)(1). The *constructive intent test* is in UVTA §§ 4(a)(2) and 5. A transfer is deemed fraudulent when the debtor receives value that is less than reasonably equivalent value and either (a) the debtor was engaged or was about to engage in a business or a transaction for which the remaining assets of the debtor were unreasonably small in relation to the business or transaction or (b) the debtor intended to incur, or believed or reasonably should have believed that the debtor would incur, debts beyond the debtor's ability to pay as they became due. UVTA § 4(a)(2)(A) & (B). Alternatively, a transfer is deemed fraudulent if the debtor made the transfer without receiving a reasonably equivalent value in exchange for the transfer and the debtor was insolvent at that time or the debtor became insolvent as a result of the transfer. UVTA § 5(a).

Subject to certain exceptions, when a fraudulent transfer is found, a creditor is entitled to obtain the avoidance of the transfer to the extent necessary to satisfy the creditor's claim. Alternatively, the creditor can receive an attachment or other provisional remedy against the asset transferred or, in certain cases, other property of the transferee. UVTA § 7(a).

Over the years, federal courts have struggled with whether the UFTA and its predecessor, the UFCA, provide relief for creditors in bankrupt companies that have recently undergone leveraged buyouts (LBOs) or other leveraged recapitalizations. See, e.g., *Pay 'N Pak Stores v. Court Square Capital LTD,* 141 F.3d 1178 (9th Cir. 1998) (jury verdict against an application of a fraudulent conveyance act to a leveraged buyout affirmed). See Chapter 1, § 5.D, for a description of an LBO. The fraudulent conveyance attack on failed LBOs has succeeded in a limited number of cases. In *Lippi v. City Bank,* 955 F.2d 599 (9th Cir. 1992), and *U.S. v. Tabor Court Realty Corp.,* 803 F.2d 1288 (3d Cir. 1986), lenders to the purchasers in an LBO had their security interests set aside as fraudulent conveyances, and in *Lippi* and *Wieboldt Stores v. Schottenstein,* 94 B.R. 488 (N.D. Ill. 1988), departing shareholders in the target had their stock sales set aside as fraudulent conveyances (they were constructive redemptions).

Boyer v. Crown Stock Distr., Inc., 587 F.3d 787 (7th Cir. 2009), represents a rare (and successful) challenge to a leveraged buyout of a target's assets, rather than of its stock. As part of the LBO, the lion's share of the target's cash was distributed to the target's shareholders. The purchaser, saddled with massive debt incurred to make the asset purchase, and having received very little cash as part of the deal (the target used its cash to pay the aforementioned dividend), limped along and eventually filed for bankruptcy. The court affirmed the bankruptcy judge's determination that the LBO constituted a fraudulent transfer. The purchaser had made payments and incurred obligations without receiving "reasonably equivalent value" in return. The court noted that even if the purchaser was not actually insolvent *ab initio,* as a result of the lack of equivalence it began life with "unreasonably small" assets given the nature of its business. Moreover, because the dividend to the target's shareholders was an "integral part" of the LBO, the court held that the dividend was also fraudulent.

Despite the cases just mentioned, most fraudulent conveyance claims fail. Plaintiffs often flounder under the heavy burden of proving that the target firm was insolvent at the time of the LBO. Parties to the LBO, the new equity owners and the new lenders (defendants in a fraudulent conveyance statute claim), do not invest unless they are convinced the firm can survive. Their return on their investment depends on the success of the re-leveraged firm. Moreover, the departing directors, to protect themselves from claims based on breach of fiduciary duty, often hire expert consultants that provide *solvency opinions,* opinions that the firm, immediately after the LBO, will be solvent. However, courts will reject the claim that new management skills and access to new credit, without more, constitute reasonably equivalent consideration. E.g., *Moody v. Security Pacific Bus. Credit, Inc.,* 971 F.2d 1056 (3d Cir. 1992) (new management skills and new access to credit not reasonably equivalent value as a matter of law, but firm solvent at time of LBO); cf. *SPC Plastics Corp. v. Griffith,* 224 B.R. 27 (6th Cir. 1998) (summary judgment for debtor affirmed on grounds that new management skills and new access to credit could not be equivalent value; summary judgment for debtor on insolvency reversed).

D. STATE BULK TRANSFER OR BULK SALES ACTS (ARTICLE 6 OF THE UNIFORM COMMERCIAL CODE)

States enacted bulk sale legislation in the early 1900s to remedy a type of fraud on creditors perpetuated by unscrupulous trading merchants. A merchant would acquire his "stock in trade" (a.k.a. inventory) on credit, then sell his entire inventory (in bulk) to a single purchaser and abscond with the proceeds, leaving creditors unpaid. The states believed that the law of fraudulent conveyances, on the books at that time, although helpful in some situations, was too narrow. When the purchaser in bulk was in league with the seller or paid less than full value for the inventory, fraudulent conveyance law enabled the defrauded creditors to avoid the sale and apply the transferred inventory toward the satisfaction of their claims against the seller. But fraudulent conveyance law provided no remedy when purchasers bought for adequate value and in good faith—without reason to know of the seller's intention to pocket the proceeds and disappear.

State legislatures responded with *bulk sales* laws. The Uniform Commissioners on State Laws simplified and codified the state laws in a *Bulk Transfer Act* added as Article 6 of the Uniform Commercial Code in the early 1950s. All 50 states adopted a version of the article. By 1987 the Commissioners had a radical change of heart and recommended that states repeal entirely the Bulk Transfer Act or replace it with a much tamer *Bulk Sales Act.* Over 40 states (including Delaware) have repealed their Bulk Transfer Act outright and close to eight states (including California) have adopted the Revised Article 6 Bulk Sales Act.

Common to all bulk sales laws is the imposition of a duty on the *purchaser* whenever it purchases the inventory of a seller, a sale *in bulk,* to notify the seller's creditors of the impending sale. The laws applied only when the seller traded in inventory (stock) and when the purchaser did not agree to assume the seller's debts in full on the acquisition of the stock. If the purchaser does assume the seller's debts, the purchaser must be solvent after the assumption and must give written notice of the assumption within 30 days of the sale. UCC § 6–103(3)(i) (1989 Text).

Original Article 6—the Bulk Transfer Act—requires that a purchaser send notice 10 days before whichever occurs first: the purchaser closes, the purchaser takes possession of the goods, or the purchaser pays for the goods. In those jurisdictions that have adopted optional § 6–106 in their Bulk Transfer Act, the purchaser also must assure that the new consideration for the transfer is applied to pay debts of the transferor.

The purchaser's failure to comply with these and any other statutory duties generally affords the seller's creditors a remedy analogous to the remedy for fraudulent conveyances: The creditors acquire the right to set aside the sale and can reach the transferred inventory in the hands of the purchaser. Like its predecessors, the Bulk Transfer Act is remarkable in that it obligates purchasers in bulk to incur costs to protect the interests of the seller's creditors, with whom they usually have no relationship. Even more striking is that the Bulk Transfer Act affords creditors a remedy against a good faith purchaser for full value without notice of any wrongdoing on the part of the seller.

Compliance with the provisions of the Bulk Transfer Act can be burdensome, particularly when the transferor has a large number of creditors. When the transferor is actively engaged in business at a number of locations, assembling a current list of creditors may not be possible. Mailing a notice to each creditor may prove costly. When the goods that are the subject of the transfer are located in several jurisdictions, the transferor may be obligated to comply with Article 6 as enacted in each jurisdiction. The widespread enactment of differing amendments makes compliance with Article 6 in multiple-state transactions problematic. Moreover, the Bulk Transfer Act requires compliance even when there is no reason to believe that the transferor is conducting a fraudulent transfer, e.g., when the transferor is scaling down the business but remaining available to creditors.

Many now believe that the benefits that compliance with the Bulk Transfer Act affords to creditors are insubstantial and do not justify the burdens and risks that the article imposes upon good faith purchasers of business assets. The Bulk Transfer Act requires that notice be sent only 10 days before the transferee takes possession of the goods or pays for them, whichever happens first. Given the delay between sending the notice and its receipt, creditors have scant opportunity to avail themselves of a remedy before the transfer has been consummated. In some cases the Bulk Transfer Act has the unintended effect of injuring, rather than aiding, creditors of the seller by discouraging the sales of inventory in the first place. Those purchasers who recognize the burdens and risks that Article 6 imposes upon them sometimes agree to purchase only at a reduced price. Others refuse to purchase at all, leaving the creditors to realize only the liquidation value, rather than the going concern value, of the business goods.

The 1987 Bulk Sales Act reduces significantly the burdens and risks imposed upon good-faith purchasers of business assets while increasing the protection afforded to creditors. There are numerous changes, among the most important: The new article applies only when the purchaser has notice, or after reasonable inquiry would have notice, that the seller will not continue to operate the same or a similar kind of business after the sale. UCC § 6–102(1)(c). When the seller is indebted to a large number of persons (over 200), the purchaser need neither obtain a list of those persons nor send individual notices to each person but instead may give notice by filing with a state official. UCC §§ 6–105(2) & 6–104(2). The notice period has also increased from 10 days to 45 days. UCC § 6–105(5). A purchaser who makes a good faith effort to comply with the requirements of Article 6 or to exclude the sale from the application of Article 6, or who acts on the good faith belief that Article 6 does not apply to the sale, is not liable for noncompliance. UCC § 6–107(3). A purchaser's noncompliance does not render the sale ineffective or otherwise affect the purchaser's title to the goods; rather, the liability of a noncomplying purchaser is for damages caused by the noncompliance. UCC §§ 6–107(1) & 6–107(8). Finally, the bulk sales law of the jurisdiction of the seller's chief executive office or place of business controls. UCC § 6–103(1) & (2).

To avoid the time, effort and potential disruption of complying with a bulk sales act, parties to asset acquisitions may agree to waive compliance based upon the seller's agreement to indemnify the purchaser against seller creditor claims. If the purchaser does not trust the indemnification protection and there is otherwise insufficient security (no escrowed funds, for example), then wise purchasers simply comply with the act.

§ 6. PURCHASING ASSETS IN BANKRUPTCY

When a target firm is in bankruptcy, a purchaser is usually limited to using an asset acquisition. The purchase of the stock of an insolvent firm makes little economic sense; the stock is worthless. Moreover, a merger of an insolvent firm into a solvent firm attaches the liabilities of the insolvent firm to the solvent firm's assets to the glee of the insolvent firm's creditors and to the pain of the solvent firm's owners. Instead, a purchaser seeks to purchase the assets of the target in bankruptcy free of the target's excessive liabilities.

The federal bankruptcy code permits insolvent firms to sell their assets in whole as well as in parcels to maximize the size of the pool of funds available for unpaid creditors. Bankruptcy Code § 1123 (all subsequent references to sections in this subchapter are to the Bankruptcy Code). During an ongoing bankruptcy proceeding, a purchaser can purchase assets from a secured lender who has foreclosed on those assets, from a bankruptcy trustee (a § 363(b) sale), or pursuant to a plan of reorganization in a Chapter 11 proceeding.

Over the past 30 years, the bankruptcy process has become a useful auction block for selling distressed companies. Instead of selling all or part of a bankrupt company through a Chapter 11 plan of reorganization (which, in most cases, requires the affirmative vote of both creditors and equity holders), however, entire companies are often sold through a § 363(b) sale (which only requires the bankruptcy judge's approval). Section 363(b) authorizes a Chapter 11 debtor-in-possession (i.e., the bankrupt firm's existing management) to use, sell, or lease its property outside the ordinary course of business, requiring in most circumstances only that a movant provide notice to interested parties and a hearing before the bankruptcy judge. The Second Circuit in *In re the Lionel Corp.*, 722 F.2d 1063 (2d Cir. 1983), held that a bankruptcy judge must be presented at a § 363(b) asset sale hearing with a *good business reason* to grant an application for a § 363(b) sale. Otherwise, the grant is an abuse of discretion.

Resort to § 363(b) has been driven by efficiency, from the perspectives of sellers and purchasers alike. The speed of the process can maximize asset value by sale of the debtor's business as a going concern. Moreover, the assets that are sold are typically burnished (or "cleansed"), because (with certain limited exceptions) they are sold free and clear of liens, claims and liabilities. See infra (discussing § 363(b) and tort issues). A § 363(b) sale can often yield the highest price for the assets because the purchaser can select the liabilities it will assume and purchase a business with cash flow (or the near prospect of it). In addition, a secured creditor can "credit bid," i.e., take an ownership interest in the company by bidding a reduction in the debt the company owes to the creditor. Bankruptcy Code § 363(k).

Today, it is typical for a Chapter 11 debtor to negotiate a binding "stalking horse bid" for some or all of its assets in anticipation of a § 363(b) sale. By doing so, the debtor is assured that a potential purchaser (the stalking horse bidder) will pay an acceptable price for the targeted assets. Moreover, the stalking horse bid itself provides the starting point against which other potential purchasers must initially bid. If additional bids do come in for the assets ("overbids"), the debtor will conduct an auction for those assets. The stalking horse bidder is entitled to participate fully in the auction but can only claim the assets if its final bid is the highest bid.

Why make a stalking horse bid? In exchange for its bid, the stalking horse bidder normally receives certain bid protections. These protections are in consideration of the time and effort expended by the stalking horse bidder in performing due diligence and engaging in the negotiations necessary to arrive at its initial bid. If the stalking horse bidder loses out on the assets, it will typically receive a breakup fee of between 1 and 3 percent of the winning bidder's purchase price as well as reimbursement of reasonable and documented expenses. Importantly, the debtor must obtain bankruptcy court approval of proposed bid protections, which is normally done by the debtor when it seeks approval of the bid and auction procedures for the § 363(b) sale.

In re Chrysler, 576 F.3d 108 (2d Cir. 2009), involves the sale of most of Chrysler through a § 363(b) sale, despite the objections of various pensioners. Pursuant to the sale, substantially all of Chrysler's operating assets would be transferred to "New Chrysler" in exchange for New Chrysler's assumption of certain liabilities and $2 billion in cash. Fiat S.p.A agreed to provide New Chrysler with certain fuel-efficient vehicle platforms, access to its worldwide distribution system, and new management that is experienced in turning around a failing auto company in return for a substantial equity stake in New Chrysler. Financing for the sale would mainly come from a "Great Recession" bailout by the United States Treasury and Export Development Canada.

The pensioners challenged the sale, labeling it a "secret" Chapter 11 plan of reorganization. Indeed, they argued that the sale so closely approximates a final plan of reorganization that it constitutes an impermissible *sub rosa* plan, and therefore cannot be accomplished under § 363(b). Nonetheless, the Second Circuit affirmed the bankruptcy judge's approval of the § 363(b) sale. The judge found "good business reasons" for the sale, including:

- The only viable alternative to the sale would be a liquidation that would net much less for the creditors. The sale of assets would yield $2 billion while a liquidation would yield a maximum of $800 million;
- Old Chrysler had circled the globe looking for potential deals, and only Fiat came forward;
- Fiat insisted the sale happen quickly, and, given that it was the only viable suitor, compliance was essential; and
- Old Chrysler was a "melting ice cube," given that its revenues were sinking, its factories were dark, and its massive debts growing.

As a general rule, Chapter 11 cleanses a debtor of its pre-Chapter 11 obligations (except to the extent they are included in the capital restructuring of the firm pursuant to a plan of reorganization). A purchaser from a debtor in Chapter 11 (whether pursuant to § 363(b) or a plan of reorganization) may nevertheless face some risk that it may succeed to certain pre-existing liabilities of the troubled seller, even where the sale purports to be free and clear of claims. In particular, there is an issue over whether a court can discharge future product liability or environmental claims in a Chapter 11 proceeding. To the extent these future claims are not dischargeable, a sale order (under § 363(b)) or order confirming a plan (discharging claims under § 1141) may be ineffective to cleanse the assets being sold. Thus, a purchaser of substantially all the assets of the bankrupt party may be subject to the risk of liability for these claims under state law successor liability doctrines.

If an asset purchaser has taken title to a contaminated property site, for example, CERCLA liability follows the asset, even if the contamination occurred prior to the bankruptcy proceeding. See *In re Chateaugay Corp.*, 944 F.2d 997 (2d Cir. 1991) (EPA cleanup orders survive bankruptcy). Such an asset purchaser is liable under CERCLA as a current owner for all contamination at the site regardless of when it occurred (unless she can use the very narrow *innocent purchaser* defense).

CERCLA is silent on two related questions: (1) the successor's liability when the environmental claim arises out of the disposal of hazardous substances off-site by a predecessor prior to its bankruptcy proceeding; and (2) the successor's liability when the claim arises out of the operation by a predecessor of a contaminated site owned by another party. Sometimes the claims are linked in one fact pattern. A purchaser in an asset acquisition may not know about the off-site disposal (it was performed by an operating unit of the seller that either no longer exists or was not acquired by the asset purchaser, for example) nor about the predecessor's operation of a contaminated site. The federal courts have not settled the question of whether a purchaser in an asset acquisition may avoid such liabilities with a disclaimer in the acquisition agreement.

Because § 363(b) on purchases from a trustee states that a sale is free and clear only of "interests" in property, some courts have suggested that assets cannot be sold free and clear of all claims. E.g., *Ninth Avenue Remedial Group v. Allis-Chalmers Corp.*, 195 Bank Rep. 716 (N.D. Ind. 1996) (no, if claim arises after the bankruptcy proceeding has been concluded). These decisions appear to be inconsistent with the approach of the vast majority of bankruptcy courts, as well as with sound bankruptcy policy. As a consequence, cautious purchasers in asset acquisitions under § 363(b) request some or all of the following: (a) adequate notice to potential claimants of the hearing at which the court will be asked to approve the sale free and clear of all claims; (b) a specific finding by the bankruptcy court that the sale is free and clear of claims; and (c) a decree in the order approving the sale enjoining claimants from pursuing the purchaser or the purchased assets.

In contrast to § 363(b), § 1141(c) of the Bankruptcy Code dealing with Chapter 11 plans of reorganization specifically refers to claims. It states that any property "dealt with" by a plan is "free and clear of all claims and interests of creditors, equity security holders, and of general partners in the debtor." Thus, the interpretive issue arising under § 363(b) creating uncertainty over the ability to sell free and clear of "claims" should not arise with respect to sales under a Chapter 11 plan of reorganization.

Hostile acquisitions (*vulture takeovers*) can be attempted when the target company is in bankruptcy. Hostile bidders attempt to do so by purchasing debt claims in the troubled company (so-called *claims trading*) (the equity interests are worthless and have little power) and seek to control the company through the creditors' committees. *In re Allegheny Int'l, Inc.,* 118 B.R. 282 (Bankr. Ct. W.D. Pa. 1990), details the facts of such an attempt. Japonica, the hostile party, sought to acquire control of the troubled company. In order to do so, it needed to "block" any proposed plan of reorganization put forth by the company itself. Therefore, Japonica purchased claims from both secured and unsecured creditors of the troubled company in order to gain sufficient voting power to do so. When the bankruptcy judge learned that Japonica's purchases were made in an attempt to gain control of the troubled company, he held that Japonica's purchases had been made in "bad faith" and refused to recognize voting rights in the purchased claims. The judge seemed to assume that Japonica would purchase the firm too cheaply if Japonica controlled the vote on the plan of reorganization. Generic claims trading is now accepted practice, but claims trading in order to do a takeover remains risky without the explicit clearance of the bankruptcy judge.

CHAPTER 6

FEDERAL LAW ON ACQUISITIONS OF OR BY PUBLICLY TRADED CORPORATIONS

Federal securities law supplements state corporate codes in regulating acquisition practice and procedure. The additional requirements are substantial whenever an acquisition involves a publicly traded company. Federal requirements in such cases are extensive and impact the basic acquisition procedure and process. Other federal provisions penalize acquisition participants for fraudulent or misleading disclosures and may apply to both publicly traded and privately held companies.

§ 1. PROXY REGULATION AND SHAREHOLDER VOTING

State Law on Disclosure. When shareholders vote on acquisitions, state law requires generally that they receive adequate information from their managers on the details of the transaction. State corporate codes often do not detail the specific kinds of information that shareholders should have when they vote. See, e.g., DGCL § 251(c). The DGCL section only requires that the directors send the shareholders a notice containing a copy of the merger agreement or a "brief summary . . . as the directors shall deem advisable." Section 251(b), however, requires that the directors' resolution approving the merger (which, along with the full agreement, is of record at the shareholder meeting on the merger) "declar[e] its advisability." Some state court case law has developed, under the rubric of a common law on fiduciary duty, on the obligation of a firm to notify its shareholders of all material facts in a transaction, particularly if the transaction creates a conflict of interest for senior managers. Management buyouts (MBOs) and parent-subsidiary mergers that cash out minority shareholders are the classic examples. Otherwise state law on the matter is basically open-ended.

Federal Proxy Regulation. Federal securities law stands in stark contrast to state law. If a firm is publicly held, then § 14(a) of the Securities Exchange Act of 1934 (hereinafter SEA) and the rules promulgated by the SEC under the section apply to the company's *proxy solicitations.* A company is publicly held if it must register one or more classes of its securities under § 12 of the SEA. A company must register any security (1) traded on a national stock exchange, (2) held by over 2,000 shareholders of record (or more than 500 non-accredited shareholders of record) when the firm has more than $10 million in assets, or (3) that has been the subject of a registered public offering. SEA § 12(a) & (g); SEA Rule 12g–1.

A proxy is a delegation of voting power by a shareholder (the principal) to the *proxy holder* (an agent, typically one or more corporate officers); it is a creation of state agency law. The SEC rules regulate the solicitation of proxies, requiring that a *proxy statement* (a disclosure document) accompany or precede all solicitations, and control the content and form of the proxy document itself, the *proxy card* (akin to an absentee ballot).

Since most large firms must solicit proxies from their shareholders in order to do business at their shareholder meetings, the rules have substantial bite. Ordinary business, such as the election of directors, requires an affirmative vote of those attending the meeting and a minimum number of shares represented at the meeting, entitled a *quorum*. The diffusion of shareholder holdings in most publicly traded firms requires that the firm actively solicit proxies to achieve a quorum. In acquisitions, since the required vote is usually a majority of all the outstanding shares entitled to vote, a proxy solicitation is necessary to gather enough affirmative votes to ratify the board's resolution on an acquisition. Moreover, even if a registered firm does not solicit proxies for a shareholder meeting, the SEA requires a firm to mail an "information statement" that is substantially the same as a proxy statement. SEA § 14(c), Reg. 14C.

While most of the popular focus on proxy regulation pays attention to shareholder voting for seats on a corporation's board of directors, the rules apply to all matters subject to a shareholder vote. Thus the regulations promulgated by the SEC specifically cover proxy solicitations for votes required by state corporate codes for mergers, asset sales, and reorganizations. The regulations are very detailed on the information that acquisition parties must disclose and also contain open-ended admonitions to add all other *material* facts as well.

Federal proxy disclosure can be important even for privately held firms, even though those firms are not covered by the federal proxy rules. A privately held firm's compliance with the federal proxy rules on disclosure—even though not legally required—provides de facto safe harbor protection from the open-ended disclosure requirements of state corporate codes. Indeed, the federal rules give guidance to privately held firm officials on what disclosure is likely to satisfy state court judges.

A. THE TIMING REQUIREMENTS OF REGULATION 14A

Regulation 14A, promulgated by the SEC under the authority of § 14(a) of the SEA, consists of twenty-one "14a" rules, two "14b" rules and one schedule (Schedule 14A (technically Rule 14a–101)). Under Rule 14a–3(a), when an acquisition is the subject of a shareholder vote, no solicitation subject to the rules may be made "unless each person solicited is concurrently furnished or has previously been furnished with a written proxy statement containing information specified in Schedule 14A." Indeed, the SEC through the rules wants shareholders to make *informed* voting decisions.

Today, shareholders of most public companies vote their shares through the internet in accordance with "e-proxy" Rule 14a–16. In that regard, companies are allowed to send shareholders a "Notice of Internet Availability of Proxy Materials." The Notice must set forth, among other information: (1) the website address where the proxy materials are available; (2)

instructions regarding how a shareholder may request a paper or e-mail copy of the proxy materials at no charge; (3) the date, time, and location of the meeting; (4) a clear and impartial identification of each separate matter intended to be acted on and the soliciting person's recommendations, if any, regarding those matters, but no supporting statements; (5) a list of the materials being made available at the specified website; (6) any control/identification numbers that the shareholder needs to access his or her form of proxy; (7) instructions on how to access the form of proxy; and (8) information on how to obtain directions to be able to attend the shareholder meeting and vote in person. SEA Rule 14a–16(d).

The SEC has recently liberalized the definition of "solicitation." SEA Rule 14a–12 permits both oral and written communications before the filing of a proxy statement. Written communications must be filed with the SEC on the date of first use, no form of proxy (e.g., a proxy card) may be furnished, and a legend must be included advising shareholders to read the proxy statement and indicating where to find participant information. Rule 14a–12 requires that a definitive proxy statement be furnished to security holders only when a form of proxy is either given to or requested from security holders.

Preliminary copies of the proxy statement and the form of proxy must be filed with the SEC under the cover of *Schedule 14A* at least 10 days before finalized materials are sent to shareholders. SEA Rule 14a–6(a). In addition, copies of all materials in *definitive* form must be filed, concurrently with its distribution to shareholders, with the SEC and sent to each exchange on which any security of the issuer is listed. Rule 14a–6(c). While the soliciting firm may mail the preliminary proxy statement to shareholders, it usually waits until the proxy statement is final or definitive because the firm can send the proxy card only with the definitive statement.

If the SEC staff decides to review a firm's preliminary proxy materials, the firm must await SEC staff comments before mailing definitive materials. Only when the SEC staff and the firm have negotiated and resolved the SEC staff's concerns can definitive materials be mailed to shareholders.

It is possible for firms to file preliminary proxy materials confidentially with the SEC. Under Rule 14a–6(e)(2), preliminary proxy material about a business combination will be confidential only if none of the parties makes any public communication relating to the transaction that goes beyond the very limited information permitted under SA Rule 135. The transaction also cannot be a "roll-up" or a SEA Rule 13e–3 going-private transaction. Rule 135 is very narrow, however; it allows disclosure of only the name of the parties involved in the exchange, the securities to be exchanged, the anticipated timing, manner, and purpose of the offering, and the basis upon which the exchange may be made. In most cases parties will make public announcements that contain more information than is specified in Rule 135, and their preliminary filing materials will then be available for public viewing through the SEC's website (www.sec.gov).

There is no federally-mandated time period between the date a soliciting company mails its proxy materials and the date of the shareholder meeting, but an often-used exception dominates practice. If a proxy statement incorporates by reference other public filings (excluding an annual report on Form 10-K), such as a current report on Form 8-K, which often is the case, then the statement must be delivered 20 days before the date of the shareholder vote. SEC Schedule 14A, Note D.3. State law provides a minimum notice requirement for shareholder meetings, however. In Delaware, for example, a corporation must mail notice to its shareholders before any meeting, annual or special, no more than 60 days nor less than 10 days before the date of the meeting (the ***60–10 Rule***). DGCL § 222(b). The proxy solicitation usually accompanies any notice of the meeting required by a state corporate code.

B. THE PROXY FORM AND ACQUISITION DISCLOSURE REQUIREMENTS OF SCHEDULE 14A

The form of proxy (i.e., proxy card) must itself indicate in boldface type whether or not the proxy is solicited on behalf of a firm's board. SEA Rule 14a–4(a)(1). Ordinarily, a proxy can confer authority to vote at only *one meeting*. Rule 14a–4(d)(2). However, in a recent SEC no-action letter addressed to

ExxonMobil Corp. (2025 WL 2649181 (S.E.C. No-Action Letter) (Sept. 15, 2025)), the SEC indicated that the SEC's Division of Enforcement would not recommend enforcement action under Rule 14a–4(d)(2) or (3) with respect to ExxonMobil's "Retail Voting Program." That Program allows investors to submit a standing voting instruction that requires ExxonMobil to vote their shares based on the recommendation of the *company's board of directors* at all *future* shareholder meetings, unless a shareholder decides to opt out of the Program or determines to vote on proposals to be considered at a particular annual meeting. The stated goals of the Program center on promoting retail voting by investors and reducing time and other burdens borne by retail investors in the proxy voting process. ExxonMobil justified the Program in part by highlighting that over the previous five years, approximately 90% of retail investors that voted at ExxonMobil shareholder meetings supported all of its board's recommendations.

A proxy must identify *clearly and impartially* any acquisition or reorganization question submitted to a vote and permit the shareholder to choose "between approval or disapproval . . . or abstention." Rule 14a–4(a)(3) & (b)(1). General discretionary proxies, proxies in which a shareholder delegates general voting authority to the proxy holder, are prohibited on acquisition votes.

The first six *items* of Schedule 14A (the numbered items detail what must be included in a proxy statement) apply to all proxy statements, regardless of the type of action proposed. They call for the date, time and place of the shareholder meeting (Item 1), information with respect to the revocability of any executed proxy (Item 2), dissenters' appraisal rights (Item 3), the identity of those soliciting the proxy, the special interest of the solicitors, and others connected with the solicitors (Item 4), a description of the issuer's outstanding securities and their principal holders (Item 5), and the number of shares of each class of stock entitled to vote, the number of votes to which each class is entitled, and the record date, if any, relating to the solicitation (Item 6).

Item 14 in the Schedule applies specifically to votes on acquisitions. Item 14 applies if any action is to be taken with respect to any transaction involving (1) the merger or consolidation of the firm into or with any other person or of any other person into or with the firm, (2) the acquisition by the firm or any of its security holders of securities of another person, (3) the acquisition by the firm of any other going business or of the assets thereof, (4) the sale or other transfer of all or any substantial part of the assets of the firm, or (5) the liquidation or dissolution of the firm.

Subsection (a) in Item 14 calls for information about the transaction at issue, and subsection (b) calls for information about both parties to the transaction. There are special rules for some types of deals: SEC rules, for example, limit the need to provide financial information in cash mergers.

The subsections of Item 14 of the Schedule incorporate by reference other SEC regulations,

Regulations S–X, S–K and M–A, and Form S-4. Regulation S–X specifies the accounting conventions that filing parties must use in their required financial documents—balance sheets, income statements, statements of shareholders' equity, and cash flow statements, and amounts to an SEC overlay on generally accepted accounting principles (GAAP). Regulation S–K is more general and contains a variety of informational requirements, including Subpart 1000 (Regulation M–A), specific to mergers and acquisitions. Form S-4 is the registration statement that firms file under the SA in connection with registering their securities for use as acquisition consideration.

The primary effect of the SEC proxy rules and schedules is to expose a firm soliciting proxies on an acquisition vote to potential litigation from either the SEC or its shareholders in the event that (1) the firm does not comply with the details of Schedule 14A, (2) the firm affirmatively misrepresents a material fact in its Schedule 14A, or (3) the firm omits a fact necessary to make a written statement in its Schedule not materially misleading. The SEC takes the position that information specifically required by Schedule 14A must be disclosed regardless of materiality.

Material misstatements or omissions by the soliciting firm subject it to liability under SEA Rule 14a–9, the antifraud rule. See, e.g., *Gerstle v. Gamble-Skogmo, Inc.*, 478 F.2d 1281 (2d Cir. 1973). When an affirmatively misleading statement or omitted information *is* material, the fact that it is not specifically called for by Schedule 14A does not foreclose the possibility of a violation of Rule 14a–9. Additionally, misstatements as to *opinions* included in proxy statements may be actionable if the person stating an opinion did not, in fact, hold that opinion. E.g., *Virginia Bankshares, Inc. v. Sandberg,* 501 U.S. 1083 (1991) (directors' statements that price to be paid to minority shareholders was "high" and "fair" was actionable if the price was not in fact "high" and "fair" and the directors knew this).

§ 2. TENDER OFFER REGULATIONS ON STOCK ACQUISITIONS: THE WILLIAMS ACT

A. THIRD-PARTY TENDER OFFERS

The 1968 Williams Act, which added several sections to the SEA, regulates *tender offers* to holders of publicly traded securities (usually voting stock). Tender offers are public announcements that a bidder (i.e., the potential acquirer) will buy securities tendered by owners to a *depositary* (a bank or trust company) acting on behalf of the bidder at a set cash price or in exchange for a set value of the bidder's securities (or a mix of both cash and securities). The price offered is usually in excess of the current market price (such excess being referred to as the *tender offer or control premium*). A tender offer may be for all shares tendered, an *any and all shares tender offer,* or for a maximum number of shares, a *partial tender offer.*

A bidder for stock generally conditions its tender offer on the receipt of financing, antitrust clearance and the like; thus, if the conditions to the tender offer are neither satisfied nor waived (by the bidder), the bidder need not purchase any tendered shares. One such common condition is the *minimum tender condition,* whereby the bidder need not purchase any tendered shares unless at least a majority of all the outstanding shares of the target have been tendered. In other words, the bidder need not purchase any tendered shares unless such purchase guarantees majority control over the target.

Importantly, the SEC has made it clear that all tender offer conditions must be based upon objective criteria and otherwise not within the bidder's control; otherwise, the offer would be illusory and may constitute a manipulative or deceptive act or practice under SEA § 14(e). The SEC has further indicated that if a bidder terminates a tender offer based on the failure of a condition(s), it must publicly identify the exact condition(s) that failed or risk violating § 14(e).

The Williams Act and its accompanying SEC regulations impose various structural requirements on a tender offer's form. The rules also require bidders to make comprehensive and detailed public disclosures when their offers are made. In addition, the Act prohibits bidders from engaging in open-market or privately-negotiated purchases while a tender offer is pending.

The form requirements for a tender offer prescribe: a 20-business day minimum offering period (SEA Rule 14e–1, designed to ensure that target shareholders are not hurried in making their tender decisions), though the typical bidder will voluntarily extend its tender offer multiple times by necessity (waiting on the satisfaction of conditions, for example); shareholder withdrawal rights coextensive with the offering period (Rule 14d–7(a)); withdrawal rights after 60 days from the initial offer if the bidder has failed to close on the tenders (SEA § 14(d)(5)); pro rata acceptance for over-subscribed partial offers (Rule 14d–8); nondiscrimination among target shareholders (Rule 14d–10(a)(1), the *all holders rule*); and the extension of any price increase during the tender offer to all shareholders who have already tendered (Rule 14d–10(a)(2), the *best price rule*).

Rule 14d–11 permits bidders in tender offers to provide for a period of between 3 and 20 business days (a *subsequent offering period*) after the expiration of a tender offer during which untendered shares could be tendered but without withdrawal rights. This period is essentially a cleanup period during which target shareholders who failed to tender their shares during a successful tender offer have another chance to tender and receive the tender offer price. By tendering during the subsequent offering period, these shareholders do not have to wait until a second-step merger is completed to get paid for their shares. The period also helps bidders achieve the percentage of target shares necessary to complete a short-form merger (typically 90 percent or more, e.g., DGCL § 253), thus avoiding the need for a vote of target shareholders in connection with a second-step merger.

Also, during the tender offer, (a) purchases by the bidder "otherwise than pursuant to such tender offer" (Rule 14e–5) and (b) any short tenders by offerees into partial tender offers (Rule 14e–4(b)) are prohibited. Indeed, the SEC views these practices as "manipulative or deceptive device[s] or contrivance[s]" and "fraudulent, deceptive or manipulative acts or practices" under § 14(e) of the SEA. Regulation M prohibits the bidder or the target from purchasing bidder securities after an exchange tender offer is commenced. SEC Reg. M, 17 C.F.R. 242.100 to 242.105.

A good example of the best price rule (Rule 14d–10(a)(2)) in action occurred in *Epstein v. MCA, Inc.*, 50 F.3d 644 (9th Cir. 1995). In 1990, Matsushita Electrical Co., Ltd. ("Matsushita") acquired MCA, Inc. ("MCA") for $6.1 billion. The acquisition was accomplished through a tender offer of $71 per share for MCA common stock. However, $71 per share was apparently not sufficient for Lew Wasserman, MCA's chairman and chief executive officer at the time, with respect to the 4,953,927 shares of MCA common stock he personally owned. Rather than tender his shares at the tender offer price along with other MCA stockholders, Wasserman instead entered into a separate agreement with Matsushita. Pursuant to that agreement, Wasserman exchanged his shares for preferred stock in a wholly-owned Matsushita subsidiary called MEA Holdings. Matsushita agreed to fund MEA Holdings by contributing 106% of the tender price multiplied by the number of MCA shares Wasserman exchanged. Essentially, through this arrangement, Wasserman would receive six percent more for his shares than his fellow MCA stockholders.

MCA plaintiff-stockholders challenged the Wasserman transaction arguing that the best price rule had been violated. Matsushita, in turn, argued that the transaction fell outside the best price rule's ambit because it closed *after* the tender offer period expired. Moreover, Matsushita contended that the Wasserman transaction could not be deemed a part of the tender offer itself because it was merely a private exchange of stock, structured to take place after the tender offer finished.

The Ninth Circuit rejected Matsushita's arguments. In the court's view, the terms of the Wasserman transaction were in several material respects conditioned on the terms of the public tender offer. The court highlighted that the redemption value of Wasserman's preferred stock incorporated the tender offer price by reference. It also noted that the entire transaction was conditioned on the tender offer's success. If the tender offer failed, Wasserman would have remained the owner of his MCA stock. Thus, in this regard the deal Matsushita made with Wasserman differed from the tender offer in only one material respect—the type of consideration provided.

The court noted that Rule 14d–10 does not prohibit transactions entered into or effected before, or after, a tender offer—provided that all material terms of the transaction stand independent of the tender offer. Thus, if in advance of the tender offer, Wasserman had become unconditionally obligated to exchange his MCA shares, the transaction would not have violated Rule 14d–10, even if Matsushita believed that acquiring Wasserman's shares was a first step in acquiring the whole of MCA. In such a case, both Wasserman and Matsushita would have assumed the burdens of their agreement despite the risk that an anticipated tender offer should fail or command a different price.

The best price rule in Rule 14d–10(a)(2) has caused recent difficulties in negotiated stock acquisitions that are executed through tender offers. Some courts had held that golden parachute payments and severance payments triggered by a tender offer and received by members of target senior management were disguised stock payments. E.g., *In re Digital Securities,* 357 F.3d 322 (3d Cir. 2004). Therefore, those payments had to be included in the calculation of the value paid on those members' shares pursuant to the tender offer and, if included, resulted in them receiving more than other shareholders in violation of the best price rule. The SEC clarified that the best price rule applies only to consideration paid for securities tendered in a tender offer and *does not* include compensation arrangements subject to two conditions. First, the compensation paid to the employee-shareholder is for past services performed, future services to be performed or future services to be refrained from performing (e.g., a non-compete). Second, the compensation must not be calculated based on the number of shares tendered or to be tendered by the employee-shareholder. In addition, the independent directors of the target, or, if the bidder is a party, the bidder must approve the arrangements. SEA Rule 14d–10(d).

All the requirements specified in § 14(d) of the SEA and the 14d series of rules promulgated by the SEC under that section (Regulation 14D) apply only to tender offers for a class of voting equity securities registered under § 12 of the SEA, that is, for voting equity securities of publicly traded corporations. The requirements in § 14(e) and the rules promulgated by the SEC under that section (Regulation 14E) apply whether or not the offer is subject to Regulation 14D. Section 14(e) is a general antifraud provision that authorizes the SEC to pass rules against fraudulent practices in all tender offers. Note, for example, that the minimum 20-business day offering period in Rule 14e–1 thus applies to all tender offers (including tender offers for debt securities), not just tender offers for the voting stock of publicly traded companies.

The Tender Offer Document Dance. The bidder typically posts a summary announcement of a tender offer in the *Wall Street Journal.* Needing to get its tender offer materials into the hands of target shareholders, the bidder also makes a Rule 14d–5 demand on the target for a list of the target's shareholders. The target must, within three days, either mail the bidder's tender offer materials to the target's shareholders (at the bidder's cost and expense) or provide a shareholder list to the bidder so that the bidder can do the mailing itself. Alternatively, a bidder also can demand a list of shareholders from the target under state law (e.g., DGCL § 220(b)), as it is highly likely that the bidder already owns a handful of shares of the target before it commences its tender offer.

A bidder will file its Schedule TO (technically found in Rule 14d–100) with the SEC, delivers a copy of the Schedule to the target and to all national exchanges on which the target's stock is traded, and on the same day mails to the shareholders of the target certain exhibits to the Schedule, namely an *Offer to Purchase* and a *Letter of Transmittal*. The Offer to Purchase, usually well over 30 pages, sets forth the terms of the offer—the number of shares to be purchased, the offer price and the length of time the offer will be open—and additional information—details on withdrawal rights, discussion of tax considerations and the conditions of the offer. A target shareholder will complete and submit a Letter of Transmittal in order to tender her shares.

Under SEC rules, a tender offer commences when the bidder first publishes or gives security holders the means to tender securities into the offer (e.g., sends a Letter of Transmittal). To deter dissemination of false offers, the SEC adopted Rule 14e–8 prohibiting bidders from announcing an offer without the intent to commence the offer within a reasonable time, with the intent to manipulate stock prices, or without a reasonable belief that the bidder will have the means (i.e., the money) to purchase the securities sought. Public announcements of a tender offer trigger an obligation to file with the SEC all written communications upon their first use.

The SEC staff reviews the filed Schedule TO and may return comments to the bidder. The bidder and the SEC negotiate the comments while the tender offer is open. If unsatisfied by the bidder's responses, the SEC may ask the bidder to send additional information to the target shareholders and may ask the bidder to extend the tender offer period so that shareholders can consider the new material.

Shareholders respond by tendering their shares through a named intermediary, usually a commercial bank or trust company, referred to as a *depositary*. They attach the Letter of Transmittal to their shares; the paying agent accumulates the shares and pays all shareholders when the offer expires and the bidder accepts the tenders. If a shareholder wishes to withdraw shares, she must submit a *letter of withdrawal* accompanied by a *signature guarantee,* verifying that the signature of the shareholder is authentic. Shareholders often wait until the last minute before tendering their shares in the hope that better offers from competing third parties will materialize. As the expiration date approaches, brokers, acting on behalf of shareholders, may submit a *notice of guaranteed delivery,* guaranteeing that the broker will deliver shares within five business days; the paying agent will consider shares so guaranteed as tendered into the offer.

The target firm, within 10 days of the commencement of the tender offer, must send a notice to its shareholders recommending, rejecting, expressing no opinion and remaining neutral, or stating that it is unable to take a position on the tender offer (Rule 14e–2). Whenever the target recommends that its security holders accept or reject the offer to tender, the firm must file a Schedule 14D-9 with the SEC and deliver a copy of that Schedule to its shareholders, the bidder and any national stock exchanges on which the stock is traded. The target's obligation to file a full Schedule 14D-9 arises on the day the target first makes a solicitation or recommendation with respect to a commenced (and not merely announced) tender offer or within 10 days of the offer, whichever is first.

B. ISSUER TENDER OFFERS

Third parties are not the only ones that can launch tender offers. An issuer itself can make a tender offer for its own outstanding securities—an *issuer (or self) tender offer*. Issuer tender offers are most often for stock, but also can be for outstanding debt securities.

Thus far in our discussion of § 14(d) of the SEA and the SEC rules promulgated thereunder, we have been assuming a third-party tender offer. Issuer tender offers for equity securities must comply with another SEC rule, Rule 13e–4. That rule imposes on issuer tender offers disclosure, form and timing requirements identical to those imposed on third-party tender offers noted above. Thus, firms launching issuer tender offers also file a Schedule TO with the SEC. In addition, all issuer tender offers, like all third-party tender offers, must also comply with the antifraud provisions of § 14(e) of the SEA.

C. GOING-PRIVATE TRANSACTIONS

The SEC has also passed a series of rules and a schedule under a general grant of authority under § 13(e) of the SEA, an open-ended antifraud provision on issuer stock repurchases, aimed at regulating *going-private transactions.* SEA Rule 13e–3 and Rule 13e–100 (a.k.a. Schedule 13E-3). In a going-private transaction, a company with publicly traded stock—that is, a company that files periodic public reports under § 12 of the SEA—buys back enough of its shares to transform itself into a company which no longer has to file public reports. The company *goes dark;* a publicly traded company becomes a privately held company once again. The consideration offered in the transaction to selling shareholders is usually cash or debt securities in the firm, or a combination of the two.

There are important differences between Schedule 13E-3 for going-private issuer repurchases and Schedule TOs for issuer and third-party tender offers. Item 8 of Schedule 13E-3 incorporates by reference Item 1014 of Regulation M–A, which requires a statement on the *fairness* of a going-private transaction with supporting rationale. By requiring a statement on fairness, the issuer becomes liable on the assertion under the general antifraud provisions of the securities acts if the statement is materially false or misleading. All material factors behind the statement must be itemized and disclosed. In particular, Item 1015 in Regulation M–A requires the disclosure of all reports or appraisals from outside parties material to the fairness of the offer. Schedule 13E-3, Item 9. In a Schedule 13E-3, the issuer, as a fiduciary to the selling shareholders, must, in essence, disclose valuation information, while outside bidders can presumably be more secretive.

Rule 13e–3 provides an exemption from a Schedule 13E-3 filing for second-step cleanup transactions occurring within one year after a tender offer by a non-affiliate, if the second-step consideration offered is at least equal to the highest consideration offered in the tender offer. See Rule 13e–3(g)(1). The rule has significant application problems, however.

D. DEFINITION OF A "TENDER OFFER"

Congress purposefully did not define the term "tender offer" in the Williams Act, as it was worried that smart investment bankers and lawyers would easily do an end run around a static definition. However, the SEC has stated that the term "tender offer" goes beyond conventional tender offers to include acquisition programs that present the type of abuses that Congress intended to eliminate when it passed the Williams Act. The SEC has proffered an eight part "flexible factors" test in various amicus briefs. E.g., *Wellman v. Dickinson*, 475 F.Supp. 783 (S.D.N.Y. 1979). Under the test, the issue of whether a given offer rises to the level of a tender offer depends on the manner in which the offer is conducted and the overall pressure, if any, it has on the purported target's shareholders to sell their shares. The eight factors are:

(1) Active and widespread solicitation of public shareholders;

(2) Solicitation made for a substantial percentage of stock;

(3) The offer to purchase stock is made at a premium over the prevailing market price for that stock;

(4) Terms of the offer are firm rather than negotiable;

(5) The offer is contingent on the tender of a fixed minimum number of shares, and is sometimes also subject to a fixed maximum number to be purchased;

(6) The offer is open for only a limited period of time;

(7) The offerees are subjected to pressure to sell their stock; and

(8) Public announcements of a purchasing program concerning the target's stock precede or accompany rapid accumulation of a large amount of the target's stock.

Unfortunately, the SEC has repeatedly cautioned that not all eight factors are entitled to equal weight and that neither all, nor even a majority, of the eight factors need be present. It has added that the eight factors really serve one ultimate purpose—to identify whether a purchasing program places pressure on shareholders to respond hastily before having a chance to consider material information.

A significantly different approach to determining whether an offer rises to the level of a tender offer is found in *Hanson Trust PLC v. SCM Corp.*, 774 F.2d 47 (2d Cir. 1985). Hanson had launched a hostile tender offer for shares of SCM Corp. SCM responded by adopting a number of anti-takeover devices, including agreeing to a leveraged buyout involving a newly-formed entity owned by SCM management and Merrill Lynch Capital Markets. SCM also entered into a "crown jewel" lock-up agreement with Merrill. That agreement allowed Merrill to purchase SCM's two most profitable businesses at bargain basement prices if an unwanted third party was successful in acquiring more than one-third of SCM's outstanding shares.

Hanson concluded that its tender offer could not be successful given SCM's defensive strategy, and thus terminated it. Nevertheless, on the *very same day* it terminated its tender offer, Hanson purchased close to one-third of SCM's outstanding shares through six separate transactions, five of which were privately negotiated purchases and one of which was an open market purchase. Hanson apparently made these purchases in an attempt to scuttle the Merrill/SCM leveraged buyout.

At issue was whether Hanson's six purchases of SCM stock in and of themselves constituted a de facto continuation of Hanson's previous tender offer. The District Court believed Hanson was making a deliberate attempt to do an end run around the requirements of the Williams Act and therefore issued a preliminary injunction against Hanson. The Second Circuit, however, disagreed.

The Second Circuit believed that embracing the SEC's eight factor test was both unwise and unnecessary. Instead, in order to determine whether a given offer was a tender offer, the court looked for guidance in *S.E.C. v. Ralston Purina Co.,* 346 U.S. 119 (1953). *Ralston Purina* was a famous U.S. Supreme Court decision which addressed the private placement transactional exemption of SA § 4(a)(2). The Second Circuit reasoned that the purpose of SEA § 14(d) is to protect the ill-informed solicitee, just as the registration requirements of SA § 5 are designed to protect those who, in the words of the U.S. Supreme Court in *Ralston Purina,* cannot "*fend for themselves*" in connection with purchasing unregistered shares directly from an issuer. Accordingly, the Second Circuit held that the issue of whether a solicitation constitutes a tender offer depends on whether, viewing the transaction in light of the totality of circumstances, it appears that, unless the pre-acquisition filing strictures of the SEA are followed, there will be a substantial risk that solicitees will lack the information needed to make a carefully considered appraisal of the proposal put before them. The Second Circuit's test is known as the *totality of the circumstances* test.

§ 3. USING SECURITIES AS CONSIDERATION: THE SECURITIES ACT OF 1933

The Securities Act of 1933 (SA) protects the purchasers of securities, broadly defined to include both debt and equity investment securities, in *public offerings.* In a classic public offering, a firm sells securities to the public as a means of raising capital to fund its business. If a firm offers securities to the public, defined roughly as over 35 or so purchasers, the firm must register the sale with the SEC under the SA. The SA also applies to all major firm acquisitions in which the target shareholders receive investment securities (stock or debt) in the bidder, rather than cash, and the number of target shareholders is large. Indeed, the SEC construes the purchaser's distribution of securities to the seller's shareholders to be a *public offering* if the number of seller shareholders is large. SA Rule 145.

A. EFFECT OF THE SECURITIES ACT OF 1933 ON EXCHANGE TENDER OFFERS

If an acquisition is an *exchange tender offer*—that is, a bidder makes a public offer to exchange stock or debt securities in the bidder (or the bidder's parent) for target stock—the offer, as noted above, is regulated under the Williams Act and the SEC rules promulgated thereunder. The Williams Act requires detailed public disclosures. Yet the SEC also construes the exchange offer to be a public offering of securities by the bidder to the holders of stock in the target. This brings into play the rules and regulations of the SA, adding a layer of SA filings to the Williams Act filings. Unless the bidder can qualify under one of the narrow exemptions to SA registration (such as the private placement offering exemption)—an unlikely event—the SA affects the form and timing of an exchange tender offer. The supplemental filings add considerable expense and timing hurdles to the Williams Act regulations that a cash tender offer does not have to satisfy.

A firm making a registered public distribution of shares must file a SA registration statement and wait for the SEC to declare that statement "effective" before the firm can actually sell the stock. The first question is whether a firm making an exchange tender offer must await the effective date of a SA registration statement before it can begin (announce) its tender offer. Prior to 2000, the answer was "yes." This effectively precluded a bidder from (a) using an exchange tender offer in a bidding contest as it would be at a distinct disadvantage from a timing standpoint and (b) commencing a *hostile* exchange tender offer because the element of surprise would be lost (registration statements generally are public documents upon filing). However, since 2000 the SEC has allowed bidders to commence their exchange tender offers upon the filing of, and *prior* to the effective date of, a SA registration statement. Security holders may tender their securities prior to effectiveness of the registration statement but the bidder cannot accept the tenders until the SEC declares the registration statement effective. SA Rule 162. Bidders who wish to commence an offer before the effective date must disseminate publicly a preliminary prospectus along with the letter of transmittal. Once a bidder has sent target shareholders a preliminary prospectus and supplements containing material changes, if any, it need not deliver a final (definitive) prospectus, however.

The second question is whether the SA adds significant disclosure requirements to those required by the Williams Act. A registration statement does indeed require the disclosure of information that is not required by a Schedule TO. The registration statement must contain specified information about the security, the issuer and the underwriters (investment bankers who place the security). In filing a registration statement, an acquirer may choose to use either Form S-1 or a special form for acquisitions, Form S-4. The parties can use a Form S-4 filing to satisfy both the acquirer's Schedule TO and the target's Schedule 14D-9 filing requirements if the parties are careful to integrate any added informational requirements in the Schedules into the S-4. Of course, combining the disclosures of the two parties is only possible when the transaction is a friendly, negotiated one.

If using Form S-4, the acquirer must include, among other things, information about the terms of the transaction (including pro forma financials for the projected combined firm), information about itself and information about the target. An acquirer does not need to provide financial statements for a non-reporting (not publicly traded) target when the acquirer's security holders are not voting on the transaction and the non-reporting target is less than 20 percent the size of the acquirer. Form S-4, Item 17(b)(7). Otherwise, the non-reporting target company disclosure requirement is limited to disclosure of one year of financial statements.

The third question is how long does it take for the SEC to declare a SA registration statement effective so a firm can close its pending exchange tender offer. Once a firm files a registration statement with the SEC, the agency reviews the materials and, if satisfied, declares the registration statement to be effective. A registration statement, according to the SA, automatically becomes effective 20 days after filing unless the SEC declares it effective sooner or takes action to toll the running of the period. In practice the SEC demands that all registrants waive the 20-day period. See SA Rule 473 (providing for a paragraph on the cover of a registration statement that effects a continuing amendment) and SEC Rule 461 (used by the SEC to condition acceleration of an effectiveness order on the issuer's filing of a delaying amendment). The delaying amendment gives the SEC time to screen registration statements and decide which ones to review thoroughly. In adopting the rules, the SEC staff noted the potential disadvantage to a bidder in an exchange tender offer if the staff review process causes a delay in declaring the registration statement effective. The SEC has publicly stated that its staff is committed to the expeditious review of exchange tender offers so that such offers could compete more effectively with cash tender offers. Recall that a bidder, in theory, can close a cash tender offer in 20 business days. See SEA Rule 14e–1.

B. EFFECT OF THE SECURITIES ACT OF 1933 ON STOCK SWAP STATUTORY MERGERS AND STOCK-FOR-ASSET ACQUISITIONS

If a purchaser uses its own stock as consideration in a stock swap merger or a stock-for-assets acquisition and the target is a publicly traded corporation, the SEC adds the disclosure requirements of the SA to the proxy solicitation rules of the SEA (see Chapter 6, § 1). The SEC construes the transactions to be a public offering of the purchaser's securities to the target shareholders. SA Rule 145.

Thus, in these transactions the purchaser must file a SA registration statement with the SEC (since it is deemed to be conducting a public offering of securities) and the seller must file a SEA proxy statement (as its shareholders are being asked to vote on the transaction). The registrants may choose to file the forms confidentially. For statutory mergers and asset sales, a Form S-4 registration statement commonly consists of the seller's proxy or information statement enclosed in the purchaser's prospectus cover; the registration statement *wraps around* the proxy statement. In those transactions in which purchaser shareholders also vote to ratify the transition, the purchaser must file a SEA proxy statement for its shareholders as well. A part of the Form S-4 thus also serves as a proxy statement for the target and, if necessary, the purchaser as well. In such a case, the disclosure is referred to as a *joint proxy statement/prospectus*.

If a purchaser uses a Form S-4 and incorporates by reference other public disclosure documents, it must send the disclosure document contained therein to the seller's shareholders at least 20 days in advance of the date of the seller's shareholder meeting. If the purchaser does not want to assume liability for the seller's representations in its proxy statement or the purchaser wants to narrow the 20-day notice requirement, then the purchaser can register the transaction on a basic Form S-1 instead of a Form S-

4. However, Form S-1 does not permit liberal incorporation by reference of other SEA reports, as does Form S-4, and thus is much more expensive and time-consuming to prepare and distribute.

If the SEC staff decides to review and comment on the filing, all is delayed until the comments are resolved. The purchaser may mail a preliminary prospectus to target shareholders but ordinarily will not because the purchaser cannot include a proxy card in the mailing. Once the SEC declares the registration statement effective, the purchaser mails the combined final prospectus/definitive proxy statement along with a proxy card to all the seller's shareholders.

C. THE EFFECT OF THE SECURITIES ACT OF 1933 ON RECAPITALIZATIONS

The SA contains a special exemption from registration for securities distributed in voluntary recapitalizations. The exemption is contained in § 3(a)(9) for "any security exchanged by the issuer with its existing security holders exclusively where no commission or other remuneration is paid or given directly or indirectly for soliciting such exchange."

Exchange transactions may occur in a wide variety of circumstances. Often outstanding bonds or preferred stock are exchanged for newly-issued common stock. To qualify for the exemption, the issuer of both securities must be identical, no part of the offering may be made to anyone other than existing security holders, and the firm cannot pay anyone for soliciting proxies.

The exemption is also important for *poison pill plans* discussed in Chapter 12, § 1. Popular poison pill plans consist of stock rights (options) distributed as an in-kind dividend on the outstanding common stock. An in-kind dividend is not a sale and does not require registration under the SA.

D. GOING PUBLIC THROUGH A REVERSE MERGER

In a *reverse merger* a privately held company *goes public* by merging with and into an existing public shell company (i.e., a public company with no real assets or liabilities). In the stock-for-stock merger, the public shell company survives and a controlling block of stock in the shell (typically 85%) is given to the owners of the privately held company, which merges out of existence. All the assets and liabilities of the privately held company are subsumed within the public shell by virtue of the merger. The Certificate of Merger changes the name of the public shell to that of the private company. The publicly held survivor then aggressively broadens its trading market to make its securities more liquid. The company courts new market makers, prepares audited financials for public reports, and eventually applies for a listing on the NASD bulletin board or the Nasdaq itself.

Several well-known firms have successfully used this procedure. The firms enjoy the benefit of a liquid market for their shares, the shares increase in value, and the market provides a valuation benchmark for the firms. The advantage of the procedure is the minimal time it takes a private company to become registered in the public capital markets. The merger into a shell takes much less time than a traditional merger because there is only minimal due diligence to conduct on the shell.

The SEC's disdain for companies "going public" through a reverse merger is palpable. The SEC believes the procedure allows "not-ready-for-prime-time" companies to go public at a time when they cannot attract a legitimate underwriter to conduct a traditional underwritten IPO. Additionally, a reverse merger does not raise any new capital. Thus, no registration statement is filed with the SEC. This, in turn, means that no registration statement has been vetted by underwriters who are subject to potential liability for a materially false and misleading registration statement under SA § 11(a).

If the surviving public firm wants to raise capital in the future for its operations, it must conduct a registered public offering or satisfy one of the offering exemptions (a private placement of public equity, a PIPE, for example). If the founders of the privately held company want to sell their newly-acquired stock in the public company (to get cash), they must do a secondary registered offering or satisfy the resale requirements of SA Rule 144 for affiliates (e.g., controlling officials can dribble out their shares to the market under the one percent rule in an effort to not disrupt the existing trading market for the shares generally).

E. SPECIAL PURPOSE ACQUISITION COMPANIES (SPACs)

Over the last 10 years, a growing number of mid-sized privately held companies agreed to mergers with *special purpose acquisition companies* (*SPACs*), formally known as *blank check companies*. A SPAC is a shell company that has no operations but has raised funds by going public through a registered *initial public offering* (*IPO*). The Form S-1 registration statement for the SPAC will list the organizer's intention of merging with or acquiring another company utilizing the proceeds of the IPO as acquisition consideration. (SPACs typically leverage their IPO funds to buy bigger companies.) Most of the proceeds from the IPO are held in a trust and released only when the acquisition is completed. The managers of a SPAC must complete an acquisition in 18 to 24 months and use at least 80 percent of the SPAC's funds in doing so. A failure to accomplish a timely acquisition means the SPAC must return those funds back to its shareholders.

The process by which a SPAC completes an acquisition is known as *de-SPACing*. Examples of companies that went public through SPACs include Lucid Motors, QuantumScape, Draft Kings, SoFi, Lucky Strike Entertainment (formerly Bowlero), Aurora, Ginko Bioworks, ChargePoint, Fisker (now bankrupt), Opendoor, Truth Social, Grindr, and even Burger King (in 2012).

Prior to completing the IPO, a SPAC may not take any steps to identify an acquisition target. Any acquisition by a SPAC requires the approval by a majority of the shares held by the SPAC's public shareholders. Holders of the shares who vote against the deal may also choose to have their shares redeemed. In practice this gives any 20 percent block of shareholders the right to wind up the SPAC. After the acquisition, the surviving company is public and must file periodic reports under the SEA.

Believing SPAC formations and transactions needed closer scrutiny and oversight, in 2024 the SEC adopted new SPAC-focused rules. At their base, the rules treat de-SPAC transactions more akin to traditional IPOs. Among other things, the rules:

- extend (via SEC guidance) statutory underwriter liability to cover de-SPAC transaction participants;
- require the target company in a de-SPAC transaction to be a co-registrant along with the SPAC with respect to a SA Form S-4 registration statement;
- eliminate the availability of the safe harbor of the Private Securities Litigation Reform Act of 1995 ("PSLRA") for projections included in de-SPAC registration statements (N.B. That safe harbor is also not available for traditional IPOs);
- expand statutory disclosure requirements for SPAC and de-SPAC transactions (including the creation of a new Subpart 1600 of Regulation S–K, setting forth specific SPAC disclosure requirements for SPAC IPOs);

- mandate a minimum dissemination period for security holder communication materials in de-SPAC transactions; and
- require a re-determination of smaller reporting company ("SRC") status following consummation of a de-SPAC transaction.

§ 4. THE DISCLOSURE REQUIREMENTS OF THE FEDERAL SECURITIES LAW

A. INTRODUCTION TO MANDATORY DISCLOSURE REQUIREMENTS IN FEDERAL SECURITIES LAW

In the U.S., the disclosure obligation of publicly traded firms is defined from the ground up by the accumulation of a constantly growing body of specific federal rules. The aggregate effect of the federal rules constitutes our mandatory disclosure system. There are other sources of disclosure obligations for publicly traded firms. Most state corporate codes include minimal disclosure obligations, e.g., MBCA § 16.20 (requiring annual reports to shareholders), as does Delaware case law, which affects over one-half of our NYSE-listed companies. E.g., *Marhart v. Calmat,* 1992 WL 212587 (Del. Ch.). And our organized stock trading markets include disclosure obligations in their private listing contracts. But the details of the Securities Exchange Act of 1934, now heavily laden with (and even, in some cases, superseded by) a thick clothing of SEC administrative rules, are the dominant source of disclosure obligations for our publicly traded companies.

The SEC pronouncements, adopted through the formal procedures of the Administrative Procedure Act, have the force of law and are multi-layered. They come in the form of *Regulations,* which contain individual *Rules,* which refer to *Forms* or *Schedules,* which contain *Items* (which often cross-reference other Schedules). SEC statements on how to interpret the rules in light of specific facts come in *Interpretive Releases, No-Action Letters,* agency enforcement proceedings, *amicus* briefs filed with federal courts, miscellaneous public comments by agency officials, and telephone conversations with SEC staff. A good securities lawyer stays informed of them all.

No General Duty to Disclose. In the U.S. there is no general overarching legal duty to disclose all material facts, plans, strategies or other information to the trading markets. The U.S. Supreme Court articulated the principle in 1980: A duty to disclose "does not arise from the mere possession of nonpublic market information. . . . When an allegation of fraud is based upon nondisclosure, there can be no fraud absent a duty to speak." *Chiarella v. U.S.,* 445 U.S. 222, 234 (1980). A precise formulation of when the duty to speak arises under federal law is hazardous, however. One reasonable classification of the duty to speak could be the following (other lawyers may have their own):

The Duty to Speak. A duty to speak arises in two contexts, the second of which is, to some degree, under the control of the issuer. First, the SEA, as heavily supplemented by SEC Regulations, requires publicly traded firms to file *periodic reports:* annual reports and quarterly reports. The SEA requires an issuer to file annual reports on Form 10-K, which must contain a full analysis of the issuer's business, audited financial statements, disclosures on pending legal proceedings, and a management discussion and analysis (MD&A) section. The SEA also requires issuers to file quarterly reports on Form 10-Q. All publicly traded firms, whether or not they solicit proxies, are also required to send a *proxy statement* to their shareholders in anticipation of the firm's required annual meeting. SEA § 14(c); Reg. 14C.

Second, an issuer must file public reports with the SEC upon the occurrence of certain specified events—so-called current reports on Form 8-K. The events include changes in control of the issuer, acquisition or disposition of assets, bankruptcy or receivership, changes in the issuer's certifying accountant, and any resignation of the issuer's directors. The form does not require the disclosure of material changes in operating results, such as sales figures or revenue trends, however.

There are also specific SEC rules that detail disclosure requirements for firms that call special shareholder meetings, announce a tender offer, respond to a tender offer, repurchase shares to go private or in response to a tender offer, make a public offering of securities, or purchase over 5 percent of the registered stock of another firm. Federal judges have held, using the open-textured SEA Rule 10b–5, that share repurchases or the existence of rumors affecting stock price that are attributable to the leaks or trades of insiders trigger a firm's obligation to disclose all material information on the firm's affairs. E.g., *Elkind v. Liggett & Myers, Inc.*, 635 F.2d 156 (2d Cir. 1980). If a firm chooses to speak voluntarily to the trading markets, Rule 10b–5 requires that the statement not contain misstatements and be sufficiently complete so as to not mislead. This duty to be complete is a subset of a third category of mandatory disclosure obligation often called the *half-truth rule.*

The Duty Not to Publish Half-Truths. Whenever a duty to speak attaches, usually as the result of an obligation to file reports with the SEC pursuant to a specific administrative regulation or schedule, an issuer must first satisfy the subject matter requirements of whatever statute, rule, regulation or schedule is appropriate. The specific information requested is presumed material. In addition, the firm must satisfy a general obligation, known among securities practitioners as the *half-truth* rule, to "add . . . such further material information, if any, as may be necessary to make the required statements, in the light of the circumstances under which they are made[,] not misleading." SEA Rule 12b–20; SA Rule 408. In other words, a half-truth, a partial disclosure of facts that may be literally correct but misleading in light of facts that are concealed, is as culpable as an affirmative misrepresentation. A definition of materiality is crucial to the doctrine. More appears below.

The half-truth rule appears in other contexts defined by case law precedent as well. If the duty to speak arises from case law under Rule 10b–5 or a similar general antifraud rule, a firm must disclose all material information with any other information necessary to make the information disclosed not misleading. Thus a firm, when obliged to correct market rumors originating with statements or trades by insiders, for example, must disclose information sufficient to satisfy the half-truth rule. If the duty to speak is triggered by a firm's voluntary statements, the statements must be truthful and supplemented by other information necessary to make the statements not misleading.

Courts have long recognized that the half-truth rule when applied to SEC forms or schedules cannot be pressed to its literal boundaries. In the context of specific disclosure schedules, the half-truth doctrine, if read literally, could require an issuer to supplement any schedule with all facts on the issuer material to investors regardless of the specific, identified items of information required by the schedule itself. In theory, any non-public material information, although not covered by a specific item in a form or schedule, could, if disclosed, make a given annual or quarterly report, in a sense, more accurate or more complete and not misleading. If the half-truth rule is so understood, all SEC required filings, whether periodic reports or event-triggered reports, would be expanded into occasions for a disclosure of all material facts. Courts seem to limit the doctrine to one requiring a disclosure only of facts that specifically contradict the statements in forms or schedules (or in press releases) rather than one requiring the issuer "to state every fact about stock offered that a prospective purchaser might like to know or that might, if known, tend to influence his decision . . . ." E.g., *Otis & Co. v. SEC,* 106 F.2d 579, 582 (6th Cir. 1939). See also *Lewis v. Chrysler Corp.*, 949 F.2d 644 (3d Cir. 1991). Information, for example, that relates only to quantification, the gravity or significance of a public statement, apparently does not have to be disclosed. *Backman v. Polaroid Corp.*, 910 F.2d 10 (1st Cir. 1990).

Of course, there is a class of cases in which the courts do appear to put a broad gloss on the half-truth obligation. The federal courts do read the half-truth language broadly if the duty to speak is triggered by firm or insider trading under SEA Rule 10b–5. In such cases, all material information on the firm must be available to third parties on the opposite side of the trade. Here the firm's option is not to trade, or to disclose fully in the context of a trade. The distinction makes sense. The ease of avoiding the disclosure obligation entirely (by not trading) is not replicated when a firm owes the SEC a periodic report, for example.

Materiality. Whenever the duty to speak attaches, a company must disclose all *material* information. The U.S. Supreme Court penned the definition of materiality in *TSC Industries, Inc. v. Northway, Inc.*, 426 U.S. 438 (1976):

> An omitted fact is material if there is a substantial likelihood that a reasonable shareholder would consider it important in deciding how to vote. . . . It does not require proof of a substantial likelihood that disclosure

> of the omitted fact would have caused the reasonable investor to change his vote. What the standard does contemplate is a showing of a substantial likelihood that, under all the circumstances, the omitted fact would have assumed actual significance in the deliberations of the reasonable shareholder. Put another way, there must be a substantial likelihood that the disclosure of the omitted fact would have been viewed by the reasonable investor as having significantly altered the "total mix" of information made available. . . .

Federal circuit courts have supplemented the definition by categorizing as not material generalized statements of optimism ("mere puffing") and statements qualified with specific risk disclosures or other cautionary statements. E.g., *Grossman v. Novell,* 120 F.3d 1112 (10th Cir. 1997) ("bespeaks caution doctrine"). The circuit courts are split, however, over whether internal financial projections (and their cousins, asset appraisals) are material. E.g., *Walker v. Action Indus.,* 802 F.2d 703 (4th Cir. 1987) (no, disagreeing with the Third, Seventh, Sixth and Ninth Circuits and following the Second Circuit).

B. PROJECTIONS OF ACQUISITION SUCCESS

It goes almost without saying that public projections of post-acquisition results by officers of participants are common in most acquisitions. The officers seek to convince their shareholders and the securities trading markets in general that a proposed deal makes good business sense. Participants negotiating an acquisition project the post-acquisition value of a combined firm and compare this value with projections of the value of the constituent firms standing alone. The SEC knows that shareholders view the projections as significant but fears that managers will misuse them and shareholders will misunderstand them (that is, overrate their importance). Moreover, the SEC is concerned that managers' misuse of projections would be difficult to police. A projection is only an opinion of future events, usually heavily qualified.

This is the debate over the public disclosure of *forward-looking* information. The SEC has created four categories of projections: predictions an issuer *must* create and disclose; predictions an issuer must disclose *if* created and available; predictions an issuer *can voluntarily* disclose, if in good faith and with a reasonable basis in fact; and finally, predictions an issuer *cannot* legally disclose even if created and available. Most lawyers, concerned about liability exposure, advise their clients not to disclose predictions unless legally required to do so in categories one and two.

1. SEC Forms and Schedules: Required Disclosure of Projections of Post-Acquisition Performance

Shareholder Voting and the Proxy Statement. There are three separate items in Schedule 14A that appear to call for the disclosure of prospective information. Item 14 calls for financial statements meeting the requirements of Article 11 of Regulation

S–X. Article 11 requires *pro forma* financial information if significant business combinations are *probable*. In essence, the pro forma financials present the combined financials of the two constituent corporations as if they had combined on the date of the last financial statements prepared by the surviving company. Thus, in a sense, the information is not prospective; it is historical in that the companies' financial performances are combined as of a past date.

At issue, however, are the obligations of the firms in an acquisition to adjust or footnote the pro forma financials if the pro formas do not accurately reflect what is likely to occur in the transaction. The SEC regulations on Article 11 contain some general language on the matter. Thus, "[i]f the transaction is structured in such a manner that significantly different results may occur, . . . additional pro forma presentations which give effect to the range of possible results" are required. Rule 11–02(a)(10) of Reg. S–X. These adjustments and footnotes to the pro forma *could* constitute a very valuable kind of prospective information for investors. Yet accountants read this language in Article 11 very narrowly. The dominant footnote to pro formas is a disclaimer. The disclaimer states that the pro formas are a "mechanical exercise": They are not an accurate indication of any real results in the acquisition, and they do not include any quantification of synergy gains and other savings that may occur in the acquisition.

Article 11 also has a little-used provision that allows a firm, if it so chooses, to file a financial forecast *in lieu of* a pro forma. The forecast is a condensed statement under Rule 11–03 of Reg. S–X. The financial forecast must cover a period at least 12 months after the estimated consummation date of the transaction and set out clearly "[a]ssumptions particularly relevant to the transaction and effects thereof." Rule 11–03(a)(3) of Reg. S–X. Although forecasts are very carefully regulated by generally accepted accounting principles, professional standards generated by accountants themselves, there is room in such forecasts to make predictions about the future results of an acquisition. In practice, accountants often advise firms not to use the forecast rule.

A second call for prospective information in Item 14 is in subsection (b)(6). It comes the closest to asking for some concrete estimates: "If a report, opinion or appraisal materially relating to the transaction has been received from an outside party, and is referred to in the proxy statement, furnish [a summary of the report, opinion or appraisal]." The requirement is readily avoidable, however. Parties to the transaction simply omit any reference to opinions and appraisals, even if available, in their proxy statements.

A third call for prospective information appears in the tame language of Item 303(a) of Regulation S–K. Item 303 is incorporated by reference in Items 13 and 14 of Regulation 14A. The instruction deals with the "Management's Discussion and Analysis" (MD&A)

section of a firm's financial statements. The MD&A is text that helps readers understand the bare numbers in the financials. Instruction 3 requires that "[t]he discussion and analysis must focus specifically on material events and uncertainties known to management that are reasonably likely to cause reported financial information not to be necessarily indicative of future operating results or of future financial condition." Major acquisition transactions would appear to qualify, but presumably such information would seem to be already contained in the pro forma financials.

The SEC has attempted to give additional substance to the hazy distinction between prospective information that an issuer *must* disclose and forward-looking information that an issuer *may* disclose through a series of double negatives. *Management's Discussion and Analysis of Financial Condition and Results of Operations; Certain Investment Company Disclosures,* SEC Rel. No. 33–6835, 1989 WL 1092885 (May 18, 1989). First, management must determine whether the known trend or event is likely to occur. If management determines that it is not reasonably likely to occur, no disclosure is required. Second, if management cannot make a determination that the event is not likely to occur, disclosure is required unless management determines that a material effect on the financial condition of the reporting company is not reasonably likely to occur.

Stock Swaps and a Prospectus. Purchasers issuing securities as consideration in stock-for-stock mergers, stock-for-assets acquisitions or exchange (stock-for-stock) tender offers are selling securities for the purposes of the Securities Act of 1933. SA Rule 145(a). If a purchaser cannot qualify under an exemption to registration, it must register the securities with the SEC and offer the securities using a selling document entitled a *prospectus*. The securities may be registered on a special Form S-4 registration statement for acquisitions or on the basic Form S-1 registration statement.

Form S-4 follows the pattern established in the proxy regulations noted above. For example, Item 5 incorporates by reference Article 11 of Regulation S–X and requires pro forma financial statements. Item 303 of Regulation S–K on MD&A text applies as well. E.g., Form S-4, Items 12(b)(3)(v), 13(a)(3)(v) & 14(h). Item 4(b) notes that "if a report, opinion or appraisal materially relating to the transaction has been received from an outside party, and such report, opinion, or appraisal is referred to in the prospectus . . .," the issuer must include information on the details of the report.

Tender Offers and Schedules TO, 13E-3 and 14D-9. Items in Schedule TO, the bidder's announcing document, Schedule 14D-9, the target's response, and Schedule 13E-3, an issuer's going-private statement, also follow the rules discussed above for proxy statements. The items require pro forma financials and a disclosure of known trends in the MD&A language. In addition, however, Regulation M–A has Item 1006(a) and (c) that requires a bidder to "state the purposes" of the tender offer including:

"any plans, proposals or negotiations that relate to or would result in" a follow-up merger (a squeeze-out, for example), the subsequent sale of the target's assets (a bust-up, for example), any change in the board or management of the target, any change in the capitalization or dividend policy, any material change in corporate structure or business, and any plans to delist the target's securities from a stock exchange.

Targets in third-party tender offers must state "reasons" for whatever recommendation they make to their shareholders in response to a tender offer. Item 4 of Schedule 14D-9 (referring to Reg. M–A, Item 1012(b)). They must also disclose negotiations with other potential acquirers in Item 7 (referring to Reg. M–A, Item 1006(d)(1)). If the target has signed an agreement in principle with another acquirer, the target must disclose the details of the acquisition, including the acquirer's future plans for the target. Reg. M–A, Item 1006(d)(2).

A series of novel provisions apply to a going-private transaction, however. Item 8 in Schedule 13E-3, referring to Item 1014 of Reg. M–A, requires a statement on the *fairness* of the transaction by the issuer. The item also requires reasonable detail on the material factors behind the statement and the weight assigned to each factor. Item 9, referring to Item 1015 of Reg. M–A, supplements Item 8. It requires that an issuer disclose any report, opinion or appraisal from an outside party (other than legal opinions)—fairness opinions from investment bankers, for example—that is materially related to the transaction, including those relating to the fairness of either the consideration or the transaction. Item 9 also requires substantial detail on the content and authors of the reports. Items 8 and 9 are unique in the SEC forms and schedules, and apply only to going-private transactions. They are reflective of the internal conflicts of interest inherent in those transactions.

2. SEC Rules on Permission to Make Voluntary Projections of Post-Acquisition Performance

If disclosure is not required, issuers can decide to disclose *voluntarily* forward-looking information. SA Rule 175 and SEA Rule 3b–6 permit a firm to disclose a short, specific list of projections in annual or quarterly reports. Rule 175(c) allows, for example, projections of "revenues, income (loss), earnings (loss) per share, capital expenditures, dividends, capital structure or other financial items" and "a statement of management's plans and objectives for future operations." Presumably each type of projection could be made about the business future of a surviving entity in an acquisition or reorganization. The safe harbor rules protect an issuer's voluntary projections only if made with a reasonable basis and in good faith.

The Rules do not specifically require the disclosure of the assumptions that underlie the forward-looking statements, but the SEC takes the position that

> [u]nder certain circumstances the disclosure of the underlying assumptions may be material to

> an understanding of the projected results. . . . [K]ey assumptions underlying a forward looking statement [may be] of such significance that their disclosure may be necessary in order for such statements to meet the reasonable basis and good faith standards embodied in the rule.

Safe Harbor Rule for Projections, SEC Rel. No. 33–6084 (July 5, 1979).

Rule 175 and Rule 3b–6 do not include and, therefore, *do not* protect projections of future stock prices or other market values of the survivor—the information probably most desired by the seller's shareholders who are deciding whether to vote on a transaction that will exchange their shares for stock in the survivor. See also SEA § 21E(i)(1) (definition of "forward-looking statement"). Indeed, SEA Rule 14a–9, the general antifraud rule applicable to proxy statements, in its list of examples of projections that may be misleading, includes "predictions as to specific future market values." The SEC is generally very suspicious of broad predictions by firm managers on post-acquisition stock prices, believing that given half a chance, managers will imitate snake oil salesmen. Indeed, the SEC fears that managers will mislead their shareholders with general, exaggerated claims that are not susceptible to correction by after-the-fact litigation based on fraud.

The definition of forward-looking information in the Rules was incorporated by Congress into the safe harbor provisions of the Private Securities Litigation Reform Act of 1995 (PSLRA). Under the provisions of the PSLRA, forward-looking statements are not fraudulent in private civil actions (the exclusion does not apply to SEC prosecutions) if they are "accompanied by meaningful cautionary statements identifying important factors that could cause actual results to differ materially from those in the forward looking statement" or if the plaintiff fails to prove actual knowledge that a statement is false or misleading. SA § 27A(c)(1)(A); SEA § 21E(c)(1)(A). The PSLRA expressly does not apply to tender offer disclosures, however. The SEC provisions that allow but do not require disclosure of certain types of prospective information are largely unused, as lawyers counsel their client to disclose only that which is required and even then only at minimal levels.

Asher v. Baxter Int'l Inc., 377 F.3d 727 (7th Cir. 2004), provides an example of a court struggling with the application of the safe harbors. Plaintiff-shareholders claimed that Baxter management made (and later doubled-down multiple times on) materially false and misleading projections. When actual numbers didn't match up with the projections, Baxter's stock price tanked. Plaintiffs claimed that Baxter management had "juiced" the numbers in anticipation of a stock-for-stock acquisition of Fusion Medical, thus effectively reducing the purchase price payable by Baxter. The court grappled with what constitutes "meaningful cautionary language" for purposes of the safe harbors relating to projections and forward-looking statements. While the safe harbors exclude certain overly broad language ("caveat emptor"), they do not rule in any specific language for use in this context. The court then analyzed Baxter's cautionary language and the factors it listed as to why its projections may not come true. Boilerplate cautionary language is clearly not enough; "cautions must be tailored to the risks that accompany the particular projections."

3. The Duty to Amend, Correct or Update Projections

The *duty to amend* is found expressly in several of the disclosure schedules pertaining to stock acquisitions. SEA Rule 13d–2(a) (disclosure of a purchase of more than 5 percent of a class of equity securities of an issuer), for example, requires the filing of an amendment disclosing any material change in the facts disclosed in an original filing within two business days after the date of such change. The duty to amend is an express direction to amend in the schedules, forms and rules. See also SEA Rules 14d–6(c) (tender offers), 14d–9(c) (issuer responses to tender offers), 13e–3(e)(2) (going-private transactions) and 13e–4(e)(3) (issuer tender offers). The *duty to correct* is the obligation of a filing company to correct promptly statements that it discovers were incorrect when originally made. See, e.g., *Gallagher v. Abbott Laboratories,* 269 F.3d 806 (7th Cir. 2001) ("[A] statement may be 'corrected' only if it was incorrect when made . . . ."). The *duty to update,* the most controversial of the three, is a general duty derived from SEA Rule 10b–5 to supplement statements (even when there is otherwise no specific duty to amend) that were accurate when made but that have become inaccurate or misleading due to subsequent events.

The duty to update attaches to forward-looking statements only (explicit firm projections and predictions made in the public filings or statements). There is disagreement among the federal circuit courts on whether the duty exists at all—the Seventh Circuit says no, the First, Second and Third Circuit Courts say yes—and, if it exists, on how broad it is. Id.; *Weiner v. Quaker Oats Co.,* 129 F.3d 310 (3d Cir. 1997); *In re Time Warner Sec. Litig.,* 9 F.3d 259 (2d Cir. 1993); *Backman v. Polaroid Corp.,* 910 F.2d 10 (1st Cir. 1990).

C. THE DUTY TO DISCLOSE ACQUISITION NEGOTIATIONS: RULE 10b–5

When must a firm disclose the existence of *preliminary* merger negotiations? The answer depends on whether the firm is under an obligation to file a periodic report (a 10-K or 10-Q) or an episodic report (a registration statement). If so, the forms each contain an explicit anti-half-truth rule (the firm must disclose whatever is necessary so the required disclosures are not misleading). The materiality standard announced in *Basic, Inc. v. Levinson,* 485 U.S. 224 (1988), for similar language in SEA Rule 10b–5, applies. The standard is a "balancing of both the indicated probability that the event will occur and the anticipated magnitude of the event in light of the totality of the company activity." Since major acquisitions are always big news, a large acquisition may be material even if the probability of it occurring is less than 50 percent.

The periodic reporting forms also incorporate by reference Regulation S–K. Regulation S–K contains Item 303 requiring MD&A statements on *known events* that could also require disclosure of preliminary negotiations. The SEC, in Rel. No. 33–6835 (May 18, 1989), however, construed Item 303 to allow parties to stay quiet if disclosure "would jeopardize completion of the transaction." Otherwise, when the negotiations (as known events) are reasonably likely to have material effects on a firm, the firm must disclose them. In the release the SEC defers to Form 8-K, requiring reporting of extraordinary events, which at the time of the release required disclosure of acquisitions only on the completion of the acquisition and since 2004 has required disclosure of a company's *signing* of an acquisition agreement. It is also not clear whether the reservations in the release apply also to the anti-half-truth language in the reporting schedules.

If no periodic reports need to be filed, is there a general disclosure obligation for material preliminary merger discussions? *Basic* is not on point. At issue in *Basic* was the materiality of *voluntarily made* disclosures, press releases and comments to the NYSE that were admittedly false. If the statements were material, Rule 10b–5 would apply without question. To define materiality, the court adopted a modified version of the materiality standard first articulated in *S.E.C. v. Texas Gulf Sulphur Co.*, 401 F.2d 833 (2d Cir. 1968) (significance of deal multiplied by its probability of occurrence), and rejected the bright-line test of *Greenfield v. Heublein, Inc.*, 742 F.2d 751 (3d Cir. 1984) (when parties reach an agreement in principle on the major terms).

Only in dicta (in footnote 17) does the court in *Basic* address the issue of whether Rule 10b–5 itself imposed a general duty to speak, and then only obliquely. Most lawyers understand that the case gives a negative answer to the question, however. As understood, the case establishes that Rule 10b–5, by itself, does not establish a general disclosure obligation for preliminary merger discussions. In footnote 17, the court penned the now often-quoted phrase: "[S]ilence, absent a duty to disclose, is not misleading." This phrase leads lawyers to believe that there is no general duty to disclose even admittedly material events. The court also noted that a "no comment" was "generally" the same as silence.

There are two significant caveats to the general rule, however. First, the *Weiner* case from the Third Circuit throws a significant wrench in the analysis using a broad form of a duty to update that requires an early disclosure of merger discussions (a firm must update outstanding public filings and public statements). *Weiner v. Quaker Oats Co.,* 129 F.3d 310 (3d Cir. 1997). Several other circuits do not follow *Weiner,* however. Second, in contrast to the requirements of Rule 10b–5 as interpreted in *Basic,* the NYSE listing requirements give a clear positive answer. In NYSE Listed Company Manual § 202.05, the exchange requires of listed companies that, if the information is likely to affect trading prices (most preliminary merger discussions, once discovered, do affect price), it must be disclosed to the public.

Section 202.05 is buttressed by § 202.01 that requires disclosure whenever leaks of sensitive information are likely and by § 202.03 that requires disclosure whenever the trading price shows unusual volatility.

Privately Held Companies. Privately held companies are not covered by the SEA's mandatory disclosure provisions. SEA Rule 10b–5 applies to all trades in securities, however, including the purchase and sale of securities of privately held companies (including those of closely held companies, a *subset* of privately held companies). The Seventh Circuit has held that, under Rule 10b–5, a privately held corporation negotiating an acquisition may not repurchase the shares of employees without a disclosure of pending merger discussions. *Jordan v. Duff & Phelps, Inc.*, 815 F.2d 429 (7th Cir. 1987). See also *Berreman v. West Publ. Co.*, 615 N.W.2d 362 (Minn. Ct. App. 2000) (fiduciary duty to disclose material information).

D. INSIDER TRADING IN ADVANCE OF ACQUISITION ANNOUNCEMENTS

The stock price of both the acquirer and the target often jump on the public announcement of an acquisition. Since target shareholders often receive an acquisition premium for their shares of around 30 percent or more, the trading price of target shares on the announcement will increase to reflect the premium. Bidder shares may lose value on the announcement if market traders believe that the bidder is overpaying for control of the target. Any person who knows of an acquisition before it has been announced can make a considerable sum of money by trading shares in either or both of the parties before the announcement. There is, therefore, often a substantial run-up in the stock price of an acquisition target before the public announcement of an acquisition. The average run-up is about thirty percent of the acquisition premium. Some of the run-up is due to legitimate trading—sleuthing by professional analysts—and street talk. Some of the run-up is due to illegal insider trading.

When a corporate insider of either a bidder or a target trades in the securities of either corporation in advance of the public announcement of an acquisition, the insider violates SEA Rule 10b–5. If the insider trades in the securities of her own company, she violates the traditional or classical theory of insider trading. E.g., *Chiarella v. U.S.,* 445 U.S. 222 (1980); *In the Matter of Cady, Roberts & Co.,* 1961 WL 60638 (S.E.C.). If an insider on one side in an acquisition trades in the stock of an opposite party to the transaction, without the authorization of her employer, she violates the "misappropriation" branch of Rule 10b–5. *U.S. v. O'Hagan,* 521 U.S. 642 (1997). Insiders include officers and directors, professionals hired to provide advice or other services on an acquisition, and any other person in a confidential or fiduciary relationship with one of the two constituent parties to an acquisition. *Dirks v. SEC,* 463 U.S. 646 (1983). Those who receive tips from insiders are also liable if an insider receives a personal benefit from tipping. Id.

The SEC also promulgated SEA Rule 14e–3 in 1980 to stop insider trading in anticipation of tender offer announcements. The rule stops insiders, whether in the bidder or target, and their tippees from trading on material information relating to a tender offer whenever a bidder "has taken a substantial step . . . to commence, or has commenced, a tender offer . . . ." The Rule is broader than SEA Rule 10b–5: In tender offers, unlike under Rule 10b–5, a party on one side of a tender offer cannot authorize its employees to trade in the stock of an opposite party.

E. DISCLOSING STOCK PURCHASES OF MORE THAN 5 PERCENT: SECTION 13(d) OF THE EXCHANGE ACT

Section 13(d) of the SEA is a portion of the 1968 Williams Act. The statute applies to the acquisition of voting stock of publicly traded companies. Once a purchaser (or cohesive *group* of purchasers) acquires more than 5 percent of such stock, it has five business days in which to file a public disclosure statement, Schedule 13D. In practice, purchasers buy 4.99 percent at their leisure and then race to buy as much as they can during the five business day "grace period" (a bidder can usually get up to 10 or 11 percent) before they file.

A purchaser who has acquired securities in the "ordinary course of his business and not with the purpose nor with the effect of changing or influencing the control of the issuer" may file a Schedule 13G rather than a Schedule 13D. Typical 13G filers are large institutional investors, such as mutual funds, that ordinarily have no interest in influencing or acquiring the public company in question. Initial 13G filings by qualified institutional investors and exempt investors are due within 45 days of the end of the quarter in which they crossed the five percent beneficial ownership threshold. Initial Schedule 13G filings by all other passive investors are due within five business days of crossing the five percent beneficial ownership threshold.

The SEC believes that the determination of whether a particular shareholder acquired or is holding securities with a purpose or effect of "changing or influencing" control of the issuer should be based on all the relevant facts and circumstances and will be informed by the meaning of "control" as defined in SEA Rule 12b–2. According to the SEC, the subject matter of the shareholder's engagement with the issuer's management may be dispositive in making this determination. Moreover, the context in which the engagement occurs is also highly relevant in making this determination.

Schedule 13D requires the disclosure of sources of funds for the purchases (Item 3) and of the acquirer's purposes, plans or proposals for the target firm (Item 4). Those who cheat try to warehouse stock in phony accounts to avoid disclosure. Ivan Boesky, the person upon whom the "Gordon Gekko" character in the movie *Wall Street* was partially based, pled guilty and went to jail primarily on § 13(d) violations.

Rondeau v. Mosinee Paper Corp., 422 U.S. 49 (1975), explains the purpose of the section, illustrates how the section can catch novice bidders unaware of the section's requirements, and deals with the question of a proper remedy for violations. In the case, officers of the target asked that the stock held by a purchaser who had violated the section be "sterilized," stripped of voting power. The Court of Appeals agreed but the U.S. Supreme Court reversed (over Justice Douglas's dissent). The purchaser, the court held, had cured by filing a Schedule 13D once he was aware of the requirement; target shareholders had the required information and the purchaser had made no further efforts to control the target. The court noted the limited scope of the holding and also reserved the question of whether shareholders, who sold stock during the period after which disclosure was required and was not made, could sue.

Unlike *Rondeau, S.E.C. v. First City Fin. Corp.*, 890 F.2d 1215 (D.C. Cir. 1989), addresses those with bad intent. In connection with its planned hostile takeover of Ashland Oil, First City Financial entered into an informal put and call agreement with Bear Stearns that covered shares of Ashland Oil stock. Bear Stearns had purchased the large number of Ashland Oil shares covered by the agreement at First City's behest. Under the agreement, First City had the right to call away the stock from Bear Stearns, while Bear Stearns had the right to put the stock to First City. Thus, First City had all the risk associated with ownership of the Ashland Oil shares covered by the agreement.

The SEC sued, believing that First City was the beneficial owner of the shares covered by the agreement for purposes of § 13(d). While First City did ultimately file a Schedule 13D, it did so much later than it should have according to the SEC. Between the time when First City should have filed its 13D and the time it actually did make that filing, First City continued to accumulate large numbers of Ashland Oil shares at artificially low prices due to the lack of disclosure on First City's part. First City saved approximately $2.7 million based on its tardy filing.

The District Court enjoined First City from further violations of § 13(d) and ordered that it disgorge its $2.7 million cost savings (what the court called First City's "profit" given that First City ultimately sold its position in Ashland Oil shares back to Ashland Oil). The D.C. Circuit affirmed. The SEC was allowed to "reasonably approximate profits" made by First City rather than provide specificity as it was impossible to determine the price at which Ashland Oil stock would have traded had First City filed its Schedule 13D in a timely fashion.

As mentioned above, § 13(d) also applies to purchases made by a cohesive "group" of purchasers. In this regard, the SEC has indicated that under its existing rules an express agreement is not necessary to find that a group exists. Instead, whether a group has been formed involves a facts-and-circumstances analysis of whether two or more persons act together for the purpose of "acquiring," "holding" or "disposing of" securities of a given company. However, the SEC has noted that some minimum indicia of agreement (such as an informal arrangement or coordination) is needed to form a group.

CSX Corp. v. The Children's Investment Fund Mgt. (UK) LLP, 654 F.3d 276 (2d Cir. 2011), is a fascinating case on the "group" doctrine and the complexities that derivative securities present in the analysis. Two "wolf pack" hedge funds purchased shares in CSX Corp. They also entered into "cash-settled total-return equity swaps" with various counterparties. To hedge their risk, the counterparties needed to purchase actual shares of CSX stock (i.e., hold long positions). The hedge funds dispersed the swaps in a way that ensured that no counterparty would have to purchase more than 5 percent of CSX's outstanding shares in order to hedge its position. This prevented drawing unwanted attention to what the hedge funds were up to.

On appeal in *CSX Corp.* was the issue of whether the two hedge funds had formed a "group" for § 13(d) purposes. Ultimately, the Second Circuit decided to remand the case for additional findings of fact to made by the District Court. However, the Second Circuit noted that it was possible that two other groups might be present in the case. One would be the hedge funds and their counterparties combined; the other would cover just the counterparties. Of course, no conclusion is provided as the District Court did not make factual findings with respect to those two other alleged groups.

Section 13(d) does have costs: it deters some purchasers at the margin by increasing the costs of purchasing control. First, it makes straight acquisitions more expensive. The lowest cost method is usually to execute quiet toe-hold purchases (negotiated private purchases and open-market purchases) until rumors flood the market. Once the rumors are wide-spread, the bidder makes a public tender offer for legal control and follows the tender offer with a back-end, cash-out merger to eliminate minority shareholders. At some point a public tender offer becomes less expensive than additional negotiated or open-market purchases. A flat public tender offer price reduces the tendency of target shareholders to hold out when rumors about a takeover are abundant in the market. Section 13(d) sets the line between private and public purchases at the acquisition of a 5 to 10 percent block, earlier than many bidders would otherwise make the shift.

Second, § 13(d) enables target managers to defend their firms by giving them an early warning of an impending takeover. Target boards can resist the acquisition, negotiate for a higher price from the bidder, or seek a second, higher bid from a new bidder. The target shareholders may receive a higher price in a given takeover but fewer bidders may bid in the first instance. At issue is a calculation of the trade-off of fewer bids against a higher price on bids that do occur.

Critics also question why passive shareholders of a target should have free access to information created by a stranger to the firm, the potential acquirer. There is no fiduciary duty of a potential acquirer, a stranger, to target firm shareholders; the stranger is not using firm assets and does not have insider information (it has developed its own information at considerable expense); and the target shareholders have done nothing to add to the value of the firm other than to elect the old managers, which may be the problem. Why, critics ask, is it fair to force those who develop information, create value, to give it away for nothing? Section 13(d) discourages outside third parties from developing valuable information on target firm value.

§ 5. THE SHORT-SWING PROFIT RULE: A TRAP FOR LOSING BIDDERS AND FOR TARGET INSIDERS

Section 16(b) of the SEA creates a right in shareholders to sue, on behalf of their corporation, officers, directors and "more than 10 percent" shareholders in the corporation for any profits (but not losses) made in trading in the corporation's own stock within any six-month period. Congress passed the section to curb speculation by insiders and controlling shareholders in company stock. Indeed, trading at a profit within a six-month period is *presumed* to have been on the basis of material, nonpublic information. That is, it is "presumed" to be *insider trading*.

Section 16(b) affects acquisition planning in several types of situations. When competing bidders each purchase stock in a target and one bidder prevails, usually by offering the highest price in a tender offer, the losing bidder can be caught by the Section. If the losing bidder holds more than ten percent of the target and tenders its target shares into the winning tender offer, or otherwise agrees to sell its shares to the winning bidder at a profit, the losing bidder violates the Section if it has held those shares for less than six months. E.g., *Texas Int'l Airlines v. Nat'l Airlines, Inc.*, 714 F.2d 533 (5th Cir. 1983). By contrast, if the losing bidder's shares are cashed out in a second-step, cash-out merger between the winning bidder and the target, the losing bidder is not in violation of the Section as it is legally forced to give up its target shares as a result of the merger. *Kern County Land Co. v. Occidental Petroleum Corp.*, 411 U.S. 582 (1973). Indeed, in that case insider trading is *not* presumed.

Another troublesome application of § 16(b) is its effect on the stock holdings of officers, directors and more than 10 percent shareholders of the target that were acquired by them from the target within six months of the time the target itself is acquired. Does the exchange of their shares for acquirer stock or cash trigger the short-swing disgorgement remedy of the Section? In 1996 the SEC promulgated SEA Rule 16b–3, a rule that exempts transfers by target officers and directors (but not more than 10 percent shareholders) if the transaction is approved by a disinterested target board of directors or by the target's shareholders. If the former officers and directors of the target receive stock in the acquirer and, as a result of the acquisition, become officers and directors of the acquirer, the acquiring board or shareholders must ratify the disposition as well.

CHAPTER 7

ACCOUNTING ISSUES IN MERGERS AND ACQUISITIONS

The financial accounting aspects of mergers and acquisitions usually focus on the post-acquisition impact on the financials of the *acquirer*.

§ 1. SOURCES OF FINANCIAL ACCOUNTING PRINCIPLES

Managerial accounting focuses on information produced for internal use in varied contexts such as pricing, budgeting and inventory planning. In comparison, *financial accounting* reports the over-all financial position of the enterprise at certain points in time (for example, December 31) and over certain periods of time (for example, quarterly or annually). This is the information upon which external users, such as lenders, labor unions, regulators, investment analysts and, of course, investors, primarily rely.

Financial accounting information must be *reliable,* accurately and neutrally reflecting the underlying transactions of the enterprise. To ensure reliability, management of publicly traded companies must adopt appropriate internal control and reporting systems. SOX § 404. Accounting information must also be *relevant,* capable of making a difference in decisions by potential users of the information. Financial accounting information should be reported in a *consistent* manner from reporting period to reporting period. Furthermore, financial accounting information should be based on common principles that make the basis for the information *comparable* from enterprise to enterprise. In that regard, reference is frequently made to *generally accepted accounting principles* or *GAAP*.

In the U.S., GAAP has been largely determined by the private sector (principally the accounting profession) through pronouncements of the Financial Accounting Standards Board (FASB) (a non-profit organization comprised of seven independent members each of whom has a concern for investors, other users, and the public interest in matters of accounting and financial reporting) and its predecessor, the Accounting Principles Board (APB), created by the American Institute of Certified Public Accountants. For publicly traded companies, the Securities and Exchange Commission (SEC), principally through the Office of the Chief Accountant, works with the accounting profession and the FASB to develop additional accounting standards for reporting companies. While the SEC has statutory authority to prescribe the accounting principles utilized in reports filed with it, it has generally relied on the accounting profession to develop such rules. The accounting rules for publicly traded companies are contained in Regulation S–X.

§ 2. THE BASIC FINANCIAL ACCOUNTING STATEMENTS

The basic financial statements for an enterprise include: (1) an *earnings statement* (a.k.a. "income statement" or "profit and loss statement") which reflects operating performance of the enterprise for a specific period of time (e.g., a quarter or a year); (2) a *balance sheet* (or statement of financial position) which reflects the assets, liabilities, and owners' equity of the enterprise as of a specific point in time (e.g., December 31); and (3) a *statement of cash flows* which reflects the cash inflows and outflows of the enterprise for a specific period of time (e.g., a quarter or a year).

The *income statement* has been compared to a motion picture of an enterprise's activities over the reporting period, accumulating the results of the sales of its goods or services and subtracting the matching costs of goods sold, overhead (such as wages and salaries, rent, supplies and depreciation), interest expense, and taxes. Thus, the income statement answers the vital question: Did the enterprise make any money during the time period in question?

Earnings per share (*EPS*), a fundamental factor in an investor's evaluation of an appropriate share price, is computed from the income statement by dividing the earnings of the enterprise by the number of outstanding shares of common stock. Outstanding shares also include shares "deemed outstanding" in connection with stock options and convertible securities under complicated "dilution" rules.

The income statement can be misleading if accepted at face value. First, it reports past results and is of limited aid in forecasting future profitability. Indeed, with a fast-growing company the focus of analysts in predicting the future price of a stock is often not on "trailing" earnings but rather on future projected earnings. Second, the income statement can report non-cash expenditures (such as depreciation of buildings and equipment) that decrease earnings but not cash flow (hence the usefulness of EBITDA analysis discussed previously in Chapter 2, § 2). Third, it would be rare for a public company to report on a simple cash receipts-and-expenditures basis (the *cash basis* of accounting). Consequently the *accrual method* of accounting is employed, whereby revenues are generally matched against the costs associated with generating those revenues (the so-called *matching principle*). However, the accrual method permits some latitude (and thus potential abuses) in the timing of revenue recognition and the deduction of costs.

The *balance sheet* accumulates, with some exceptions, the historical "book" accounting value of assets, subtracting liabilities to arrive at the equity or net worth of the enterprise. Like the income statement, the balance sheet can present information that is potentially misleading. First—with some exceptions for cash, accounts receivable, and marketable securities—historical cost, rather than current fair value, is reported for assets. In an industry with declining asset values book value may overstate the value of assets. By contrast, in an industry with increasing asset values book value may understate the current fair value. Second, the balance sheet amounts may not include valuable assets, such as internally developed goodwill, going concern value, or important innovations, and may exclude substantial liabilities, such as certain lease obligations (substituting footnote disclosures perhaps for line numbers).

The *statement of cash flows* (once referred to as the statement of changes in financial position, the sources and uses of financial resources statement, or the funds statement) presents changes in an enterprise's financial position that are normally generated from operations and summarizes the financing and investing activities of the enterprise for the same period.

§ 3. ACQUISITION ACCOUNTING: THE COST METHOD—ACQUISITIONS OF LESS THAN 20 PERCENT OF THE TARGET'S OUTSTANDING COMMON STOCK

If an acquirer purchases less than 20 percent of a target's outstanding common stock, when and how should the acquirer's income statement reflect the earnings of the target? Moreover, how should the acquirer's balance sheet reflect the investment in the target?

Under the *cost method* of accounting, the separate accounting identity of a target is respected and the acquirer reports income from the target's operations only when and if dividends are distributed by the target to the acquirer. Dividends from the target in excess of its earnings subsequent to the acquisition date are a return of the acquirer's investment and reduce the reported amount of the investment. When the acquirer sells the stock of the target, the acquirer will record as gain or loss on its income statement the difference between the cost basis of the investment (as adjusted for any dividends in excess of earnings) and its sales price. However, as discussed in the following paragraphs, unrealized holding gains and losses of certain equity securities must also be included in current earnings.

On the issue of how to present a less than 20 percent acquisition on the balance sheet, it depends on the purpose of the investment. See FASB Statement 115 (FAS 115), Accounting for Certain Investments in Debt and Equity Securities. Equity securities that are bought and held principally for the purpose of selling them in the near term are *trading securities*. Trading is the active and frequent buying and selling of securities with the objective of producing profits on short-term differences in price (buy low, sell high). Equity investments that are not classified as trading securities are *available-for-sale* securities. Most strategic investments in companies like an acquisition target would fall into this category. FAS 115 does not apply to investments in equity securities, however, unless the fair value is *readily determinable,* with reference to bid-and-asked quotations that are currently available on a securities exchange registered with the SEC or in the over-the-counter market.

If FAS 115 does not apply to an equity investment, it is reported on the balance sheet at the original acquisition cost with adjustment only for other than temporary impairment of value (e.g., a series of operating losses of the target or other factors may indicate that a decrease in value has occurred which is other than temporary and should be recognized).

Under FAS 115, trading securities are classified as current assets on the balance sheet. Unrealized holding gains and losses are included in current earnings.

Under FAS 115, available-for-sale securities are classified as either current or non-current assets. If the investment in a target is a marketable security representing the investment of cash available for current operations (assuming it is not already characterized as a trading security), the stock would be classified as a current asset. In the more likely case of a strategic investment in a target, the stock would be classified as a non-current asset. Dividend income, as well as realized gains and losses, are included in earnings. Unrealized holding gains and losses are generally excluded from earnings, but reported as a separate component of shareholders' equity until realized. If an available-for-sale security suffers a decline in fair value below cost that is other than temporary, the cost basis is written down to fair value, and the amount of the write-down is included in earnings, accounted for as a realized loss.

§ 4. ACQUISITION ACCOUNTING: THE EQUITY METHOD—ACQUISITIONS OF 20 PERCENT UP TO 50 PERCENT OF THE TARGET'S OUTSTANDING STOCK

APB Opinion 18 discusses the *equity method* of accounting, which applies if an acquirer is able to exercise significant influence over the operating and financial policies of a target. While 20 percent or greater ownership produces a presumption of influence (and influence is presumed not to exist for ownership of less than 20 percent), both presumptions may be overcome by predominant evidence to the contrary (e.g., the presence of a majority shareholder).

If the equity method applies, an acquirer records an investment in the stock of the target at cost on the balance sheet, but subsequently increases or decreases that investment by the acquirer's share of the earnings or losses of the target arising after the date of acquisition. Moreover, the acquirer reports its share of the target's earnings or losses on its income statement. The acquirer makes adjustments to its balance sheet and income statement irrespective of whether or when any dividend distributions are received from the target. Dividends received from the target, however, are not income, but reduce the amount of the investment account on the balance sheet. APB Opinion 18 requires that a loss in value of an investment which is other than a temporary decline should be recognized the same as a loss in value of other long-term assets.

In sum, if the business of a partially owned subsidiary is profitable, and the acquirer's share of the profits exceeds dividend distributions, the acquirer's reported investment in the target will grow and exceed its cost. However, losses of the subsidiary have an immediate impact on the acquirer's income statement as well as its balance sheet. Therefore, the potential accounting impact on the acquirer's reported profits may influence the size of the planned stake in the target.

§ 5. ACQUISITION ACCOUNTING: ACQUISITIONS OF GREATER THAN 50 PERCENT OF THE STOCK OF THE TARGET

If an acquirer owns more than 50 percent of the target, control of the target is assumed. Thus, the accounting results of both companies must be *consolidated* into a single set of numbers. FAS 94, Consolidation of All Majority-Owned Subsidiaries.

A. FUNDAMENTALS OF ACQUISITION ACCOUNTING

In July 2001, the FASB issued two statements on 50 percent or more acquisitions that substantially rewrote the consolidation rules: FASB Statement 141, Business Combinations (later superseded by FAS 141(R), a 2007 revision, which was then codified into Accounting Standards Codification (ASC) 805 in 2009), and FASB Statement 142, Goodwill and Other Intangible Assets (later codified into ASC 350-20 in 2009).

In FAS 141(R), the FASB ruled that only the acquisition method of accounting is permitted for business combinations initiated after June 30, 2001. Under *acquisition accounting*, the acquisition of the target is treated as an arm's-length purchase of the target by the acquirer, reflecting the *fair values* of the acquired assets and liabilities. The fair values allocated to the acquired assets and liabilities are the basis for accounting in the future and are reported on the acquirer's balance sheet—the target's book values are not relevant. The lack of symmetry is remarkable in that the other assets and liabilities of the acquirer remain at historical cost amounts and are not adjusted to reflect their market values.

Critical to the figures then is the identification of which of the two combining companies is the acquirer. Consequently, all pertinent facts are examined in determining which party is considered to be the acquirer, including relative voting power in the combined enterprise, composition of the board of directors and senior management, and which company received a premium as an inducement for the combination.

The income statements of an acquirer reflect only the post-acquisition earnings of the target. If the acquirer is acquiring the target for a premium price, the purchase price in excess of the amounts assigned to the target's identifiable assets will be ascribed to *goodwill*. However, if the acquirer acquires the assets at a bargain price, below the target's historical cost, the negative goodwill is eliminated by reducing the historical cost of certain classes of the target's assets, to zero if necessary, with any remaining negative goodwill reported as an extraordinary gain.

In FAS 142, mandatory amortization of goodwill is abolished. Amortization is the expensing of a portion of the value listed on the firm's balance sheet of an intangible asset (an asset that lacks physical substance) with a limited useful economic life. Intangible assets include, among others, goodwill recognized in connection with an acquisition. Under FAS 142, the mandatory amortization of goodwill has been replaced by a write-down of goodwill only in the event of a demonstrated impairment of its fair value.

Under ASC 350-20, an acquirer is required to identify and evaluate goodwill impairment triggering events *when they occur* to determine whether it is more likely than not that the fair value of a previous acquisition is less than its carrying amount. If an acquirer determines that it is more likely than not that goodwill is impaired, it must test goodwill for impairment using the triggering event date as the measurement date. If, in fact, impairment has occurred, the acquirer must write-down the value of its previous acquisition to its fair value.

FASB provides privately held companies more flexibility on goodwill than their publicly traded counterparts. Privately held companies, unlike publicly traded companies, have the option of amortizing goodwill over a period of ten years or less. See Accounting Standards Update (ASU) 2014-02. Moreover, privately held companies that do not choose to amortize goodwill have the option of measuring goodwill impairments only at the end of a given reporting period in recognition of the costliness of the measurement process. See ASC 350-20.

The benefit to publicly traded companies of not amortizing goodwill turned into a mixed blessing after the collapse of the dot.com bubble in 2002. Publicly traded companies that had purchased scores of high-tech, smaller companies found themselves faced with huge write-offs, as the smaller companies' values evaporated. WorldCom posted over $80 billion in goodwill write-offs in 2002, a record that may never be broken. AOL Time Warner Inc. reported a 2002 net loss of $98.7 billion after taking a fourth quarter charge of $45.5 billion, mostly to write down the value of its troubled America Online unit. The write-down created the biggest annual corporate loss in history until American International Group (AIG) posted a $99.3 billion loss in 2008.

B. POOLING ACCOUNTING: A HISTORICAL ACCOUNT

APB Opinion 16, Business Combinations, from the time of its release in 1970 until its rescission by FAS 141(R), generally permitted two methods of accounting—the *acquisition method* described above and the *pooling method.* The parties to the transaction could, as a practical matter, elect acquisition or pooling treatment through the manner in which the transaction was structured.

Although pooling has been eliminated as a permitted method of acquisition accounting, it was a significant chapter in the story of acquisition accounting that requires some elaboration to understand pre-2001 acquisition structure. When pooling accounting applied, the combined enterprise was treated as a merger of the acquirer and the target (not as an arm's-length transfer of assets at fair value), and the book values of the separate enterprises carried over to the surviving entity. The numbers in the consolidated financial statements were simply the addition of the numbers in the financial statements of the previously separate enterprises (after inter-company eliminations and adjustments). No goodwill was created or necessary.

The advantage of not recognizing goodwill in a pooling transaction was significant as goodwill created in an acquisition accounting transaction (pre-2001) had to be amortized over forty years, thus reducing income on the acquirer's income statements. A transaction done with pooling accounting, therefore, would show significantly more income over time on an acquirer's income statements than one done with acquisition accounting.

Qualifying an acquisition for pooling treatment required that a transaction satisfy twelve criteria prescribed by APB Opinion 16. One requirement in particular shaped the structure of many acquisitions. With very limited exceptions for fractional shares and dissenting shareholders, target common shareholders had to receive only common stock in the surviving enterprise; there could not be a pro rata distribution of cash. This requirement reflected the premise on which pooling was based: that the surviving enterprise was a continuation of the two separate enterprises, and the target shareholders continued their undisturbed investment in the form of stock in the surviving entity. As discussed later in Chapter 8, §§ 1 and 3, this "solely stock" requirement also had federal income tax consequences, as it often permitted the transaction to be treated as a tax-free transaction.

§ 6. ACQUISITION ACCOUNTING: THE IMPACT OF THE ACCOUNTING RULES ON THE SIZE OF AN ACQUISITION

The size of an acquirer's stake in the target will dictate the accounting treatment for the investment. The equity method of accounting is likely to apply once a 20 percent ownership threshold is achieved. For example, an acquirer might choose to avoid the equity method by purchasing less than a 20 percent stake in a high risk start-up company in order to avoid sharing in potential losses. By contrast, an acquirer might wish to hold more than 20 percent of a non-dividend paying, but profitable, target. Once in the neighborhood of a 50 percent ownership, an acquirer should weigh the advantages of the equity method that permits only the net investment in a subsidiary to be reported and not the liabilities. The liabilities are *off the balance sheet*. If the acquirer and the subsidiary are consolidated, the subsidiary's debts would appear in the consolidated financial statements.

CHAPTER 8

FEDERAL INCOME TAX TREATMENT OF M&A TRANSACTIONS

§ 1. THE *TAXABLE* VERSUS *TAX-FREE* DISTINCTION

A. DEFINITIONS

Most publicly held corporations are so-called "C" corporations (i.e., they are taxed under Subchapter C of the IRC). Thus, their profits are subject to a double tax. The federal government imposes a *corporate-level* income tax on the corporate profits and a *shareholder-level* income tax upon the shareholders' receipt of a portion of the profits (in the form of dividends or liquidation proceeds). Due to the two levels of taxation, an acquisition planner must consider the effect of an acquisition structure on the tax bill of every constituent corporation in the deal and of the shareholders in each as well. In most acquisitive reorganizations there are *four potential taxpayers*—two corporations, an acquirer and a target, and two sets of shareholders, those of the acquirer and those of the target, to consider.

A general principle of federal income taxation is that a disposition of assets (whether corporate stock by a target shareholder or the underlying enterprise assets by the target itself) will presumptively cause the disposing party to realize and recognize immediately taxable income. The tax-free corporate reorganization provisions discussed below provide an exemption from immediate recognition (but not realization) of taxable gain or loss by the various parties to a corporate acquisition. See IRC §§ 354, 355, 356, 361 & 368.

Viewed through an income tax lens, the structure of mergers and acquisitions is divided into *taxable* transactions, on the one hand, and *tax-free* or *tax-deferred* transactions, on the other hand. In the absence of special factors (such as a tax-exempt seller or stock purged of its built-in gain under IRC § 1014 on account of the death of a shareholder), the tax-deferred label is more accurate for the tax-free category of transactions. A consequence of tax-free reorganization treatment is a *substituted* or *carryover* adjusted basis for stock or assets received by a party to the reorganization that preserves the built-in gain or loss in the asset, postponing the tax until a follow-up resale of the stock or assets occurs (see Chapter 8, § 3.E below).

B. THE CHOICE

Due to the *time value of money*, money in one's hands now has a higher value than money received in the future. If income tax consequences were the sole consideration, it would seem that the opportunity to defer income taxes into future years would channel most all acquisitions into a tax-free structure. An investor could take the tax money not paid to the government and invest it, keeping the returns until such time as the tax is due. A taxable transaction does come with a sizable benefit—a *cost* (fair market value) *adjusted basis* (rather than a substituted basis) that can be used by the acquirer (see IRC § 1012) to avoid future taxes. But the future taxes avoided due to the cost basis do not usually outweigh the higher, current tax bill. In a taxable transaction the parties must pay a tax in the year of the acquisition while the income tax benefits of the cost basis may be realized by the acquirer only in future years through cost recovery (i.e., depreciation or amortization) deductions or a subsequent taxable disposition of the assets.

Business considerations prevent some transactions from qualifying for a tax-free structure, however, and some acquirers, targets and target shareholders may have special characteristics that diminish the benefits of a tax-free structure.

To qualify for a tax-free reorganization, a significant percentage of the seller's shareholders must receive stock in the acquirer as consideration for their shares; a tax-free transaction is a stock swap. As discussed in Chapter 8, § 3 below, tax-free structures generally require a level of continuing proprietary (i.e., equity or stock) investment in the reorganized enterprise by the target's shareholders.

Target shareholders may not want to take equity in the purchaser. As discussed later in Chapter 8, § 3.D below, even if the overall transaction is accorded tax-free treatment, target shareholders can receive debt securities with tax-free consequences only in limited circumstances. Further, even if target shareholders would accept an equity stake in the reorganized enterprise, the acquirer might prefer to pay in cash or with debt securities. Indeed, the acquirer may not want to dilute its outstanding equity with a sizeable group of new shareholders or might want more flexibility in allocating deal assets and liabilities. Moreover, an acquirer might desire the financial leverage and income tax deductions for the interest that debt consideration offers.

Some target shareholders or sellers of a business unit may have a special tax status and, therefore, may not pay taxes even in a taxable transaction. For example, a foreign person generally can avoid U.S. income taxes on the outright sale of shares of stock in a U.S. corporation (unless the corporation holds significant U.S. real estate assets). See IRC § 897. Likewise, a tax-exempt entity, such as a pension plan or charitable organization, would generally not be taxed on gains from the sale or other disposition of corporate stock held for investment. See IRC § 512(b)(5). Such shareholders may prefer a taxable transaction to a tax-free one.

With respect to a sale of enterprise assets, the target could have expiring net operating losses (see IRC § 172) or credits that could be used to offset taxable gains. Moreover, sales of lackluster business units can produce recognizable losses that could offset any gains. Such a target may prefer a taxable transaction over a tax-free one.

§ 2. TAXABLE TRANSACTIONS

A. BASIC CASH-FOR-ASSETS ACQUISITION

In a cash-for-assets acquisition, the target sells all or a portion of its assets to the acquirer for cash, notes, debt assumptions and other consideration. If the target receives stock of an acquirer, it will transform the transaction into a tax-free transaction only if the acquirer's stock comprised at least a majority of the consideration received by the target; this discussion will assume that is not the case.

The target will recognize gain or loss on each asset sold, based on the purchase price allocable to each asset, reduced by the asset's adjusted basis. At this time there is no reduced income tax rate for capital gains income recognized by a corporation, so any net gain on the sale could be taxed at rates as high as 21 percent (35 percent before the Tax Cuts and Jobs Act of 2017). If the target receives purchase money debt obligations qualifying for installment sales method reporting, the target may be entitled to defer recognition of gain until payments are received. See IRC §§ 453 & 453A.

The acquirer will receive a basis in each purchased asset equal to an allocable amount of the purchase price. Consequently the seller's gain or loss with respect to each asset sold, and the acquirer's basis in each asset purchased, turn upon the allocation of the purchase price among the various assets sold and purchased. As discussed in Chapter 8, § 6.A below, IRC § 1060 prescribes rules for such purchase price allocations among asset classes.

B. BASIC CASH-FOR-STOCK ACQUISITION

If the business unit is a subsidiary of the target, the acquisition can be structured as a sale by the target of the subsidiary's stock. If the target itself is the focus of the acquisition and its stock is widely held, the acquisition could be structured as a cash tender offer for the target's outstanding stock. A seller of stock under either scenario will recognize taxable gain or loss, computed as the difference between the selling price and the adjusted basis of the shares sold. If the sellers of stock receive purchase money debt obligations, they may be permitted to defer recognition of gains until payments are received using the installment method described in the previous section. Portions of gains from the sale by taxpayers (other than corporations) of qualified small business stock issued after August 10, 1993 may be permanently exempted from income taxation (see generally IRC § 1202) or subject to deferral if the proceeds are reinvested in similar stock (see generally IRC § 1045).

While the acquirer receives an adjusted basis in the shares purchased equal to the purchase price, the adjusted basis in the underlying assets of the target generally remain unchanged (assuming the absence of a "section 338 election" discussed in Chapter 8, § 2.C below). An acquirer of stock should demand a discount in the purchase price (as compared with an acquisition of raw assets) to reflect: (1) the implicit cost of foregone cost recovery deductions that the target could have claimed in the future if the adjusted basis of its assets had been increased to reflect the purchase price; and (2) the explicit cost of an income tax on the unrealized built-in gain in the assets of the target that could be due upon a future disposition, in whole or in part, of those assets.

C. SOME PLANNING CHOICES FOR STOCK ACQUISITIONS

Sale of Stock of a Subsidiary with a Bootstrap Dividend. A corporation that receives dividends from other domestic (and some foreign) corporations is allowed a *dividends-received deduction* computed as 70, 80 or 100 percent of the dividend (the percentage being determined primarily by the degree of ownership in the distributing corporation; see IRC § 243). A "bootstrap dividend" plan takes advantage of the dividends-received deduction through the declaration of a dividend by a subsidiary to its parent prior to the parent's sale of its stock in the subsidiary to an acquirer. The parent and the acquirer wager that much of the dividend income will be eliminated by the dividends-received deduction. The structure has been given a mixed reception by the courts: The timing of the dividend declaration versus the stock sale is a critical factor. See, e.g., *Waterman Steamship Corp. v. Comm'r,* 430 F.2d 1185 (5th Cir. 1970) (finding that the dividend was in substance part of the sales price and denying a dividends-received deduction); *TSN Liquidating Corp. v. U.S.,* 624 F.2d 1328 (5th Cir. 1980) (respecting the dividend characterization); *Litton Indus., Inc. v. Comm'r,* 89 T.C. 1086 (T.C. 1987) (respecting the dividend characterization).

Sale of Stock with a § 338 Election. A stock sale does not affect the adjusted basis of the assets held by the target. A pure asset sale can provide the purchaser with a fair market value adjusted basis in purchased assets, but it can be cumbersome, involving numerous documents of transfer, transfer fees, third-party approvals and other complications. In response IRC § 338 generally permits a sale of stock to be treated as a *sale of assets* for income tax purposes, even though only shares of stock are changing hands. If an asset purchase is otherwise desirable, an IRC § 338 election can simplify the mechanics of the acquisition while producing equivalent income tax consequences.

The IRC § 338 election does not generally offer a better income tax result than a simple stock sale, however, because it generates an immediate tax liability that must be paid by the target. Target assets, in the hands of the acquirer, have a purchase price adjusted basis but the target itself must recognize gain or loss and pay an immediate tax. In the absence of special circumstances (e.g., a net operating loss carryover in the target, particularly one that could be of limited use after the acquisition due to the net operating loss limitation rules of IRC § 382 (as discussed later in Chapter 8, § 6.G)) or a target that is an S corporation (i.e., it is taxed under Subchapter S of the IRC) which, unlike a C corporation, is generally subject to only one layer of taxation imposed directly on the shareholders, the acquirer would usually not choose to incur the immediate tax.

If the acquirer makes an IRC § 338 election, the target is treated for income tax purposes as if it sold all of its assets to a new corporation for the "aggregate deemed sales price" or "ADSP," and the target recognizes gains or losses accordingly.

Ignoring a number of complications, the ADSP can simply be the selling price of the target stock (reduced by any selling expenses of the shareholders) plus the liabilities of the target assumed by the purchaser. The fictional "new" corporation likewise takes a new adjusted basis in the assets corresponding to the purchase price, the "adjusted grossed-up basis" or "AGUB." In the simplest case, AGUB is computed by adding the basis of the target stock to the liabilities of the target. The allocation of the purchase price among the "purchased" assets is made under rules that also govern asset sales (see Chapter 8, § 6.A).

There are a number of requirements to an IRC § 338 election, and two of them are of fundamental importance in structuring an acquisition. First, the election can be made only within a narrow time window. It may be made not later than the 15th day of the ninth month, beginning after the month in which the *acquisition date* occurs (see IRC § 338(g)). The acquisition date is the first day on which there is a *qualified stock purchase* (see IRC § 338(h)(2)). Second, the election window opens only if there is a qualified stock purchase, which is limited to any transaction or series of transactions in which stock that is at least 80 percent of the voting power of the corporation and at least 80 percent of the total value of the stock of the corporation is acquired, *by purchase* (this excludes, among other transactions, tax-free stock-for-stock exchanges), *during the 12-month acquisition period*. See IRC § 338(d)(3). If, for example, the purchasing corporation acquired more than a 20 percent position in the target at some time in the past in a *toehold* or *creeping* acquisition, but subsequently acquires the balance of the shares in one or more transactions that do occur within a 12-month period, IRC § 338 may not apply because an 80 percent position was not purchased entirely within the 12-month period.

Sale of Stock with a § 338(h)(10) Election. In the IRC § 338 election discussed above, two layers of tax are imposed. First, the target computes gain or loss on the sale of its assets through the deemed sale produced by the IRC § 338 election. Second, the seller of the shares computes gain or loss on the shares sold by subtracting the adjusted basis of the shares from the sales price. Although IRC § 338 may offer little advantage under the current corporate income tax provisions, IRC § 338(h)(10) has continued usefulness.

The IRC § 338(h)(10) election is made jointly by the seller and the acquirer, and can be made only if the target is part of an affiliated group of corporations (generally speaking, it must be at least an 80-percent-owned subsidiary of another corporation) or is an S corporation (the special treatment of S corporations and shareholders is otherwise beyond the scope of this work).

If the IRC § 338(h)(10) election is made, two results follow. First, the target can be included as a member of a consolidated group that includes the selling corporation, so that the gains and losses from the deemed asset sale could be combined with other losses, income or credits of the consolidated group. See IRC §§ 338(h)(9) & (h)(10)(A). Second, no gain or loss is recognized on the sale of the stock of the target. In many cases, the only gain or loss recognized is that produced by the deemed asset sale, so only one layer of tax is imposed.

In weighing the desirability of an IRC § 338(h)(10) election to a C corporation seller, one generally would compare the taxable gain produced by a sale of the target stock (without an IRC § 338 election) with the taxable gain produced by a sale of the target's assets (the practical tax result of the IRC § 338(h)(10) election). However, since the target stock (without an IRC § 338 election) and the target's assets with a fair market value tax basis have different after-tax values to the acquirer, those potential price differences also must be considered in the calculation.

Liquidating the Target: The § 332 Alternative. The IRC § 338(h)(10) election permits the sale of a subsidiary's stock to be treated as a sale of assets, but without the need for transferring each of the assets individually (as required in a true asset acquisition). If the seller is not troubled by the costs of asset transfers, and indeed, if the acquirer insists on receiving a transfer of assets rather than accepting stock in the subsidiary, a similar income tax result can be achieved by first liquidating the subsidiary into the parent corporation and then selling the assets to the acquirer (or selling the assets to the acquirer and then liquidating the subsidiary with a distribution of the cash proceeds). The liquidation of an 80-percent-controlled subsidiary is generally not a taxable event to either the subsidiary or the parent corporation. See IRC §§ 332 & 337. The parent corporation receives the subsidiary's basis in each of the assets received (see IRC § 334(b)); the parent corporation's basis in the subsidiary's stock is irrelevant. As with an IRC § 338(h)(10) election, the parent corporation's gain or loss on the sale of the assets will be determined with reference to the subsidiary's adjusted basis in the assets. Since the parent need not sell all of the assets to the acquirer, this approach may be preferable to an IRC § 338(h)(10) election if the target holds assets that the acquirer does not want.

D. CASH-OUT MERGERS

A sale of all of the target's assets, and the elimination of the target as a corporation, may be accomplished through a cash-out forward merger, in which the target is merged with and into the acquirer, and target shareholders receive cash and/or debt in exchange for their stock in the target. Although considered a statutory merger for state law purposes, the IRS may view the transaction as a taxable sale of the assets of the target, followed by a liquidation of the target, for which target shareholders will recognize gain or loss as if they had sold their shares. See IRC § 331; Rev. Rul. 69–6, 1969–1 C.B. 104. If the target's shareholders receive debt obligations of the acquirer, installment sales reporting of the gain may be available. See IRC § 453(h).

Likewise, the equivalent of a taxable sale of stock can be achieved through a cash-out reverse subsidiary merger, a triangular merger (see Diagram 9 in Chapter 1, § 5.C), in which the acquirer forms a subsidiary that merges with and into the target, with the target surviving and with the target's shareholders receiving cash and/or debt in exchange for their stock in the target. If the acquirer's cash or debt obligations are used to buy out the target's shareholders, the transaction may be treated for income tax purposes as a purchase of the target shareholders' stock. See, e.g., Rev. Rul. 73–427, 1973–2 C.B. 301.

§ 3. TAX-FREE TRANSACTIONS: AN OVERVIEW

A. IRC § 368: THE BASE DEFINITIONS

IRC § 368 is the definitional base of tax-free acquisitions. The definitions in the section unlock the related non-recognition provisions found elsewhere in the Code. There are seven principal reorganization categories defined in IRC § 368(a)(1)(A)–(G), and the income tax paragraph designations are used to identify the transactions in common usage. For example, it is quite common to hear or read about a "*B reorganization*" (or *B reorg,* for short) without elaboration, referring to IRC § 368(a)(1)(B).

The section begins by defining the term "reorganization" and then defines who is "a party to a reorganization," which is a key phrase used throughout the companion non-recognition provisions. The transactions must also proceed pursuant to a "plan of reorganization." See Treas. Reg. § 1.368–1(c).

B. IRC § 1032: NON-RECOGNITION FOR AN ACQUIRING CORPORATION

An acquirer will often issue its own shares (or use its repurchased stock, *treasury stock*) in exchange for assets of the target. The issuance or transfer of shares for this purpose is not a taxable event (see IRC § 1032).

C. IRC § 361: NON-RECOGNITION FOR A TARGET CORPORATION

The target will often exchange its assets solely for stock or securities of the acquirer. This is not a taxable event. See IRC § 361(a). Even if the target receives other property, such as cash, it still will not be a taxable event to the target if it distributes all of the property so received pursuant to a plan of reorganization. See IRC § 361(b). Although there are potential complications, generally IRC § 361 immunizes the target from recognition of gain or loss on the transfer of its assets to the acquirer in exchange for stock, securities or cash, which are in turn distributed to the target's shareholders pursuant to a plan of reorganization.

D. IRC §§ 354 & 356: NON-RECOGNITION FOR SHAREHOLDERS AND BONDHOLDERS

Security holders do not recognize gain or loss if securities in a corporation that is a party to a reorganization are exchanged solely for similar securities in the corporation (for example, in a recapitalization of a single corporation) or in another corporation that is an opposing party in the reorganization (for example, in an acquisitive merger). See IRC § 354(a)(1). If the shareholder receives cash or other property, gain may be recognized, but in an amount not to exceed the sum of such money and the fair market value of the other property received. The gain may be treated as a capital gain or as a dividend, depending upon whether the exchange "has the effect of the distribution of a dividend." See IRC § 356(a); *Comm'r v. Clark,* 489 U.S. 726 (1989); Rev. Rul. 93–61, 1993–2 C.B. 118.

When a shareholder exchanges stock for stock, there will almost always be a non-recognition transaction if the other reorganization requirements are met. However, if a shareholder receives other securities (i.e., debt), the fair market value of the securities will be treated like the receipt of cash, triggering income to the recipient. If a debt holder exchanges debt for debt and the principal amount of the securities received exceeds the principal amount of the securities surrendered, the fair market value of such excess is likewise treated like the receipt of cash. See IRC § 356(d).

Because the receipt of stock usually enjoys non-recognition treatment while the receipt of debt securities may trigger gain, acquisition planners use preferred stock as consideration to get target shareholders tax-free consideration that has debt-like characteristics. The Taxpayer Relief Act of 1997 responded to potential abuses by treating most "non-qualified preferred stock" as the equivalent of cash, so its receipt will produce income to the recipient. Non-qualified preferred stock generally means preferred stock having debt-like features such as: shareholder put rights; mandatory redemption provisions; corporation call rights if, as of the issue date, it is more likely than not that such right will be exercised; or a dividend rate varying with reference to interest rates, commodity prices, or similar indices.

E. IRC §§ 362 & 358: ADJUSTED BASIS RULES

To preserve the gain or loss otherwise deferred by IRC § 361, the acquirer's basis in the property acquired is the same as it would be in the hands of the target, increased by any gain recognized by the transferor on the transfer. Likewise, a shareholder's basis in stock or securities received in a reorganization is the basis of the property exchanged decreased by the fair market value of any other property or money received by the taxpayer and increased by the amount of income recognized in the transaction. See IRC § 358(a).

§ 4. THE REORGANIZATION CATEGORIES OF IRC § 368

A. "A" REORGANIZATIONS

This is one of the most widely-used acquisition forms. The "A" reorg is described simply as "a statutory merger or consolidation." See IRC

§ 368(a)(1)(A). The regulations state that the merger or consolidation must be "effected pursuant to the corporation laws of the United States or a State or Territory or the District of Columbia." See Treas. Reg. § 1.368–2(b)(1). State law is not conclusive, however. The IRS, for example, has ruled that to qualify as an A merger, the reorganization must end the target's existence and must result in a single acquiring corporation acquiring the target's assets. See Rev. Rul. 2000–5, 2000–5 I.R.B. 436; Treas. Reg. § 1.368–2(b)(1)(ii).

Continuity of Proprietary Interest. Although not expressly required by the statute, courts and the IRS require "continuity of proprietary interest" in the acquirer by the target shareholders. See Treas. Reg. § 1.368–1(e)(1). The requirement reflects the premise that the tax-free reorganization provisions represent only a change in the form of ownership by, and not a "cashing out" of, target shareholders. The target shareholders must reinvest in the reorganized corporation. The IRS requires that at least 40 percent of the consideration received by target shareholders in the acquisition must be in the form of stock in the acquirer. See Rev. Proc. 77–37, 1977–2 C.B. 568. An early U.S. Supreme Court decision recognized a transaction in which only 38 percent of the consideration was in the form of stock (see *John A. Nelson Co. v. Helvering,* 296 U.S. 374 (1935)), but publicly traded companies are often reluctant to proceed at levels close to or below 40 percent without a favorable IRS letter ruling.

Even if the overall reorganization qualifies for tax-free status, shareholders will usually be required to recognize income to the extent of other non-qualifying consideration received. See IRC § 356, discussed in Chapter 8, § 6.D.

In 1998 the IRS issued regulations (amended in 2000) that have liberalized the proprietary interest requirement:

> a mere disposition of stock of the target corporation prior to a potential reorganization to persons not related . . . to the target corporation or to persons not related . . . to the issuing corporation is disregarded and a mere disposition of stock of the issuing corporation received in a potential reorganization to persons not related . . . to the issuing corporation is disregarded.

Treas. Reg. § 1.368–1(e)(1)(i). Target shareholders can now generally dispose of the acquirer's stock they will receive prior to or following the reorganization to third parties without jeopardizing the overall tax-free reorganization treatment for those shareholders who wish to retain equity. If an acquirer or a target corporation buys the stock sold by target shareholders outside the acquisition, however, the sales may destroy continuity of proprietary interest.

Continuity of Business Enterprise. The IRS also requires "continuity of business enterprise." The acquirer must either continue the target's historical business or use a significant portion of the target's historical business assets in the acquirer's business. See Treas. Reg. § 1.368–1(d)(1).

Forward Triangular Merger. This is the most common form of tax-free reorganization for publicly traded companies. In a forward triangular merger, an acquirer creates a subsidiary, the target merges with and into the subsidiary (with the target disappearing), and the target shareholders receive at least 40 percent of the acquisition consideration in the form of stock of the acquirer/parent corporation (the balance can be cash, debt securities or other property). This is a tax-free acquisition so long as: (1) the acquirer/parent corporation controls the subsidiary; (2) stock of the acquirer/parent corporation is used and no stock of the subsidiary is used; (3) the transaction would otherwise have qualified as an A merger had the merger been directly into the acquirer/parent corporation itself (i.e., the transaction is under a State statutory merger law, and continuity of proprietary interest and business enterprise is satisfied); and (4) substantially all of the properties of the target are acquired.

As compared with a merger of the target directly into the acquirer, the fourth requirement represents the additional restriction. The IRS finds the "substantially all" test is satisfied if "assets representing at least 90 percent of the fair market value of the net assets and at least 70 percent of the fair market value of the gross assets held by the target corporation immediately preceding the transfer" are, indeed, transferred. See Rev. Proc. 77–37, 1977–2 C.B. 568.

One must also respect the potential application of the *step transaction doctrine.* The IRS uses the doctrine to reclassify reorganizations if their technical form does not match their economic substance. For example, in Revenue Ruling 72–405 (1972–2 C.B. 217) the IRS ruled that if the acquisition subsidiary is transitory by plan and subsequently liquidated into the parent corporation, the overall transaction will be viewed as a "C" reorganization (discussed below). The requirements of a C reorg are more restrictive than those for a forward A reorg; a C reorg, for example, requires the use of *voting stock* of the acquirer as acquisition consideration.

Reverse Triangular Merger. The transaction is initially structured in the same manner as a forward triangular merger except that the target, rather than the acquisition subsidiary, survives the merger to become a subsidiary of the acquirer. Planners use the form if the continued existence of the target is necessary to acquire licenses, leases, loan covenants, and government licenses or permits that are subject to anti-assignment restrictions. The structure is not as popular as a forward triangular merger, however, because the reverse form has more restrictions. The use of cash, debt securities and other property is limited to 20 percent of the consideration for the acquisition.

A reverse triangular merger is tax-free so long as: (1) the parent corporation controls the subsidiary which is to be eliminated in the transaction; (2) stock of the parent corporation is used as consideration for the merger; (3) the corporation surviving the merger holds substantially all of its properties and the properties of the merged corporation (other than the stock of the parent corporation used as acquisition consideration); and (4) in the transaction former shareholders of the surviving target exchange, for an amount of *voting stock* of the parent corporation, an amount of stock in the surviving corporation which constitutes control of the target. Not only must the reorganization meet the "substantially all properties" test, but the fourth requirement mandates that the target shareholders receive *voting* stock in the parent corporation *and* that in the aggregate the target shareholders must relinquish, in exchange for such voting stock, stock which represents control (i.e., 80 percent) of the surviving target.

B. "B" REORGANIZATIONS

In a B reorg, one corporation, in exchange solely for all or part of its voting stock, purchases the stock of another corporation and, immediately after the acquisition, the acquirer has control (generally at least 80 percent ownership as defined in IRC § 368(c)) of the other corporation. The statute permits a triangular stock acquisition in which a subsidiary controlled by the acquirer uses stock of the acquirer in the exchange.

This structure is the most restrictive of the acquisitive reorganizations. The acquiring corporation must use *solely its voting stock.* While there are some administrative exceptions for the payment of some of the target's transactional expenses, such as legal and accounting fees (see Rev. Rul. 73–54, 1973–1 C.B. 187) and for the cash redemption of fractional shares (see Rev. Rul. 66–365, 1966–2 C.B. 116), the voting stock requirement is otherwise strictly applied. The reorganization is disqualified if the target's shareholders receive any cash, debt securities (except for exchanges or purchases of debt securities apart from, and not constituting indirect additional consideration for, the stock acquisition; see Rev. Rul. 98–10, 1998–1 C.B. 643), non-voting stock or other property. Early toehold acquisitions of small amounts of target stock for cash, followed by a later acquisition of control solely for voting stock are risky unless the taxpayer can demonstrate that the toehold acquisition was unrelated to the subsequent acquisition of control for stock. Public corporations may be reluctant to risk a "creeping" B reorg with cash consideration for any of the target stock. See, e.g., *Chapman v. Comm'r,* 618 F.2d 856 (1st Cir. 1980) (holding that "solely for stock" applies to all acquisitions of stock pursuant to the plan, even if the 80 percent control stake in the target were solely for stock, but not reaching the issue of whether the toehold was a severable transaction).

The acquirer's assumption of target obligations personally guaranteed by target shareholders must be approached with care to avoid treatment as disqualifying *boot* (money or the fair value of other property received by a taxpayer that is *taxable* in an otherwise tax-free exchange), particularly if the target is inadequately capitalized. Compare Rev. Rul. 79–4, 1979–1 C.B. 150 (assumption treated as consideration for target stock) with Rev. Rul. 79–89, 1979–1 C.B. 152 (contribution of cash by acquiring corporation to discharge debt obligations of target not treated as consideration for target stock).

C. "C" REORGANIZATIONS

A "C" reorg is the acquisition by one corporation, in exchange solely for all or a part of its voting stock, of substantially all of the assets of another corporation. See IRC § 368(a)(1)(C). The section permits triangular structures that allow a subsidiary to acquire target assets in exchange solely for voting stock of a parent corporation. Id. Alternatively, the parent corporation can acquire the assets of the target and then push part or all of them down into a subsidiary. See IRC § 368(a)(2)(C). Unless a waiver is granted by the IRS, which is unusual, a target must dissolve and liquidate. That is, the target must distribute to its shareholders all the stock, securities and other properties it receives from the acquirer pursuant to the plan of reorganization. See IRC § 368(a)(2)(G).

Although the result of this reorganization resembles a merger of the target with and into the acquirer, the C reorg requirements are more restrictive than the A reorg requirements (although not as restrictive as the B reorg requirements). First, the acquirer must use its voting stock as consideration. Second, the acquirer must acquire substantially all of the properties of the target. Third, under the so-called "boot relaxation rule," the acquirer is very limited in how much consideration other than its voting stock it may use. Target liabilities that the acquirer assumes are ignored if no consideration other than voting stock is used. See IRC § 368(a)(1)(C). However, if even $1 of other consideration is utilized, all assumed liabilities count as boot.

Consider the effect of the boot relaxation rule on most acquisitions. In a C reorg, voting stock in the acquirer must be exchanged for assets of the target, the fair market value of which is at least 80 percent of the fair market value of all of the property of the target, and debts assumed are treated by the parties as money paid for the property. Even a modest level of debt assumed (normal on encumbered property, for example) can exceed the 20 percent limit of the boot relaxation rule. So any cash consideration offered in addition to the voting stock may disqualify the entire transaction from tax-free status. Moreover, toehold acquisitions for cash are risky: The money or other property to which the 20 percent rule is applied can include money or other property paid to acquire toehold positions in the target unless the stock was, for example, "purchased several years ago in an unrelated transaction." See Treas. Reg. § 1.368–2(d)(4).

D. SINGLE-FIRM REORGANIZATIONS: "D," "E," "F," AND "G" REORGANIZATIONS

The A, B and C reorgs are *acquisitive.* Other reorganizations may only involve a single corporation. When a single corporation is shedding assets in a tax-free reorganization, it is a *divisive* reorg.

D Reorgs. A "D" reorganization is described as a transfer by a corporation of all or part of its assets to another corporation if, immediately after the transfer, the transferor, one or more of its shareholders, or any combination thereof, is in control of the corporation to which the assets are transferred and the stock or securities of the transferee corporation are distributed in a transaction that qualifies under IRC §§ 354, 355 or 356. See IRC § 368(a)(1)(D). The required distribution avenues create two principal types of D reorganizations, governed by IRC § 354 or 355.

For our purposes the § 355 D reorg is important; under the section a corporation can create a subsidiary and distribute stock in the subsidiary to the parent's shareholders (a *divisive reorganization*). IRC § 355 permits a single corporation to be split, free of immediate tax, into multiple corporations. If IRC § 355 applies, neither the distributing corporation nor its shareholders recognizes income upon the distribution of the stock of a subsidiary. Tax-free treatment is available if: (1) the distributing corporation distributes stock of a corporation (the subsidiary) that it controls immediately before the distribution; (2) the transaction was not used principally as a device for the distribution of earnings and profits; (3) the distributing corporation and the controlled corporation are engaged immediately after the distribution in the active conduct of a trade or business that has been actively conducted throughout the previous five-year period (this may be difficult for emerging companies); (4) the distributing corporation distributes all of the stock of the controlled corporation held by it; and (5) there is a business purpose for the transaction.

The disguised dividend test in (2) provides difficulties for closely held corporations, but if the distributing corporation is publicly traded and widely held, with a no-greater-than five percent shareholder, there is a presumption of legitimacy. Treas. Reg. § 1.355–2(d)(3)(iii).

The most common divisive reorganization for public corporations is the *spin-off*. In a spin-off, the corporation places the assets of a business unit (such as a division) in a newly-formed subsidiary using a D reorganization. If the business unit is already in a subsidiary, then the preparatory D reorganization is unnecessary. The parent corporation then distributes stock of the subsidiary to the parent's shareholders pro rata as an *in-kind* (or *in specie*) dividend. At the conclusion of the transaction, the same shareholders continue to own shares of the parent (sans the former subsidiary) plus shares of the newly-spun off former subsidiary (now a stand-alone company), and both companies may now be publicly traded as separate stocks, hopefully enhancing the aggregate market value of the two stocks. eBay's 2015 spin-off of its PayPal subsidiary is a good example. If IRC § 355 applies, the transaction is tax-free as to the distributing corporation as well as its shareholders. Most public companies will request a private ruling from the IRS confirming that the transaction is tax-free.

The Taxpayer Relief Act of 1997 placed complex new limitations on the use of so-called "*Morris Trust*" transactions (*Comm'r v. Morris Trust,* 367 F.2d 795 (4th Cir. 1966)), in which spin-off transactions are used prior to a merger to dispose of target assets that the acquiring merger party does not desire. See IRC § 355(e). *Reverse Morris Trust* transactions involve a parent placing assets into a new subsidiary which the parent then spins off to its shareholders under § 355. The former subsidiary then merges with a target company. The parent shareholders receive a majority stake in the survivor to qualify for tax-free treatment under § 368(a)(1)(A), while the management of the target manages the survivor.

There are two other common divisive structures. In the *split-off* transaction, the stock of the subsidiary is not distributed pro rata, but is instead distributed only to some of the distributing corporation's shareholders in complete redemption of their stock. At the conclusion of the transaction, one group of shareholders owns the distributing corporation, and another group of shareholders owns the distributed corporation. This technique is often employed to split corporate assets, on a tax-free basis, among feuding shareholders in a closely held corporation. The *split-up* transaction involves the creation of multiple subsidiaries, the stock of which is distributed to all of the shareholders in liquidation of the original corporation, which ceases to exist.

E Reorg. An E Reorg is a single corporation capital-side restructuring and is defined in the IRC simply as "a recapitalization." See IRC § 368(a)(1)(E). The section is very flexible, and the regulations permit the issuance of preferred shares to bondholders, the surrender of preferred stock for no par value common stock, the issuance of preferred stock for outstanding common stock, and the exchange of preferred stock with various priorities for a new issue of common stock having no such rights. See Treas. Reg. § 1.368–2(e). One can encounter transactions of this nature in reorganizing the capital structure of a corporation in anticipation of an initial public offering.

Bonds may also be exchanged for bonds, mindful of the rule that if the principal amount of the bonds received exceeds that of the bonds surrendered, the fair market value of the excess will produce taxable gain to the recipients. See IRC § 356 (discussed earlier in Chapter 8, § 3.D). Furthermore, with the issuance of stock to bondholders or bonds for bonds, the corporation must consider the income tax consequences of a cancellation of indebtedness. See IRC § 108(e)(10). Bonds received for stock are troublesome, because it is likely that this transaction will be treated as a taxable redemption of the stock. See *Bazley v. Comm'r,* 331 U.S. 737 (1947); IRC § 356.

F Reorg. An "F" reorganization is "a mere change in identity, form, or place of organization of one corporation, however effected." See IRC § 368(a)(1)(F). While extending to mundane transactions such as corporate name changes, this provision is also helpful in changing the place of incorporation. For example, a Nevada corporation can be merged into a newly-formed Delaware shell as an F reorganization. While that would also qualify as an A reorganization, F reorganization status can avoid certain limitations on the use of corporate attributes, such as net operating losses.

G Reorg. "G" reorganizations are reorganizations in insolvency proceedings, such as Chapter 11 of the Bankruptcy Code.

§ 5. TAX-FREE ACQUISITIONS UNDER IRC § 351

A small but notable number of tax-free acquisitions after 1991 use IRC § 351 for tax free treatment. In such deals, an A reorg is not appropriate because the target shareholders are receiving less than 40 percent of the consideration in acquirer stock. Yet, the stock held by controlling shareholders in the target may have a very low basis. Can the controlling shareholders receive tax-free treatment if they exchange their shares for shares in the acquirer, even if the shares they receive represent less than 40 percent of the purchase price? Planners have devised a very clever "*double dummy*" deal structure under the section to accommodate them.

The acquirer and target form a new holding company with two shell subsidiaries. One shell merges into the acquirer, exchanging stock of the holding company for stock in the acquirer on a one-to-one ratio; the second shell merges into the target, exchanging stock in the holding company for some of the target stock (30 percent) and paying cash (or debt) for the remainder. The entire transaction qualifies as a § 351 transfer to a controlled corporation. Target shareholders recognize tax only to the extent they have received cash (or debt securities). Those target shareholders who take only stock in the holding company do not recognize tax.

The disadvantage is that the surviving company must use a holding company structure for some reasonable length of time.

§ 6. COLLATERAL INCOME TAX PROVISIONS IMPACTING MERGER AND ACQUISITION TRANSACTIONS

While the taxable versus tax-free distinction is the principal income tax consideration in deal structure, other income tax provisions (such as the amortization of goodwill and limits on interest expense deductibility) also play roles in acquisition planning. Some of the provisions are relevant only to taxable transactions, and some are relevant only to tax-free transactions. Others impact both groups of transactions.

A. PURCHASE PRICE ALLOCATIONS

Special income tax considerations apply to the transfer of a group of assets that constitute a trade or business in the hands of either the seller or the acquirer (a so-called "applicable asset acquisition"). First, the seller and the acquirer can agree in writing as to the allocation of the consideration or fair market value of any assets, and it will be binding on both parties unless the IRS determines that the parties' allocations are not appropriate. See IRC § 1060(a). Second, the seller and the acquirer are each required to furnish information about the transaction, particularly the allocation of the purchase price among the assets transferred, to the IRS. See IRC § 1060(b). Third, IRS regulations prescribe a method of allocating the purchase price among the assets transferred. Those regulations are found under IRC § 338, but the allocation methods apply to outright asset sales as well as deemed asset sales under IRC § 338.

The allocation regulations designate seven classes of assets. Class I assets are highly liquid cash, demand deposits and similar items. Class II assets include certificates of deposit, U.S. government securities, foreign currency and readily marketable stock or securities. Class III assets include accounts receivable, mortgages and credit card receivables from customers arising in the ordinary course of business. Class IV assets are inventories. Class V assets are assets not in any other class. Class VI assets are IRC § 197 intangibles (discussed below), but excluding goodwill and going concern value. Class VII assets are goodwill and going concern value.

The regulations first apply some of the purchase price to the Class I assets transferred by the seller. The remaining consideration is apportioned among the Class II assets, Class III assets and so on in order, such that Class VII becomes a residual category. As discussed below, goodwill purchased after 1993 can be amortized over 15 years, and that has reduced the negative income tax consequences of allocating residual value to that category.

Section 197 Intangibles. IRC § 197 permits amortization of a "section 197 intangible" over a 15-year period, beginning with the month in which the intangible is acquired. IRC § 197 specifically includes as a section 197 intangible a broad list of property interests, including goodwill, going concern value, workforce in place, business books and records, operating systems, customer lists, patents, copyrights, formulae, processes, designs, patterns, know-how, licenses or permits, covenants not to compete, franchises, trademarks, trade names, customer-based intangibles, supplier-based intangibles, and the deposit base of a financial institution. "Covenants not to compete" must be amortized over the full 15-year period even if their term of effectiveness is considerably less (often two years).

B. GREENMAIL PAYMENTS

IRC § 5881(b) defines "*greenmail*" as any consideration transferred by a corporation (or any person acting in concert with such corporation) to directly or indirectly acquire the corporation's stock from any shareholder if the shareholder has held the stock for less than two years before entering into the agreement to make the transfer. In addition, at some time during the two-year period ending on the date of the acquisition, *the shareholder (or any person acting in concert with the shareholder or any related persons) must have made or threatened to make a public tender offer for the stock of the corporation.* The acquisition also must be pursuant to an offer that was not made on the same terms to all of the corporation's shareholders.

Thus, greenmail payments are payments made by a besieged company to a corporate raider who is threatening a hostile takeover of that company. The company pays the raider a premium price (essentially a bribe) for the shares held by the raider to make the raider leave the company alone. Typically a *standstill agreement* is entered into between the company and the raider at the time of the payment. In the standstill agreement, the raider agrees to leave the company alone for a set period of time (typically two years) in exchange for the greenmail payment.

IRC § 162(k) denies a deduction for any amount paid or incurred by a corporation in connection with the reacquisition of its stock or the stock of certain related persons. The denial includes greenmail payments. Some related expenditures, such as interest expense and loan costs, are still deductible. Moreover, IRC § 5881 imposes an excise tax of 50 percent of gain or other income on the recipient of greenmail (i.e., the corporate raider). As a result of IRC §§ 162(k) and 5881, greenmail payments have become scarce.

C. IRC § 279 DEBT

The Tax Reform Act of 1969 added IRC § 279 with the aim of curbing the deductibility of interest on debt used for corporate acquisitions. The provision limits a corporation's interest deduction on account of "corporate acquisition indebtedness" to a maximum of $5 million. The provision generally applies only if the debt is: (1) subordinated to the claims of trade creditors or any substantial amount of unsecured indebtedness of the corporation; and (2) convertible into stock of the issuing corporation. (Convertible subordinated debt is also referred to as "high-yield" or "junk" bonds.) Furthermore, as of the last day of the taxable year of the year of issue, the debt-to-equity ratio of the issuing corporation must exceed 2:1 or the projected earnings must not exceed three times the annual interest to be paid or incurred. The use of "straight" debt that is not convertible into the issuer's stock has reportedly rendered IRC § 279 inapplicable to most transactions.

D. JUNK BONDS: HIGH-YIELD DISCOUNT OBLIGATIONS

The Omnibus Budget Reconciliation Act of 1989 introduced another limit on the use of high-yield ("junk") bonds in corporate acquisitions where the payment of interest is significantly postponed into later years. In the case of an "applicable high-yield discount obligation" (AHYDO) issued by a corporation, no deduction is allowed for the "disqualified portion" of the original issue discount on the obligation, and the remainder of the original issue discount is not deductible until actually paid. See IRC § 163(e)(5). An "applicable high-yield discount obligation" is a debt instrument with a term of more than five years, a yield to maturity that exceeds the applicable federal rate in effect under IRC § 1274(d) (tied to government securities) for the calendar month of issuance plus 500 basis points, and the instrument has "significant" original issue discount. Original issue discount is significant if the amount of original issue discount that would be accrued in the first five years of the instrument exceeds the sum of the aggregate amount of interest to be paid during such period plus the product of the issue price of the instrument and its yield to maturity.

The disqualified portion of the original issue discount is the lesser of the original issue discount or the total return on such obligation multiplied by a fraction, the numerator of which is the "disqualified yield" and the denominator of which is the yield to maturity. The disqualified yield is the yield to maturity in excess of the applicable federal rate in effect under IRC § 1274(d) for the calendar month of issuance plus 600 basis points.

E. TAX CUTS AND JOBS ACT OF 2017: CAP ON INTEREST EXPENSE DEDUCTION

The Tax Cuts and Jobs Act of 2017 presents challenges to private equity firms that load up acquired firms with debt in order to boost returns. The Act caps the amount of interest expense that companies can deduct from their taxes at 30 percent of "adjusted taxable income." IRC § 163(j). Before January 1, 2022, "adjusted taxable income" consists of taxable income *without regard to* (1) items of income or loss not allocable to the trade or business, (2) any business interest or business interest income, (3) any net operating loss under IRC § 172, (4) any deduction for certain pass-through income under IRC § 199A, and, *importantly,* (5) any deduction for depreciation, amortization or depletion. On or after January 1, 2022, "adjusted taxable income" is calculated the same way *but without* the adjustment for depreciation, amortization and/or depletion.

As a result of the interest expense cap, private equity firms will likely avoid targets with cyclical earnings. During down cycles, the ability of those targets to take advantage of a lower corporate income tax rate as well as deduct interest payments will be diminished. Thus, private equity firms should favor targets with more consistent earnings.

F. NET OPERATING LOSS CARRY-BACK LIMITATIONS: CERT

IRC § 172 permits a corporation that has experienced net operating losses to carry those losses back to two prior years (and obtain a tax refund if those years were profitable), and then forward 20 years. See IRC § 172(b). A corporation incurring large amounts of interest expense in connection with an acquisition, or simply to leverage assets to produce cash for dividends and stock repurchases, could create a net operating loss that could be carried back to prior years, securing tax refunds for those years. The Omnibus Budget Reconciliation Act of 1989 introduced a narrow provision aimed at limiting the use of debt in these situations.

Under the section the amount of a net operating loss of a corporation is reduced by a portion of the interest deductions attributable to a "corporate equity reduction transaction," known as a "CERT." See IRC § 172(h). A CERT includes the acquisition by a corporation of stock in another corporation representing 50 percent or more (by vote or value) of the stock in the target. The statute does not apply to asset purchases or to stock purchases for which an IRC § 338 election is made or to purchases of stock of corporations that are already affiliated with the acquirer. A CERT is also an excess distribution, defined as aggregate distributions (including redemptions) made during a taxable year by a corporation with respect to its stock in excess of the greater of 150 percent of the average of such distributions over the three immediately preceding taxable years or 10 percent of the fair market value of the stock of such corporation as of the beginning of the year. This provision could apply to a leveraged going-private (LBO) transaction.

G. LIMITATIONS ON A PURCHASER'S USE OF A TARGET'S NET OPERATING LOSS CARRY-FORWARDS

As noted above, a net operating loss (NOL) can be carried forward 20 years from the taxable year in which it arose. If the target owns that loss, the potential shelter from taxation can be valuable to the target if its fortunes improve or to an acquiring corporation that might be entitled to offset target losses against acquiring firm profits (subject to consolidated income tax return considerations).

Section 382. IRC § 382 limits the use of a net operating loss for the periods following an acquisition. Companion IRC § 383 places limitations on the use of certain tax credits following an acquisition. The limits apply irrespective of whether the acquisition takes the form of a taxable or a tax-free acquisition (except that if an IRC § 338 election is made, the net operating losses are extinguished).

The limits are triggered by an ownership change in the target. Speaking very generally, there is a triggering ownership change if the percentage of stock of the loss corporation owned by one or more 5 percent shareholders has increased by more than 50 percentage points (not simply 50 percent) over the lowest percentage of stock of the loss corporation owned by such shareholders at any time during a "testing period" which, subject to exceptions, generally looks back three years. See IRC § 382(g). In publicly traded corporations, pre-acquisition minority target shareholders may be treated as a single 5 percent shareholder for this calculation.

Subject to various exceptions, if the successor corporation does not continue the business enterprise of the target at all times during the two-year period beginning on the date when the 50-percentage-point change of ownership occurred, none of the net operating loss may be used in post-change years.

Even if the business enterprise is continued, the "section 382 limitation" for any post-change year is, subject to exceptions, limited to the product of the value of the target immediately before the ownership change multiplied by the "long-term tax-exempt rate" (a rate tied to long-term government securities, adjusted for differences between taxable and tax-exempt obligations). The amount of the IRC § 382 limitation is fixed at the time of the acquisition. The use of the tax benefits from the net operating loss in excess of the annual § 382 limitation is consequently deferred into future years and therefore has less present value. Moreover, at some point the overall carryover limitation of a maximum of 20 years prescribed by IRC § 172 will apply, denying the further use of any remaining losses.

Acquisitions by the Loss Company. Rather than it being acquired, the target might consider the acquisition of another corporation (or the assets of such a corporation in a tax-deferred A, C or D reorg) that holds appreciated assets, so that the gain from a post-acquisition disposition of those assets could be absorbed by the operating loss carry-forwards. IRC § 382 could apply to this transaction if the relative values of the acquiring and acquired corporations are such that the shareholders of the acquired corporation hold more than 50 percent of the surviving post-acquisition entity. Even if IRC § 382 does not apply, IRC § 384 would deny application of the pre-acquisition net operating loss carry-forwards of the acquiring corporation to built-in gains of the acquired corporation recognized within five years after the acquisition. IRC § 384 has a number of exceptions and qualifications.

Section 269. Acquisition of a corporation, the principal purpose of which is evasion or avoidance of federal income taxes, may also run afoul of the broad sweep of IRC § 269, with possible disallowance of the claimed deduction or credit. While this section is a noted acquisition risk factor in dealing with a target that possesses losses or credits, IRC §§ 382, 383 and 384 are more certain in application and often a greater concern for acquirers.

H. GOLDEN PARACHUTE PAYMENTS

IRC § 280G denies a deduction "for any excess parachute payment." See IRC § 280G(a). A "parachute payment" includes any compensation to or for the benefit of employees, independent contractors, officers, shareholders or highly-compensated individuals if the payment is contingent on a change in the ownership or effective control of the corporation or in the ownership of a substantial portion of the assets of the corporation. If the aggregate present value (determined using the government securities applicable federal rate of IRC § 1274) of the parachute payments exceeds an amount equal to three times the base amount, it constitutes an "excess payment." The "base amount" is the annualized compensation which was includable in the gross income of the individual for the most recent five taxable years ending before the date on which the change in ownership or control occurs (or such portion of such period during which the individual performed personal services for the corporation). Exceptions apply if a taxpayer establishes by clear and convincing evidence that the compensation is reasonable for personal services actually rendered or to be rendered, before, on or after the date of the change in control or ownership.

I. DEDUCTIBILITY OF ACQUISITION EXPENSES

The costs of an acquisition (e.g., fees to attorneys, accountants and underwriters) can be substantial.

For the acquiring corporation, the costs of obtaining debt financing can be amortized over the term of the applicable obligations. See Rev. Rul. 70–359, 1970–2 C.B. 103. The expenses of obtaining equity financing, however, are neither deductible nor amortizable and are therefore more costly from an income tax perspective. See Rev. Rul. 69–330, 1969–1 C.B. 51. However, maintenance costs of stock such as registrar and transfer agent fees (Rev. Rul. 69–615, 1969–C.B. 26) and SEC reporting (Rev. Rul. 65–13, 1965–1 C.B. 87) are generally deductible currently. The costs of acquiring specific target assets will usually be added to the basis of the acquired property and can be amortized or depreciated if that is otherwise allowed for the acquired asset.

For a target's expenses, there is some uncertainty. The U.S. Supreme Court has held that the costs of a friendly takeover are capitalized and not immediately deductible if there are future benefits from the transaction. See *INDOPCO, Inc. v. Comm'r*, 503 U.S. 79 (1992). Amortization of those costs may not be allowed if a specific asset with a definite useful economic life cannot be identified.

In the view of the Tax Court, the costs of a hostile takeover are capitalized if the target succumbs to the acquisition and it offers future benefits. See, e.g., *A.E. Staley Manufacturing Co. v. Comm'r,* 105 T.C. 166 (T.C. 1995). However, the Seventh Circuit reversed the Tax Court, finding that a hostile takeover can produce deductible expenses in countering the offer at the outset, as well as capitalized costs for costs incurred later to consummate the acquisition. *A.E. Staley Manufacturing Co. v. Comm'r,* 119 F.3d 482 (7th Cir. 1997).

This is still an evolving area. However, the 15-year amortization treatment of IRC § 197 (discussed in Chapter 8, § 6.A) cannot be an independent basis for amortizing such costs in a nontaxable transaction, since it cannot be utilized for "fees for professional services, and any transaction costs, incurred by parties to a transaction" for which any portion of the gain or loss is deferred. IRC § 197(e)(8).

PART III

THE LEGAL DUTIES OF BOARDS AND CONTROLLING SHAREHOLDERS

CHAPTER 9

THE BOARD OF DIRECTORS' DUTY OF CARE IN ACQUISITIONS

The Delaware Supreme Court uses five basic tests for judging the actions of a board of directors in an acquisition:

(1) the basic *business judgment rule* applied in *Smith v. Van Gorkom*, 488 A.2d 858 (Del. 1985);

(2) the *reasonableness and proportionality* test, a type of *enhanced scrutiny review*, which applies when (a) a target employs takeover defenses to block an unwanted stock acquisition, established in *Unocal Corp. v. Mesa Petroleum Co.*, 493 A.2d 946 (Del. 1985), (b) deal protection measures are employed in connection with a stock swap merger with no one shareholder controlling the survivor post-transaction, established in *Omnicare, Inc. v. NCS Health Care, Inc.*, 818 A.2d 914 (Del. 2003), or (c) a board or management interferes with the shareholder voting franchise, established in *Coster v. UIP Cos., Inc.*, 300 A.3d 656 (Del. 2023);

(3) the *best price on sale of control test*, another type of *enhanced scrutiny review*, which applies when a seller favors one bidder over another, established in *Revlon, Inc. v.*

MacAndrews & Forbes Holdings, Inc., 506 A.2d 173 (Del. 1986);

(4) the *entire fairness test,* applied when directors are operating under conflicts of interest, e.g., *Weinberger v. UOP, Inc.*, 457 A.2d 701 (Del. 1983); and

(5) the *coercion test* for tender offers by controlling shareholders, created in *Solomon v. Pathe Comm.*, 672 A.2d 35 (Del. 1996).

If one were to add the historical but lightly used *waste* and *entrenchment* tests (*Cheff v. Mathes,* 199 A.2d 548 (Del. 1964)), a good argument could be made that there are really seven basic tests. Some states follow the lead of the Delaware courts on some of the tests, while others have rejected the doctrines entirely.

This Chapter, as well as the next three, describes when each test applies, the standards employed in each test, and the consequences of each test.

§ 1. A BOARD'S DECISION TO SELL A FIRM

Corporate law in the U.S. has developed a distinction between standards of conduct for directors and standards of court review of the conduct of directors. The *standards of conduct* are what are expected of directors, while the *standards of review* determine whether a director may be held liable for their actions or a transaction may be enjoined or set aside by a court.

The basic standard of conduct for a director is that he or she act in good faith and in a manner that he or she reasonably believes to be in the best interests of the corporation. MBCA § 8.30(a). When becoming informed in connection with their decision-making function or devoting attention to their oversight function, directors must discharge their duties with the care that a person in a like position would reasonably believe appropriate under similar circumstances. MBCA § 8.30(b). See also *Graham v. Allis-Chalmers Mfg. Co.,* 188 A.2d 125 (Del. 1963).

The standard of review for a director's conduct in an acquisition starts with the *business judgment rule.* The business judgment rule protects decisions of the board of directors from being set aside by courts. It also protects directors from personal liability should a business decision lead to unfortunate results. The rule is a *legal presumption* that courts will not interfere with, or second-guess with the benefit of 20/20 hindsight, business decisions made by directors. Thus, it is a *pro-director* legal presumption. In *Smith v. Van Gorkom,* 488 A.2d 858 (Del. 1985), the Delaware Supreme Court stated that, under appropriate circumstances, it would apply the business judgment rule (BJR) to evaluate the conduct of the board of directors of the selling corporation in a negotiated acquisition.

According to *Brehm v. Eisner,* 746 A.2d 244 (Del. 2000), the business judgment rule *does not apply* if

> . . . directors are interested or lack independence relative to the decision, do not act in good faith, act in a manner that cannot be attributed to a

rational business purpose or reach their decision by a grossly negligent process that includes the failure to consider all material facts reasonably available.

Cases in which there are conflicts of interest are termed *duty of loyalty* cases. These cases are discussed in Chapter 11. Cases that do not involve fraud or conflicts of interest are termed *duty of care* cases. If the business judgment rule is not available, the Delaware courts evaluate the merits of the deal under the *entire* or *intrinsic fairness test. Cede & Co. v. Technicolor, Inc.,* 634 A.2d 345 (Del. 1993). In those instances, the defendant directors have the burden of proving that the deal is entirely or intrinsically fair to the shareholders. The details of the entire fairness test are discussed in Chapter 11, § 1.

Other states may use a *basic* negligence test for agents harvested from the common law of agency as the fall back test for a breach of the duty of care when the business judgment rule does not apply (and there are no conflicts of interest). E.g., *Barnes v. Andrews,* 298 F. 614 (S.D.N.Y. 1924). In other words, without the protection of the business judgment rule, courts would evaluate whether senior officers and directors acted with the care that an ordinarily prudent person in a like position would use under similar circumstances. A damage award would also require proof of damage proximately caused by a failure to act with due care.

On the facts of *Van Gorkom,* the court found that the selling board had not made an informed business decision when it approved the sale of the company. The initial board meeting to consider the sale was hastily called, was concluded very quickly (only two hours), and featured only a brief, oral description of the deal and recommendation from the target CEO and a lukewarm, general endorsement from the target CFO. Moreover, because no valuation of the company was undertaken, the board did not know the intrinsic per share value of the company. Thus, they had no way of truly knowing whether the price being offered was a fair price.

The *Van Gorkom* holding led to a change in board procedures for selling a company. Most target boards now require *fairness opinions* from independent investment bankers on whether the price offered is within a range of fairness. Moreover, most boards hold lengthy meetings to gather information from both inside and outside experts on the merits of the offer before the board will vote to accept any offer. The meetings are often recorded to show courts that directors were attentive and asked informed questions before they voted in favor of an acquisition.

§ 2. A BOARD'S DECISION TO BUY A FIRM

When an acquisition does not work out well for the acquirer, shareholders of the acquirer may sue their board for its approval of the acquisition. However, the decision of the board of the acquirer is also protected by the business judgment rule. E.g., *Ash v. McCall,* 2000 WL 1370341 (Del. Ch.).

The sorry performance of many large acquisitions in the late 1990s has led some to call for a strengthening of legal standards applied to the managers of acquirers in an effort to discourage large-scale acquisitions. Some argue for an ordinary negligence standard, unprotected by the business judgment rule; others argue for more shareholder voting rights for the shareholders of an acquirer. The reforms seem unnecessary in light of the market correction of 2001 that now has managers much more reluctant to propose acquisitions and boards more reluctant to approve them. Purchasers have sobered up.

§ 3. EXCEPTIONS RELATING TO DEAL PROTECTIONS

Negotiated purchase agreements, especially merger agreements, often contain *deal protection measures* that serve two purposes. First, they provide some economic compensation to the jilted suitor in the event that the target chooses not to close. Second, the measures obstruct disruption of the deal by another potential purchaser. Common covenants include the following measures: (1) a limitation on the target providing confidential information to other potential purchasers (a *no-talk* clause); (2) a limitation on the target soliciting offers from other potential purchasers (a *no-shop* clause); (3) a requirement that target managers and directors use their *best efforts* to close the merger; and (4) a *termination fee* compensating the jilted suitor if the transaction does not close (a *goodbye kiss*). Occasionally one also sees: (5) a covenant that the target managers will recommend to their shareholders that they approve the deal and will call a shareholder meeting to ratify the transaction (or the softer version that the managers will call a ratifying shareholder meeting even if they no longer can recommend a deal to their shareholders); (6) an option granted to the purchaser to acquire stock or assets of the target if the deal does not close (a *lock-up option*); or (7) a promise to allow the purchaser a few days to *match* any higher bid that another potential purchaser may make.

The deal protection measures contained in purchase agreements are often softened by *fiduciary out* clauses that provide targets with an escape hatch. The provision protects the directors of a target from having to choose between violating their fiduciary obligation to shareholders and breaching an executed purchase agreement. Under the language of a fiduciary out provision, the directors are excused from any action that would constitute a violation of their fiduciary duty. For example, such a clause would allow a target board to negotiate with a third party despite a no-shop clause or waive the requirement that a board recommend a deal to its shareholders. As a check on the breadth of the clause, purchasers may demand language requiring that the target board receive an opinion from outside legal counsel stating that any action foregone under the authority of the clause would constitute a breach of fiduciary duty.

Bidders deterred by deal protection measures (e.g., a termination fee deemed to be excessive) often sue to have them enjoined. The Delaware courts, sensitive to the argument that deal protection measures are similar in effect to classic takeover defenses, have applied the *enhanced scrutiny* review of takeover defense cases to deal protection measures. In *Omnicare, Inc. v. NCS Health Care, Inc.,* 818 A.2d 914 (Del. 2003), the Delaware Supreme Court held that because deal protection measures inherently favor one bidder over other bidders, a form of an *enhanced* scrutiny test should apply. Takeover defenses are more fully discussed in Chapter 12. We note here how the two prongs of enhanced scrutiny review, the *Unocal* and the *Revlon* tests, apply to deal protection covenants.

A. DEAL PROTECTION MEASURES WHEN THERE IS NO "CHANGE IN CONTROL": *UNOCAL*

In applying the enhanced scrutiny test to the facts of the case in *Omincare,* the court dealt with a case in which there was no "change in control." The basic *Unocal* test and not the more stringent *Revlon* test applied. See Chapter 12, § 3. In essence, the *Unocal* test is a reasonableness test, while the *Revlon* test requires targets which put themselves up for sale to sell the company for the highest price. *Omnicare* involved a stock swap merger with no one shareholder controlling the survivor post-transaction. The facts of the case are unusual.

The controlling shareholders of the target had signed a side agreement with the bidder promising to vote for a deal with the bidder. The target board agreed to put the deal to a vote regardless of whether it recommended the deal. There was no fiduciary out clause in the board promise. The side agreement plus the board agreement locked up the deal for the bidder. The court held that the lack of a fiduciary out clause was a violation of the target board's duties under the *Unocal* test.

Thus, the Delaware courts evaluate a board's decision to engage in a stock swap merger under the basic business judgment rule but will evaluate the board's decision to use deal protections in the merger under an enhanced scrutiny test. The *Omnicare* case does not preclude the use of deal protection devices in negotiated agreements; however, it does raise doubts about which devices will be upheld. Subsequent opinions of the Chancery Court have upheld limited use of deal protection devices. E.g., *Orman v. Cullman,* 794 A.2d 5 (Del. Ch. 2002). Former Vice Chancellor and later Chief Justice Strine tells attorneys not to worry—the enhanced scrutiny test leaves considerable room for the continued use of deal protections. Under the enhanced scrutiny test,

> well-motivated directors ought to have the right to present a strategic merger to their stockholders and to give their merger partner substantial contractual protections to induce them to contract. Unlike in the *Revlon* context, the court will defer to director decisions to give a preferred merger partner bidding and timing advantages over later emerging rivals. This deference to directors, as a practical matter, may mean that courts will give scant weight to whether deal protection measures are preclusive

> of other bids as a short-term matter. That is, if all that the board is asking for is to go first and to require other bidders to await the outcome of an unfettered stockholder vote, it seems likely to get that opportunity.

Leo E. Strine, Jr., *Categorical Confusion: Deal Protection Measures in Stock for Stock Merger Agreements,* 56 BUS. LAW. 919, 941–42 (2001).

Again, other states may not follow Delaware's example. States that have more respect for the acquirer's contract rights may decide that a target board's compliance with its fiduciary duties should be judged at the time it enters into the contract and that its ability to act subsequently, in response to new events, should be governed in part by the terms of the acquisition agreement. In other words, a board that signed a merger agreement would breach the contract by taking a later appearing, higher offer from another bidder. E.g., *Jewel Cos., Inc. v. Pay Less Drug Stores Northwest, Inc.,* 741 F.2d 1555 (9th Cir. 1984). A decision to breach would itself be evaluated under fiduciary duty principles.

B. DEAL PROTECTIONS WHEN THERE IS A CHANGE IN CONTROL: *REVLON*

In takeover contests in the 1980s, managers often sought to favor one bidder, a *white knight,* over others, particularly a *hostile raider*. Often a white knight would promise to retain incumbent managers while a hostile raider sought to replace them. The most direct method of favoring one bidder over another was to apply takeover defenses to the raider and waive them for the white knight. Takeover defenses are discussed in more detail in Chapter 12. A second, more subtle, method of favoring one bidder over another is to give one bidder deal protections to deter other bidders from making topping offers. Since the effect of a target's successful discrimination among bidders is a negotiated deal with the favored bidder, however, the standard of review on the target board's decision to sign a deal with the favored bidder needs to be discussed briefly in this Chapter.

When a target corporation is in what lawyers now refer to as the *Revlon* zone, the Delaware courts will analyze the board of directors' conduct using an *enhanced level of scrutiny* that focuses on whether the directors acted reasonably in obtaining the *best value* for target shareholders. The case of *Paramount Comm. Inc. v. QVC Network Inc.*, 637 A.2d 34 (Del. 1994), explained that a target enters the *Revlon* zone when target managers agree to a *change in control.* A change in control occurs when the target is broken up (an LBO), sold for cash, or sold for a minority allotment of stock in a controlled corporation. In a controlled corporation context, a person (or affiliated group) has a fifty percent or more controlling position in the acquiring corporation's stock after the acquisition (a change in control).

Once in the *Revlon* zone a target board must select the highest bidder for its shares absent very strong justifications to do the contrary. Deal protection covenants must be justified solely as directed at the object of getting the highest price. A common justification is that the deal protections are necessary to encourage the last topping bid from a balky bidder. E.g., *In re Toys "R" Us, Inc. Shareholder Litig.*, 877 A.2d 975 (Del. Ch. 2005). Also a possible justification, but with more risk for the target board, is the argument that deal protection measures were necessary to encourage the first bid from a balky bidder who did not want to be a *stalking horse* for other bidders.

In *Arnold v. Society for Savings Bancorp,* 650 A.2d 1270 (Del. 1994), the Delaware Supreme Court provided important guidance as to *when* a board has put its company up for sale. The court stated that *Revlon* duties apply in *at least* the following three scenarios:

(1) *Initiation of Active Bidding Process.* A company's board initiates an active bidding process seeking to sell the company or to effect a business reorganization involving a clear break-up of the company.

(2) *Responsive Break-Up.* In response to a bidder's offer, a target company's board abandons its long-term business strategy and seeks an alternative transaction involving the break-up of the company.

(3) *Change in Control.* A company's board approves a transaction resulting in a sale or change in control.

Importantly, where a potential sale of control is *not* the consequence of actions taken by a company's board, the board is entitled to resist a third party's unsolicited acquisition proposal or offer. In other words, only the actions of the board itself—not those of a third party—can result in the company being put up for sale. *Paramount Comm., Inc. v. Time Inc.,* 571 A.2d 1140 (Del. 1989).

According to the Delaware Supreme Court in *Malpiede v. Townson,* 780 A.2d 1075 (Del. 2001), *Revlon* neither creates a new type of fiduciary duty in the sale of control context nor alters the nature of the fiduciary duties that generally apply. Rather, *Revlon* emphasizes that the board of a Delaware corporation must perform its *existing* fiduciary duties in the service of a *specific objective:* maximizing the sale price of the enterprise. Although the *Revlon* doctrine imposes enhanced judicial scrutiny of certain transactions involving a sale of control, it *does not* eliminate the requirement that plaintiffs plead sufficient facts to support underlying claims for breach of fiduciary duties in conducting the sale.

Thus, in *Lyondell Chem. Co. v. Ryan,* 970 A.2d 235 (Del. 2009), shareholders mounting a *Revlon* challenge alleged that the defendant directors breached their fiduciary duties, including the duty of good faith, in connection with the sale of their company. The shareholders alleged that the defendant directors failed to maximize the sales price due to their "two months of slothful indifference" to a potential sale of their company despite *knowing* that their company was "in play." They further alleged that the defendant directors "languidly awaited overtures" from potential suitors.

The company's charter contained an exculpatory charter provision which exonerated directors for breaches of the duty of care. However, such a provision is impotent against breaches of the duty of loyalty through a failure to act in good faith. Based on the shareholders' allegations, the Chancery Court denied the directors' motion for summary judgment on the issue of bad faith.

In reversing the Chancery Court, the Delaware Supreme Court stated that, in a transactional context like the one involved in this case, an *extreme set of facts* is required to sustain a disloyalty claim premised on the notion that disinterested directors were intentionally disregarding their duties. The Chancery Court asserted that the defendant directors' " 'unexplained inaction' " had prevented it from determining that the directors had acted in good faith (and thus granting their motion for summary judgment). But, according to the Delaware Supreme Court, "if the directors failed to do all that they should have done under the circumstances, [then] they breached their duty of care." According to the court, "[o]nly if they knowingly and completely failed to undertake their responsibilities would they breach their duty of loyalty." The court determined that the Chancery Court had approached the record from the wrong perspective. Indeed, according to the court: "Instead of questioning whether disinterested, independent directors did everything that they (arguably) should have done to obtain the best sale price [for their company], the inquiry should have been whether those directors utterly failed to attempt to obtain the best sale price."

As noted in Chapter 12, § 3.D, other states may not follow the *Unocal/Revlon* distinction.

§ 4. STATE LEGISLATION MODIFYING THE BASIC STANDARDS OF COURT REVIEW

A. LIABILITY WAIVERS IN THE CHARTER

The outcry over the holding in *Smith v. Van Gorkom*, 488 A.2d 858 (Del. 1985), led the Delaware legislature to respond in 1986 with a new statute enabling Delaware corporations to nullify the effect of the holding on director liability (later expanded to also cover officer liability). DGCL § 102(b)(7) authorizes corporations to put in their certificates of incorporation an *exculpatory charter provision*

> eliminating or limiting the personal liability of a director or officer to the corporation or its stockholders for monetary damages for breach of fiduciary duty as a director or officer, provided that such provision shall not eliminate or limit the liability of:
>
> (i) A director or officer for any breach of the director's or officer's duty of loyalty to the corporation or its stockholders;
>
> (ii) A director or officer for acts or omissions not in good faith or which involve intentional misconduct or a knowing violation of law;
>
> (iii) A director under DCCL § 174 of this title [Unlawful Distributions];

(iv) A director or officer for any transaction from which the director or officer derived an improper personal benefit; or

(v) An officer in any action by or in the right of the corporation.

Over 40 states have adopted a version of the Delaware *opt-in* provision (e.g., NYBCL § 402(b)), although few have expanded their provision to exculpate officers as well (the MBCA has not, for example).

Most publicly traded Delaware corporations have accepted the invitation of the statute and passed charter amendments waiving director liability to the full extent allowed under the provision. The Model Business Corporation Act has a stronger version of the Delaware section in § 2.02(b)(4) (there is no express reservation for a breach of the duty of loyalty, and the reservation for intentional misconduct does not include as an alternative ground a lack of good faith). Ohio has made its waiver of liability section the default rule for Ohio corporations by statute; Ohio corporations can choose to *opt out* of the liability waiver, returning to a business judgment rule analysis, by a charter amendment. OGCL § 1701.59(D). The Ohio statute also applies to actions to set aside transactions as well as the personal liability of directors.

In two *Arnold* decisions—*Arnold v. Society for Savings Bancorp,* 650 A.2d 1270 (Del. 1994), and *Arnold v. Society for Savings Bancorp,* 678 A.2d 533 (Del. 1996)—the Delaware Supreme Court demonstrated that it will parse the allegations and facts carefully in cases involving the board's adoption and use of takeover defenses. The court will apply § 102(b)(7) to some allegations and not others, depending on whether the court classifies the claim as one for a breach of the duty of care or loyalty. The courts in a state adopting the MBCA language need only classify the claim as not alleging personal gain or intentional misconduct.

There has been some confusion in Delaware cases about how a director asserts a § 102(b)(7) defense. In *Emerald Partners v. Berlin,* 726 A.2d 1215 (Del. 1999), the court noted that § 102(b)(7) was "in the nature of an affirmative defense." Thus, defendant directors must include the provision in their pleadings, as the Chancery Court will not raise it *sua sponte.* However, a later case, *Malpiede v. Townson,* 780 A.2d 1075 (Del. 2001), held that the section enables a court to dismiss claims on summary motion if the plaintiff's complaint asserts only a due care claim. To get by a summary motion when the section applies, the plaintiff's complaint must allege well-pled facts that, if true, constitute breaches of the duty of loyalty or good faith.

B. CONSTITUENCY STATUTES

Constituency statutes authorize boards to consider non-financial matters and constituencies other than their shareholders in deciding whether to accept a takeover offer. In other words, the "best interests of a corporation" includes, by statute, the welfare of groups other than target shareholders. Nearly 30 states have adopted some version of a constituency statute. Significantly, Delaware has as yet refused to adopt a constituency statute and the drafters of the Model Business Corporation Act have refused to put such a provision in the Model Act.

Although Delaware does not have a constituency statute, the Delaware Supreme Court in *Revlon, Inc. v. MacAndrews & Forbes Holdings, Inc.*, 506 A.2d 173 (Del. 1986), has opined on the ability of a Delaware board of directors to take the interests of constituencies other than shareholders into consideration when adopting takeover defenses:

> The Revlon board argued that it acted in good faith in protecting the noteholders because *Unocal* permits consideration of other corporate constituencies. Although such considerations may be permissible, there are fundamental limitations upon that prerogative. *A board may have regard for various constituencies in discharging its responsibilities, provided there are rationally related benefits accruing to the stockholders*. However, such concern for non-stockholder interests is inappropriate when an auction among active bidders is in progress, and the object no longer is to protect or maintain the corporate enterprise but to sell it to the highest bidder. (emphasis added).

Constituency statutes in several states—e.g., Connecticut, Iowa, Louisiana, Missouri, Oregon and Tennessee—apply only to change in control contests and the rest apply to all board decisions. Most constituency statutes permit directors to *consider* the interests of constituencies other than shareholders—typically employees, creditors, suppliers, customers and communities, among others (other *stakeholders*)—and a few allow for consideration of the national and state economies. See, e.g., NYBCL § 717(b); OGCL § 1701.59(F). Cf. *Herald Co. v. Seawell,* 472 F.2d 1081 (10th Cir. 1972) (taking into account public interest in sale of locally-owned newspaper to New York publishing chain).

Some permissive statutes contain simply a laundry list of groups, including shareholders, whose interests a board *may* consider. Two statutes, those of Indiana and Pennsylvania, direct that a board ought not to consider the interests of any one group (an oblique reference to shareholders) as dominant. Ind. Code § 23–1–35–1(d); PBCL § 1715(b). Connecticut's statute mandates that the board *shall* consider interests of non-shareholder groups. Conn. Gen. Stat. § 33–133(e).

CHAPTER 10

THE LEGAL DUTIES OF CONTROLLING SHAREHOLDERS IN ARM'S-LENGTH ACQUISITIONS

The duties of controlling shareholders in arm's-length acquisitions (acquisitions with an independent party) are considered in this Chapter. The following Chapter considers cases in which a controlling shareholder is a party to the acquisition itself, as in a merger of a parent corporation with a controlled subsidiary, or when a controlling shareholder holds shares in both parties to an acquisition, as in a merger of brother and sister corporations.

§ 1. THE OBLIGATION TO SHARE THE PROCEEDS FROM THE SALE OF A CONTROLLING BLOCK OF STOCK

A. NO GENERAL DUTY TO SHARE

The general rule in the common law is that a controlling shareholder who sells her block of stock to a third party and thereby control in a corporation does not have to share any part of the sale proceeds with the minority shareholders or otherwise give the minority shareholders an opportunity to participate in the stock sale. *Zetlin v. Hanson Holdings,* 397 N.E.2d 387 (N.Y. 1979). There is no "*equal opportunity*" rule (or "*tag along*" rule) in the common law that benefits minority shareholders when a controlling shareholder sells control to a third party.

This is true even if the controlling shareholder receives a control premium for her shares. (If the stock is trading at $100 a share and the price for a 51 percent controlling block of shares is $130 a share, the control premium is $30 a share.) A maverick Second Circuit case, *Perlman v. Feldman,* 219 F.2d 173 (2d Cir. 1954) (sale of control of a company operating under war time price controls), often featured in basic corporations courses, has been limited to its unique facts. See, e.g., *Mendel v. Carroll,* 651 A.2d 297 (Del. Ch. 1994).

A controlling shareholder may not, however, in anticipation of a pending acquisition of the *entire company* by an acquirer, purchase or cause the company to purchase shares held by minority shareholders so as to deprive them of a portion of the control premium. Courts have held, for example, that a closely held corporation negotiating an acquisition may not repurchase the shares of minority shareholders without a disclosure of pending merger discussions. *Lawton v. Nyman,* 327 F.3d 30 (1st Cir. 2003); *Jordan v. Duff & Phelps, Inc.,* 815 F.2d 429 (7th Cir. 1987); *Berreman v. West Publ. Co.,* 615 N.W.2d 362 (Minn. Ct. App. 2000). In such cases, an acquirer is attempting to buy complete ownership of the company.

In a twist on the basic doctrine, the Delaware Supreme Court has held that when a parent corporation sells the stock it owns in a subsidiary, and the subsidiary board participates in *signing* the deal, the subsidiary board itself has a fiduciary duty to protect the interests of the minority shareholders in the subsidiary. *McMullin v. Beran,* 765 A.2d 910 (Del. 2000). If the subsidiary board is not a party in the sale of a parent (or of a parent's stock in the sub), however, the subsidiary's board does not have an obligation to negotiate on behalf of minority subsidiary shareholders. *In re Digex, Inc.,* 789 A.2d 1176 (Del. Ch. 2000).

The SEC has established an equal treatment rule of sorts for tender offers in SEA Rule 14d–10. A public tender offer for over 5 percent of registered voting stock in a public company must include all shareholders; it cannot include, for example, only the large institutional shareholders. See Chapter 6, § 2. Moreover, the bidder in a public tender offer cannot purchase shares privately once the tender offer has been publicly announced (which announcement may occur before the tender offer is actually commenced). SEA Rule 14e–5.

B. THE DUTY NOT TO USURP A CORPORATE OPPORTUNITY

The *corporate opportunity doctrine,* the duty of senior managers and directors not to usurp business opportunities that belong to the firm, see *Guth v. Loft,* 5 A.2d 503 (Del. 1939), can apply to acquisition offers. In the classic case, a purchaser approaches a CEO and asks to buy her corporation. The CEO, rather than present the offer formally to the corporation's board, offers to sell the purchaser the CEO's personal, controlling block of stock in the corporation. The CEO's actions violate the corporate opportunity branch of the duty of loyalty doctrine.

Thorpe v. CERBCO, 676 A.2d 436 (Del. 1996). The scenario described is to be distinguished from offers to buy a control block that go directly to controlling shareholders in the first instance. These are not corporate opportunities. See, e.g., *Broz v. Cellular Inf. Sys., Inc.*, 673 A.2d 148 (Del. 1996).

In *Thorpe*, the purchaser wanted to purchase a subsidiary of a parent corporation. The officers of the parent corporation convinced the purchaser to buy their controlling stock in the parent instead. As often happens, the officers lied to their board about the purchaser's interest in the sub. In an odd twist, the officers had the voting power, however, to block any sale of the sub to the purchaser. The court held that the voting power of the officers meant that the corporation could not take advantage of any purchase offer for the sub and that the officers therefore did not harm the company. No "transactional damages" were available. The court held that the officers' actions violated their fiduciary duty to the parent, however, and had to disgorge any benefits received. The court held, in essence, that the defendants were entitled to act as shareholders and obtain a control premium for their shares, but only after presenting the offer to the corporation, withdrawing from further action on behalf of the corporation, allowing outside directors to negotiate on the corporation's behalf, and then voting against the acquisition when the outside directors asked for shareholder ratification.

§ 2. THE OBLIGATION NOT TO HARM THE REMAINING SHAREHOLDERS BY SELLING TO A LOOTER

California courts have pioneered a duty of a majority shareholder not to sell to someone known, or who should be known, to be a *looter*. *Debaun v. First Western Bank and Trust Co.,* 120 Cal. Rptr. 354 (Cal. Ct. App. 1975). The Delaware Chancery Court seems to have accepted the rule as well. *Harris v. Carter,* 582 A.2d 222 (Del. Ch. 1990); see also *Insuranshares Corp. of Del. v. Northern Fiscal Corp.,* 35 F.Supp. 22 (E.D. Pa. 1940) (owners of control are under a duty not to transfer it to outsiders if the circumstances surrounding the proposed transfer are such as to awaken suspicion and put a prudent person on his or her guard, unless a reasonably adequate investigation discloses such facts as would convince a reasonable person that no fraud is intended or likely to result). In *Debaun,* the selling controlling shareholder had seen an unfavorable Dunn & Bradstreet report on the purchaser and the structure of the sale was fishy. Installment payments on the purchase price were to be made out of corporate distributions (an *earn out* provision) that were larger than the firm's after-tax profits.

§ 3. NO PURE SALES OF A CORPORATE OFFICE

A controlling shareholder may not agree with a purchaser to sell a board position in the company unless the agreement is accompanied by a sale of effective control of the company itself. *Essex*

Universal Corp. v. Yates, 305 F.2d 572 (2d Cir. 1962). In the case, a 28-percent shareholder sold his block of stock with the understanding that he would cause a majority of the board to resign one at a time, with the remaining directors agreeing to appoint new directors, one at a time, selected by the purchaser. The court held that the contract provision was legal as long as the stock represented effective control of the firm. If the seller did not have effective control, the contract was an illegal sale of a pure corporate office. The dissent said that the stock had to represent legal control, 51 percent, otherwise the shareholders were deprived of their right to vote on the election of directors.

CHAPTER 11

THE BOARD OF DIRECTORS' DUTY OF LOYALTY IN RELATED PARTY TRANSACTIONS

Many transactions are between entities in which some of the same parties have ownership stakes or management interests in both parties to the acquisition. The managers are operating under a *conflict of interest;* they are said to be *conflicted.* The deals are termed *related party transactions.* The cases present the danger that non-controlling shareholders will be cheated when conflicted managers sell the corporation at discounted prices to themselves or buy the corporation from themselves at exorbitant prices—thus putting their own needs ahead of those of the shareholders. Managers in such cases are held to a high standard of conduct, labeled the *duty of loyalty.* The business judgment rule and liability waiver charter provisions (e.g., DGCL § 102(b)(7)) do not apply in pure duty of loyalty cases.

The practical effect of the distinction between a duty of care claim and a duty of loyalty claim in litigation is that a duty of care claim may be subject to dismissal on summary motions if the business judgment rule applies; a duty of loyalty claim, if well pled, can usually be resolved only through a trial on the merits. In other words, plaintiff shareholders can win on duty of loyalty claims and usually lose pure duty of care claims. Plaintiffs try to style their claims as duty of loyalty claims and defendants try to recast the claims as duty of care claims. Similarly, acquisition transaction lawyers attempt to erect procedures that protect directors in related party transactions from duty of loyalty claims and transform any claims brought into duty of care claims.

§ 1. GENERAL PRINCIPLES: THE ENTIRE FAIRNESS TEST

When a firm's senior managers have a stake in the acquiring entity engaged in a leveraged buyout (LBO), a *financial* acquisition, see Chapter 1, § 5.D, the takeover is more properly referred to as a management buyout (MBO). Managers of the target may also have an interest in the acquiring firm in *strategic* acquisitions (between two operating companies). If a party to the transaction has a conflicted majority of directors or has a conflicted controlling or dominating shareholder, the deal, without more, must meet a strict *entire* or *intrinsic fairness* test. The business judgment rule does not apply.

The entire fairness test requires both fair dealing (a fair process) and a fair price. See *Weinberger v. UOP, Inc.*, 457 A.2d 701 (Del. 1983). If the board violates a duty of candor, however, it is a *per se* violation of the entire fairness test. See, e.g., *Sealy Mattress Co. of N.J., Inc. v. Sealy, Inc.*, 532 A.2d 1324 (Del. Ch. 1987).

In conflict of interest transactions, however, the courts apply a less rigorous standard of review if the transaction is (1) ratified by a disinterested, independent board of directors (or subcommittee) or

(2) by disinterested shareholders. In both circumstances, the courts condition the application of the less rigorous standard on candor by the conflicted directors; the conflicted directors must disclose to the board or shareholders the nature of the conflict. MBCA § 8.62. There is some confusion on which standard applies to which facts, however, in Delaware and among other states.

It is difficult for defendant directors to satisfy the entire fairness standard of review if a transaction triggers it. However, it certainly is not impossible. Such was the case in *In re Tesla Motors, Inc. Stockholder Litig.*, 298 A.3d 667 (Del. 2023). Elon Musk, the CEO, board member and significant stockholder of Tesla, coveted SolarCity Corporation in order to help achieve his strategic vision. Indeed, one of the pillars of the "Tesla Motors Master Plan" was achieving sustainable energy generation from clean sources, such as solar power. SolarCity, therefore, was a worthy acquisition target in light of that pillar.

The proposed transaction suffered from innumerable conflicts of interest. Musk was deemed to be a controlling stockholder of Tesla by the Delaware Chancery Court. Musk's brother also served on Tesla's board. SolarCity was founded by two of Musk's cousins. There was a partial interlocking directorate between the boards of Tesla and SolarCity. And, of course, Musk really wanted the deal to happen.

After the deal was consummated, plaintiff-stockholders of Tesla sued the Tesla board alleging that Tesla overpaid for SolarCity. Their allegation was based on their belief that SolarCity was insolvent at the time of the closing. All Tesla board members other than Musk reached a settlement with the plaintiffs, leaving Musk as the only defendant.

Given the inherent conflicts of interest present in the transaction, the Delaware Chancery Court applied the entire fairness test. In this regard, the court observed that "a controlling stockholder [like Musk] brings with him into the boardroom an element of 'inherent coercion.'" However, the court found "that any control [Musk] may have attempted to wield in connection with the Acquisition was effectively neutralized by a board focused on the *bona fides* of the Acquisition, with an indisputably independent director leading the way."

Focusing on the "fair process" prong of the entire fairness test, the court noted that there were several significant flaws in the process, mostly due to Musk's personal involvement (e.g., several of Musk's communications with SolarCity's management about the proposed transaction were not disclosed to the Tesla board). However, the court noted that there were some admiral aspects of the process as well (e.g., the board's insistence that the deal structure include a majority-of-the-minority stockholder vote provision). Ultimately, the court held that the process was fair, concluding that the "Tesla Board meaningfully vetted the Acquisition" and Musk "did not *impede* the Tesla Board's pursuit of a fair price."

Focusing on the "fair price" prong of the entire fairness test, the court pointed to six factors and categories of evidence it relied upon in reaching its determination on fair price. First, the court rejected the plaintiffs' contention that SolarCity was insolvent based on the evidence presented. Second, the court found that the proffered discounted cash flow models presented by two of Musk's experts were unhelpful and, thus, the court disregarded them. Third, the court considered three pieces of market evidence which supported its finding of fair price: SolarCity traded in an efficient market, Tesla paid, at most, a small premium for SolarCity, and Tesla stockholders overwhelmingly voted in favor of the acquisition. Fourth, the court determined that SolarCity derived most of its value from long-term cash flows, and that benefit would flow to Tesla after the acquisition. Fifth, the court relied on the fairness opinion of Tesla's financial advisor, finding that the work performed by that advisor was credible and that the advisor was not beholden to Musk. Lastly, the court found that the potential synergies between the two companies weighed in favor of finding that the price paid was fair.

The court acknowledged that "where there are process infirmities, the court is obliged to study fair price even more carefully." However, its review of the evidence put forth at trial regarding the price Tesla paid for SolarCity led it to conclude that the price was, indeed, fair. As a result, the court found that Musk satisfied the entire fairness standard and, as a result, did not breach his fiduciary duty.

On appeal, the Delaware Supreme Court affirmed the Chancery Court's decision, noting that the record supported the conclusion that the acquisition was entirely fair. The court highlighted that the Chancery Court's opinion was replete with factual findings and credibility determinations, and those determinations had not been challenged and decidedly weighed in favor of Musk. The court underscored that a determination that a transaction must be subjected to an entire fairness analysis is not an implication of liability. Indeed, under Delaware's entire fairness standard, a finding of perfection is not a *sine qua non* in an entire fairness analysis. While the court stated that the process that the Tesla board followed was not "pitch perfect," it did not need to be. The question is whether the acquisition was entirely fair. The court agreed with the Chancery Court that it was.

§ 2. SANITIZING A RELATED PARTY DEAL: BOARD OR SHAREHOLDER RATIFICATION

A. RATIFICATION BY DISINTERESTED, INDEPENDENT DIRECTORS

Ratification by *disinterested, independent directors* must be either (1) by a majority of those directors or (2) by a special subcommittee of the board consisting entirely of those directors. MBCA § 8.62(a) (majority must consist of at least two disinterested directors). The most common method of ratification is the *special negotiating (or transactional) committee* (sometimes termed simply a *SC*), a subcommittee of the board consisting entirely of disinterested, independent directors. The SC is charged by the full board with exclusive authority to act in a transaction on behalf of the corporation. The SC has the power to hire (and absolutely should hire) its own independent legal counsel and investment advisor.

Courts prefer the SC structure in acquisitions because they expect the disinterested, ratifying directors to actively participate in the negotiation of the acquisition price; the SC is the most effective negotiating vehicle. See *Weinberger v. UOP, Inc.*, 457 A.2d 701, n. 7 (Del. 1983) (heavily cited footnote). When a majority of the disinterested directors vote at the full board level to support a transaction, the court is suspicious of the influence of the other conflicted directors on the content of the deal and the ratifying vote; the interested directors can be found to *dominate* the other directors. Or some of the disinterested directors may "go along to get along" by voting yes.

There are three scenarios for a sanitizing vote of disinterested directors at the *full* board of directors level (i.e., without using a SC). A quorum for board action is usually a majority of the entire authorized board ignoring any vacancies (the bylaws can reduce the requirement to one-third). Assuming a quorum of directors has been achieved, a majority of those directors actually present (either in person or through electronic means) must vote in favor of a resolution.

In scenario one, assume the number of disinterested directors is sufficient to constitute a majority of the full board. Thus, by themselves they constitute a quorum and can approve the transaction if they wish. The interested directors need not attend the meeting, although they often do to properly explain the conflict of interest to the disinterested directors.

In scenario two, assume the number of disinterested directors is not sufficient to constitute a majority of the full board. In that case, some interested directors must also attend the meeting to help achieve a quorum. DGCL § 144(b). If the number of disinterested directors is sufficient to be a majority of a bare quorum, the interested directors who also appear to achieve the quorum may abstain on the vote.

In the third scenario—a rare case—assume that the number of disinterested directors is too small to make even a majority of a bare quorum. Thus, not only must some interested directors attend the meeting to help achieve a quorum, but some may have to vote to help approve the deal. In this case, the disinterested directors simply *contribute* to the majority vote on the deal.

In each of the three scenarios, the vote of a majority of the disinterested directors (as long as there are at least two) could protect the transaction in theory. See MBCA § 8.62(c) (to the same effect; defines majority of disinterested directors, if two or more, to be a quorum). In practice, the courts seem to respect ratification only when disinterested directors constitute a *majority* of the full board (i.e., scenario one). *Orman v. Cullman,* 794 A.2d 5 (Del. Ch. 2002). In any event, the entire quorum/vote counting exercise is mercifully rendered moot through the use of a SC.

Traditionally, a director is *disinterested* if she has no personal stake in the outcome of the transaction at issue. In March 2025, the Delaware General Assembly substantially amended DGCL § 144 (Delaware's interested director and officer statute) to include a common sense definition of "disinterested director": he or she "is not a party to the act or transaction and does not have a material interest in the act or transaction or a material relationship with a person that has a material interest in the act or transaction." DGCL § 144(e)(4). "Material interest" is defined to mean an actual or potential benefit, including the avoidance of a detriment, other than one which would devolve on the corporation or the stockholders generally, that would reasonably be expected to impair the objectivity of the director's judgment when participating in the negotiation, authorization, or approval of the act or transaction at issue. DGCL § 144(e)(7). "Material relationship" is defined to mean a familial, financial, professional, employment, or other relationship that would reasonably be expected to impair the objectivity of the director's judgment when participating in the negotiation, authorization, or approval of the act or transaction at issue. DGCL § 144(e)(8).

A director is *independent,* by contrast, if not beholden to an interested party due to family, business or other relationships—i.e., she votes her mind freely. Cf. *Beam v. Stewart,* 845 A.2d 1040 (Del. 2004) (discussing independence in derivative action pre-suit demands). In Delaware the test for independence is fact and context specific—it is largely *subjective.* Additionally, newly-amended

DGCL § 144 now includes a presumption that a director of a public corporation is independent with respect to a given transaction if he or she is not a party to the transaction and the board determines that he or she is independent under applicable stock exchange rules (e.g., NYSE Listed Co. Manual § 303A.02; Nasdaq Marketplace Rule 5605). DGCL § 144(d)(2). The independence presumption is rebuttable only if there is "substantial and particularized evidence" that the director has a material interest in the transaction or a material relationship with an interested party.

The MBCA uses different terminology with respect to directorial disinterest and independence. It employs the concept of "qualified directors" to include a requirement of both disinterest and independence. MBCA §§ 8.62(a) & 1.43.

The effect of a valid ratification by directors on the judicial standard of review differs by state and, in Delaware, by the type of conflict. In Delaware, if there is a conflicted transaction involving a controlling shareholder (who is either on both sides of the transaction or is otherwise competing with the common stockholders for transaction consideration), a special committee process shifts the burden of proof to the plaintiff to demonstrate that the special negotiating committee's decisions are not entirely fair. *Kahn v. Lynch Comm. Sys., Inc.*, 669 A.2d 79 (Del. 1995). But "[t]he presence of a controller in the midst of a corporate transaction, *without more*, does not automatically subject [the controller's conduct] to entire fairness review." *In re Viacom Inc.*

Stockholders Litig., 2020 WL 7711128, at *11 (Del. Ch.) (emphasis added). In that situation, valid board ratification or a legitimate SC may resuscitate a business judgment rule analysis for the ratifying directors. *Orman v. Cullman,* 794 A.2d 5 (Del. Ch. 2002).

Other jurisdictions may apply a traditional business judgment rule analysis to all valid director ratifications. E.g., MBCA § 8.61(b).

B. RATIFICATION BY SHAREHOLDER VOTE

If the disinterested shareholders vote to ratify a transaction and the shareholders are fully informed of any conflicts, courts will respect the ratifying vote. *Solomon v. Armstrong,* 747 A.2d 1098 (Del. Ch. 1999); MBCA § 8.63. In *Solomon,* the Chancery Court held that a fully-informed shareholder vote in favor of a classic self-dealing transaction "maintains the business judgment rule presumptions." However, in such cases plaintiff-shareholders often attack the integrity of the vote itself to undermine the outcome of the vote.

When enhanced scrutiny under *Revlon, Inc. v. MacAndrews & Forbes Holdings, Inc.,* 506 A.2d 173 (Del. 1986), presumptively applies to a sale transaction, the Delaware Supreme Court has held that defendant fiduciaries can lower the standard of judicial review to an irrebuttable version of the business judgment rule. See *Corwin v. KKR Financial Holdings LLC,* 125 A.3d 304 (Del. 2015). However, to lower the standard, no controller must exist and the transaction must have been approved by a fully informed, uncoerced majority of the disinterested stockholders. Importantly, a single disclosure deficiency will defeat *Corwin* cleansing. The plaintiff bears the initial burden of identifying alleged disclosure problems, but the defendants bear the burden of proving at trial that the stockholder vote was fully informed. See Chapter 12, § 3.C for more on *Revlon*.

§ 3. GOING-PRIVATE TRANSACTIONS

In a "*going-private*" (or "*going dark*") transaction, a purchaser seeks to buy all the stock in a publicly traded company so as to escape the public reporting obligations of the federal securities laws. SEA § 12. In other words, a publicly traded corporation is converted back into a privately held corporation. The acquisition vehicle can be funded by a buyout group (an LBO) that may include senior managers as participants (an MBO). More commonly, the purchaser is already a controlling shareholder, usually a parent corporation, that is purchasing all minority interests in a subsidiary. Both MBOs and controlling shareholder acquisitions present conflict of interest problems.

A. MANAGERS AS PURCHASERS: MBOs

When a target's senior managers, board members or controlling shareholders have major stakes in the acquirer, the courts take a much closer look at the transaction. And rightfully so. In acquisitions in which senior managers are on both sides of the deal, there is a conflict of interest and the business judgment rule is normally unavailable. The board's decision must then meet the entire or intrinsic fairness test.

For example, in *Weinberger v. UOP, Inc.*, 457 A.2d 701 (Del. 1983), the Delaware Supreme Court applied the entire fairness test to a squeeze-out (or cash-out) merger. In a squeeze-out merger, a majority shareholder eliminates the minority shareholders. The court explained the entire fairness test as having two parts, an investigation into the procedure of the deal (*fair process*) and an investigation into the deal price (*fair price*). In this case the court held that the process (a.k.a. procedure) was not fair because members of the target subsidiary board, who were also officers of the parent acquirer, used their special access to target company information to the advantage of the acquirer. The court also noted in dicta its support for a legitimate special committee decision-making structure for the target.

If the plaintiff alleges with particularity facts indicating the existence of a conflict of interest, the business judgment rule is disabled and the burden of proving the deal is entirely fair shifts to the defendants. If, however, the defendants can prove that fully-informed shareholders ratified a board's decision or that a board delegated decision-making power to a subcommittee of disinterested directors (a SC) that acted independently and with adequate information, then the standard of judicial review shifts. The nature of the shift may depend on the facts. If there are multiple bidders and the management group wins the auction, a SC may only shift from the defendants to the plaintiffs the burden of proof on the entire fairness test.

In *Mills Acquisition Co. v. Macmillan, Inc.*, 559 A.2d 1261 (Del. 1989), the special committee ran a rigged auction between a leveraged buyout group that included senior managers of the target (a classic MBO) and an independent bidder. The committee tipped the MBO group on the content of its competitor's bids. The court held that the special committee's actions did not meet the entire fairness test. For SC auctions that courts have respected, see *Barkan v. Amsted Indus., Inc.*, 567 A.2d 1279 (Del. 1989); *In re RJR Nabisco, Inc. Shareholders Litig.*, 1989 WL 7036 (Del. Ch.).

B. CONTROLLING SHAREHOLDER PURCHASES OF MINORITY INTERESTS

A parent corporation of a partially owned subsidiary seeking to make the subsidiary wholly owned must purchase the minority shareholder interest in the sub. The parent corporation has four choices: (1) a squeeze-out merger (either an upstream or triangular merger); (2) an upstream asset acquisition; (3) a reverse stock split; or (4) a combination tender offer/short-form, back-end merger. The first and last choices are the most frequent. In the last option, the parent's tender offer for the minority shares is conditioned upon the parent obtaining enough stock through the tender offer to give the parent at least 90 percent ownership of the subsidiary. If achieved, the parent can merge the subsidiary with and into the parent through

DGCL § 253, Delaware's short-form merger provision.

In a classic squeeze-out merger (choice 1), as noted in the previous section, the entire fairness test of *Weinberger* normally applies. Ratification by a disinterested special committee merely shifts the burden of proof under the test from the defendants to the plaintiff shareholders. In 2014, however, the Delaware Supreme Court allowed controllers pursuing single-step mergers to enjoy the benefits of the business judgment standard of review so long as stringent conditions were met.

Kahn v. M & F Worldwide Corp., 88 A.3d 635 (Del. 2014), involved Ronald Perelman's MacAndrews & Forbes Holdings, Inc. ("MacAndrews"). In 2011, MacAndrews sought to acquire the 57 percent of the equity in M & F Worldwide Corp. ("MFW") that it did not already own by means of a single-step merger. From the outset, MacAndrews' proposal to take MFW private was made contingent upon two shareholder-protective procedural conditions. First, MacAndrews required the merger to be negotiated and approved by a special committee of independent MFW directors. Second, MacAndrews required that the merger be approved by a majority of shareholders unaffiliated with MacAndrews (a.k.a., an affirmative vote of a "majority of the minority").

Plaintiff-shareholders (the "Appellants") initially sought to enjoin the merger from taking place, but were unsuccessful. The merger closed in December 2011 after it was approved by holders of 65.4 percent of MFW's minority shares. Appellants then sued

MFW's directors (including the members of the SC) for breach of fiduciary duty. The defendants moved for summary judgment, which the Delaware Chancery Court granted.

The Chancery Court proffered a new structure which, if followed by a controller, would allow its single-step merger to be reviewed under the *business judgment rule* rather than the entire fairness test. The Delaware Supreme Court embraced this new structure, thus allowing controllers going forward to avail themselves of the business judgment rule standard of review *if* they followed the roadmap laid out in *M & F Worldwide.*

According to the Delaware Supreme Court, the business judgment standard of review will apply *if and only if:*

(1) the controller conditions *ab initio* (from the beginning) the procession of the transaction on the approval of *both* a special committee and a majority of the minority shareholders;

(2) the special committee is independent;

(3) the special committee is empowered to freely select its own advisors and to say no to the deal definitively;

(4) the vote of the minority is informed; and

(5) there is no coercion of the minority.

The two approval requirements in clause (1) above are referred to as the *dual procedural protections* by the Delaware Supreme Court.

As recognized by the Delaware Supreme Court, the beauty of the new structure is that the controller must voluntarily relinquish control over the process so that the transaction's negotiation and approval process replicates one typically involved in a merger with an unaffiliated third party. Indeed, the court highlights that the use of a functioning special committee *and* a majority of the minority vote operate to replicate an *arm's-length* merger.

Assuming a controller utilizes the new structure, a plaintiff-shareholder would have to plead a reasonably conceivable set of facts showing that any or all of the enumerated conditions did not exist before the court would apply an entire fairness review. If the plaintiff-shareholder's complaint does state a claim for relief, the plaintiff-shareholder would be entitled to proceed and conduct discovery. If, after discovery, triable issues of fact remain about whether either or both of the dual procedural protections were established, or if established were effective, the case will proceed to a trial in which the court will conduct an entire fairness review.

In *Flood v. Synutra Int'l, Inc.,* 195 A.3d 754 (Del. 2018), the Delaware Supreme Court clarified *M & F Worldwide* in two respects. First, a controller need not include the dual procedural protections of *M & F Worldwide* in its initial offer (i.e., ab initio), so long as it modifies its offer to include them before the special committee convenes, before any substantive negotiations with the special committee commence, and before the special committee initiates its due diligence process. In other words, *M & F Worldwide*'s "ab initio" (from the beginning) requirement can still be satisfied even if the controller does not include the dual procedural protections in its very first offer. See also *Swomley v. Schlecht,* 2014 WL 4470947 (Del. Ch.). Second, while a plaintiff can plead a duty of care violation under the business judgment rule in connection with the special committee's approval of the controller's offer, to succeed the plaintiff must show that the special committee acted with gross negligence. Merely questioning the sufficiency of the price was held insufficient by the Delaware Supreme Court.

A threshold issue to address in this context is who qualifies as a "controller" in the first instance. While it is a safe bet to label a stockholder holding a majority of a corporation's voting stock a "controller" (as well as a "majority stockholder"), do others qualify? What if a given stockholder does not own a majority of a corporation's voting stock, but does hold a significant block of stock as well as other indicia of control (e.g., a board position or certain contractual veto rights)? Is he, she or it a controller? Delaware case law on point has been far from clear. See, e.g., *Tornetta v. Musk,* 310 A.3d 430 (Del. Ch. 2024) (controller status at 21.9%); *Sciannella v. AstraZeneca UK Ltd.,* 2024 WL 3327765 (Del. Ch.) (no controller status at 26.7%); *In re Oracle Corp. Deriv. Litig.,* 2023 WL 3408772 (Del. Ch.) (no controller status at 28.8%); *In re GGP, Inc. S'holder Litig.,* 2021 WL 2102326 (Del. Ch.), (no control at

35.3% with unexercised right to increase stake up to 45% because stockholder's power was diminished due to contractual standstill arrangements).

In light of the lack of clarity in Delaware case law, in March 2025 the Delaware General Assembly substantially amended DGCL § 144. Among other welcomed changes, Section 144 now sets forth parameters for identifying "controlling stockholders." Specifically, the "controlling stockholder" designation is limited to only those that (i) control a majority in voting power of the outstanding stock entitled to vote generally in the election of directors, (ii) control the election of directors possessing a majority of the board's total voting power, or (iii) possess the functional equivalent of majority control by having both control of *at least one-third* in voting power of the outstanding stock entitled to vote generally in the election of directors and the power to exercise managerial authority.

Amended § 144 also alters the *M & F Worldwide* framework to provide more predictability, give greater deference to independent directors and rebalance litigation incentives. Indeed, on the litigation point, good-faith corporate actors now have greater ability to either obtain dismissal of stockholder litigation at the pleading stage or avoid having to face litigation in the first instance. Specific changes include:

(a) *non*-squeeze out mergers with controllers and other interested transactions have to satisfy only one of the dual procedural protections of the *M & F Worldwide* framework to receive the more favorable business judgment standard of judicial review;

(b) controller mergers where minority stockholders are squeezed out ("going private" transactions) must satisfy both of the dual procedural protections of the *M & F Worldwide* framework to receive the more favorable business judgment standard of judicial review, but such transactions benefit from all of the modifications to that framework set forth in clauses (c) through (g) below;

(c) "disinterested director" is now defined in a common sense way as a director who lacks a "material interest" in the transaction at hand or a "material relationship" with a person that has a material interest in that transaction;

(d) a presumption now exists that a director of a public corporation is independent with respect to a given transaction if he or she is not a party to the transaction and the board determines that he or she is independent under applicable stock exchange rules. The independence presumption is rebuttable only if there is "substantial and particularized evidence" that the director has a material interest in the transaction or a material relationship with an interested party;

(e) with respect to the use of a special committee, only a majority of its members, rather than every member, is required to be disinterested;

(f) the *ab initio* requirement is now eliminated, thus allowing special committee review or a "majority of the minority" vote to occur any time during the deal process;

(g) in the context of a "majority of the minority" vote, a "majority of the votes *cast* by minority stockholders" standard has now replaced the former "majority of the outstanding stock *held* by minority stockholders" standard for controller transactions and other interested transactions (thus lowering the voting threshold and providing more certainty for obtaining the requisite vote); and

(h) a safe harbor now exists that affords protection from liability and equitable relief for a controlling stockholder or other interested transaction if the transaction is "fair as to the corporation" (defined to mean that the transaction, as a whole, is beneficial to the corporation or its stockholders taking into account whether the transaction is fair in terms of the relevant fiduciary's dealings with the corporation and approximates an arm's-length transaction).

Turning back to the four choices noted at the beginning of this section, with respect to choices 2 and 3, the entire fairness test of *Weinberger* would also apply to parent acquisitions of the minority interest in a subsidiary through an upstream asset acquisition and a reverse stock split. *Levco Alt. Fund Ltd. v. The Reader's Digest Assoc. Inc.*, 803 A.2d 428 (Del. 2002).

With respect to choice 4, the Delaware Supreme Court applies a different test to the tender offer/short-form merger. The tender offer is subject only to a "*coercion*" test; the controlling shareholders cannot coerce or threaten minority shareholders to induce them to tender. *Solomon v. Pathe Comm. Corp.*, 672 A.2d 35 (Del. 1996). The Delaware Chancery Court has also held that the coercion test requires that the tender offer be subject to a "majority of the minority" tender condition, that the back-end merger price equal the tender offer price, and that no retributive threats occur. *In re Pure Resources, Inc., Shareholders Litig.*, 808 A.2d 421 (Del. Ch. 2002). The minority shareholder's exclusive remedy in the back-end merger is the appraisal procedure under DGCL § 262. *Glassman v. Unocal Expl. Corp.*, 777 A.2d 242 (Del. 2001).

Prior to *M & F Worldwide,* parent corporations preferred to use the tender offer/back-end merger procedure rather than the single-step, squeeze-out merger procedure when purchasing a minority interest in a subsidiary. Indeed, defendants, using proper procedures, could win on summary motions when using a tender offer/short-form merger but could not win on summary motions when using a squeeze-out merger. Now, if a parent complies with the stringent conditions espoused in *M & F Worldwide* when conducting a squeeze-out merger, the Delaware courts will apply the business judgment rule as the standard of review. This is even more true today given the substantial codification of *M & F Worldwide* in newly-amended DGCL § 144.

CHAPTER 12

THE TARGET BOARD OF DIRECTORS' POWER TO BLOCK TAKEOVERS

Statutory mergers and asset acquisitions require the approval of the target board of directors to proceed. In both types of acquisitions, the target board typically signs an acquisition agreement and recommends ratification by target shareholders. An acquirer must negotiate with the board on acquisition terms (a *negotiated* or *friendly* acquisition). One form of acquisition, a *pure stock* acquisition, does not—in theory—need the approval of the target board of directors to succeed. The acquirer purchases shares directly from the hands of target shareholders, who do not need the approval of the target board to sell their shares. If an acquirer purchases control from target shareholders and the target board does not support the control change, it is a *hostile* acquisition or *hostile takeover.*

Clever firm maneuvers and state statutes have all but doomed hostile acquisitions by establishing a practical requirement for target board approval in stock acquisitions. Takeover offers may start hostile, that is, without target board approval, but most by necessity end friendly (i.e., on a negotiated basis). The hostile offer is now often used merely to secure bargaining leverage over the target board by inviting target shareholders to pressure their board to accept an acquisition offer. The last remaining truly hostile acquisition is one that first replaces the members of a balking target board through a hostile proxy solicitation and then closes the acquisition with a new, now friendly, board. E.g., *Hilton Hotels Corp. v. ITT Corp.,* 978 F. Supp. 1342 (D. Nev. 1997) (combination tender offer/proxy contest).

§ 1. FIRM-SPECIFIC HOSTILE TAKEOVER DEFENSES

Firms concerned about reducing their vulnerability to unwanted takeovers have fashioned a growing number of defenses. There are three different kinds of takeover defenses relevant to our study of board power. The categories are defined by the role of shareholders in the creation of each defense: first, takeover defenses that require specific shareholder ratification (e.g., "shark repellent" certificate amendments); second, takeover defenses put in place by the board using very general grants of authority contained in a firm's certificate of incorporation (e.g., a firm uses a charter provision authorizing the issuance of "blank check" preferred stock to promulgate a poison pill plan); and third, takeover defenses based on the board's general powers as granted in a state corporate code (e.g., a board uses a code provision authorizing a board to contract for the sale of firm assets to erect a crown jewel defense).

In the first category, shareholders must vote to approve the specific defense in question. In the second category, shareholders, unless the general grant is in a firm's original charter, must vote to amend a firm's charter to give the board the general power. And in the third category, shareholders do not necessarily vote at all, unless they vote to amend a charter to remove the board's power to use the defense.

The shareholders are not powerless, however, with respect to defenses promulgated without specific ratification (categories two and three). They can, using the shareholder resolution procedure provided under SEA Rule 14a–8 (Shareholder Proposals), vote to recommend that a board withdraw specific defenses that it has chosen to put in place. Moreover, a board deciding to use a takeover defense in categories two or three could choose to ask for shareholder ratification, although unnecessary, to protect them from shareholder-derivative litigation.

Shark Repellant Amendments to Certificates of Incorporation. Certificate amendments that require a specific shareholder vote are called *shark repellent* amendments. Drafters of early shark repellent amendments designed them to retard the ability of someone with newly-acquired voting power from taking control of the firm's board of directors. The amendments often provide for a staggered or classified board of directors (only a minority, usually one-third, of the board seats are the subject of an election in any given year), for eliminating shareholder voting through the written consent procedure (a method of voting that does not require a formal shareholder meeting), for limiting the right of shareholders to call a special meeting of shareholders, for prohibiting the removal of a sitting director unless for cause, for limiting the creation of new seats on the board of directors, and for giving the remaining members of the board the sole authority to appoint new directors if a director resigns, becomes incapacitated or dies mid-term.

First-generation shark repellent charter amendments proved to be only marginally effective. Once an acquirer gained voting control of the stock, existing board members owed the new owner fiduciary duties, and most board members who could not respond to the new owner's requests simply resigned rather than continue in an uncomfortable lame duck capacity, at constant risk of being the object of a suit brought by the new controlling shareholder. Moreover, courts prohibited the existing board from finding ways of diluting the ownership of a new controlling owner once the new owner acquired the controlling block of stock. *Condec Corp. v. Lukenheimer Co.*, 230 A.2d 769 (Del. Ch. 1967) (the court enjoined the issuance of a large block of new shares to a friendly party after an unwanted purchaser had otherwise obtained control).

Lawyers, therefore, designed a second round of certificate amendments with much more punch. The more powerful amendments contain provisions for a super-majority vote for all business combinations between a controlling shareholder and the firm if the controlling shareholder acquired control without the specific approval of a pre-existing board of directors or if the controlling shareholder did not meet fair price criteria in the merger. Some charter amendments give non-tendering shareholders in hostile acquisitions the right to put (i.e., sell) their stock to the firm for a specified period of time at a generous price after a successful stock acquisition. Others reduce the voting rights of the acquirer's purchased target stock unless the acquisition meets specified fair price requirements or is approved by non-selling shareholders.

The most extreme form of this sophisticated class of certificate amendments is one that changes the voting rights of outstanding common stock. In *time-phased* or *tenure* voting plans, a firm—through a charter amendment—changes the voting rights of its common stock. Upon the effectiveness of the amendment, all outstanding shares are deemed to have multiple votes per share. However, the multiple votes disappear (reverting back to a single vote per share) upon the sale or transfer of the underlying stock and reappear when a shareholder holds the stock for three or four consecutive years. See *Williams v. Geier,* 671 A.2d 1368 (Del. 1996). In *capped voting* plans, a firm limits the voting power of shares based on the number of shares owned. Shareholders who purchase shares in excess of the triggering amount do not get voting rights on the excess shares.

A firm can also recapitalize, amending their certificate of incorporation to create two classes of common stock (*two-tier voting stock*). Shares of one class, sold exclusively to insiders, have concentrated voting power (often 10 votes per share). Shares of the other class, typically held by public shareholders, have limited voting power (typically one vote or even no votes per share). Alphabet, Inc. (a.k.a. Google) employs two-tier voting stock, while Snap, Inc. (SnapChat) employs *three-tier* voting stock (no votes per share for the public, one vote per share for early investors, and 10 votes per share for the founders!).

Finally, in the same vein as two-tiered voting stock is an "identity-based" voting system, which provides more votes to certain shareholders based on who they are. In *Colon v. Bumble, Inc.*, 305 A.3d 352 (Del. Ch. 2023), the Delaware Chancery Court upheld Bumble, Inc.'s identity-based voting system contained in two charter provisions after a plaintiff shareholder had challenged those provisions. The provisions essentially provided that each share of common stock would carry one vote, unless the share was owned by a "Principal Stockholder" (defined to include the parties to a publicly disclosed stockholders agreement), in which case it would carry ten votes.

The plaintiff argued that the identity-based voting system violated statutory law (specifically DGCL § 151(a)) and sought a declaration that the challenged charter provisions were invalid. The court, however, disagreed. It noted that the provisions set forth a formula that applies to all the shares and specified how voting power was calculated, and thus were in compliance with § 151(a). The court emphasized that the formula made the quantum of voting power that a share carried dependent on a fact ascertainable outside of the certificate of incorporation, namely the identity of the owner. The court added that nothing in § 151(a) prohibits a provision that creates a closed set of holders who can exercise certain rights. The court, however, noted that its decision expressed no view on whether an identity-based voting system could be inequitable, as that issue was not before the court.

Poison Pill Plans. The major disadvantages of charter amendments adopted by shareholder vote are: first, they take time to put in place; second, they are not flexible; and third, the firm must justify them in comprehensive disclosure documents required by the federal proxy rules. In response, clever corporate lawyers designed new defenses that can be implemented without a shareholder vote—the firms can employ them in less time and do not have to justify them in proxy statements.

The most popular of these defenses is a *poison pill plan* (a.k.a. a *shareholders' rights plan*). The plan involves a target company (particularly one believing it is vulnerable to a bidder's hostile takeover attempt) making a distribution to existing shareholders of stock, stock rights or other securities (notes, for example) that have special redemption or conversion provisions. The redemption or conversion options in these instruments are activated by a stock acquisition—*not* approved in advance by the target's board—by a bidder of a specified percentage of the target's stock (a *trigger,* typically 15, 20 or 25 percent of outstanding shares, depending on the pill in question), as would occur in the case where the bidder closes a successful hostile first-step tender offer for target shares.

Triggering the pill makes the target *prohibitively expensive* for the bidder to buy. This is accomplished through the dilution of the value of the target shares in the hands of the bidder. When the bidder triggers the pill, all target stockholders (*other than the bidder itself*) is entitled to purchase additional shares of target stock from the target at a bargain basement price (typically at a 50 percent discount) (a pill feature known as the "flip in"). The introduction of these cheap shares into the marketplace *devalues* the existing shares in the marketplace. Target stockholders other than the bidder can protect themselves from this dilution by exercising their poison pill rights and purchasing their allotment of cheap shares. The bidder, prevented from purchasing cheap shares, suffers massive value dilution with respect to the target shares it just purchased. Due to the *in terrorem* effect that the triggering of a pill has, to date no bidder has ever triggered a traditional, defensive poison pill. That is, no bidder has triggered such a pill and purchased the target anyway—a strategy known as "buying through the pill."

As mentioned above, only stock acquisitions that the target board has *not approved* (i.e., hostile acquisitions) trigger the pill. A target board will carve out from the pill a friendly, negotiated deal that it has approved. That is, a target board retains the right to waive the effects of the pill, usually through a right to redeem the outstanding securities for a nominal fee. Given the *in terrorem* effect that the triggering of a pill has, a bidder must negotiate with the target board *before* acquiring a triggering block of target stock, seeking the target board's approval of the acquisition and the target board's agreement that it will redeem the outstanding conversion rights. In other words, poison pill plans *force bidders to negotiate* with the target board in stock acquisitions—acquisitions that the bidder could otherwise consummate (through a successful tender offer) without the target board's approval.

Negotiations between the bidder and the target board, however, inevitably lead to the bidder offering to pay *more per share* for the target's shares in order to secure the target board's approval. Thus, poison pills typically force bidders to negotiate with target boards and, if those bidders wish to secure the target, agree to pay more per target share than they otherwise would. When deals become too rich for bidders, they either have to walk away empty handed or seek to replace members of the target's board with new members who are sympathetic to doing a deal. In the latter case, bidders will launch *hostile proxy contests* to oust incumbent target directors and install replacements who will look favorably upon a deal between the bidder and the target. Bidders often launch hostile proxy contests contemporaneously with hostile tender offers to exert maximum pressure on target boards to approve deals. See, e.g., *Air Products and Chem., Inc. v. Airgas, Inc.*, 16 A.3d 48 (Del. Ch. 2011).

The poison pill plans, which began as distributions of convertible preferred stock, have evolved into distributions of stock rights (options to purchase stock from the firm) and convertible debt (convertible debentures). Some firms, concerned about the legality of any one plan in a given jurisdiction and hedging their bets, will put in place two or even three plans—each based on a different underlying security.

A board, to be able to create one of the popular poison pill plans, must have the authority to issue rights, debt or preferred stock with rights and privileges set by board resolution at the time of issuance.

A charter provision that empowers the board to issue novel kinds of preferred stock is called a *blank check preferred provision.* Most states require an express declaration in a firm's certificate of incorporation that its board can issue preferred stock with rights and privileges set at the time of issuance. E.g., DGCL §§ 102(a)(4) & 151(a). This means that at some point the shareholders must have voted to authorize the blank check provision (assuming incorporators did not include one in the original charter). Moreover, most state corporate codes provide that boards have a default power (absent a contrary provision in the certificate) to issue stock rights and to place debt with the terms set by the board at the time of issuance. DGCL §§ 122(13) & 157. Stock rights and convertible debt plans do not require even a general form of shareholder authorization and therefore belong in category three.

Firm Exchange Offers. A second member of this category of defenses, which requires general but not specific shareholder authorization, is less popular and more controversial—stock exchange offers or stock dividends that put in place a two-tier voting stock system. In the exchange tender offer, a firm offers stock with diluted voting power and concentrated claims on equity for its outstanding common stock. The insiders do not tender, the outsiders do, and the insiders end up with concentrated voting power. A board must have authorization in its charter, or must amend the corporation's certificate to grant the board authorization, to issue the non-voting or diluted voting common stock. Again, many publicly traded firms have amended their charters to give their boards this authority and, even though unused, the provisions are available should the need arise.

In the stock distribution form of this defense, a firm issues super-voting stock as a stock dividend on its common stock with a transfer restriction that converts the super-voting stock to lower voting common stock if the new stock is sold or transferred. Insiders hold and outsiders trade.

Lock-Ups and Other Asset-Based Strategies. The third category of defenses—those that do not require any shareholder vote, even at the most general level of authorization—is the most wide-ranging. Boards of directors use their inherent power over firm assets to make the firm unattractive to unwanted bidders. These defenses are often less attractive than a poison pill plan, because the defenses in category three usually require that the board expend assets or make major changes in the capital structure of the firm.

The board sells or gives contingent rights to the key firm asset to a third party (the *crown jewel* or *asset lock-up* defense), buys its own stock back from the hands of an unwanted bidder (*greenmail*), gives top managers handsome severance payments contingent on control changes (*golden parachutes*), or issues stock or contingent stock rights (a *stock lock-up*) to a friendly party (a *white squire*) subject to reselling restrictions (a *standstill agreement*). The firm makes acquisitions of its own to create antitrust problems for the bidder (the *Clayton defense*), to create national defense concerns if the bidder is foreign (the *Pentagon play*), or to acquire control of the *bidder* in a reverse acquisition (the *Pac-Man defense,* the little fish turns around and tries to swallow the big fish!).

The most common modern defense in this category is a radical restructuring, the *leveraged recapitalization*. This defense entails the target releveraging itself by selling debt and passing the cash proceeds of the placement back to its own shareholders in a huge, one-time cash dividend. By releveraging, the target exhausts its debt capacity and its cash reserves so that a bidder (e.g., a private equity or leveraged buyout firm) cannot use the target's own assets to finance an acquisition. In other words, the target beats an acquirer planning on using junk bond financing to the punch.

The Most Effective Defenses. Two-tier common stock plans are bullet proof. A purchaser must acquire the super-voting stock to get control of elections of directors and the super-voting stock is held exclusively by incumbent managers and founders. Also very effective are poison pill plans combined with staggered or classified boards. The poison pill plan stops stock acquisitions that a target board has not pre-approved, while the staggered or classified board severely impedes proxy contests to replace a majority of the incumbent target board members. Indeed, a hostile bidder's nominees would have to win at least two annual elections to replace a majority of the target's incumbent directors. A poison pill plan without a staggered or classified board could be removed if the hostile bidder replaces a majority of the target's incumbent directors with the hostile bidder's nominees; a staggered or classified board without a poison pill does not stop a more than 50 percent stock acquisition by a new controlling shareholder who can then demand that hold over directors either change allegiance or resign.

§ 2. STATE ANTI-TAKEOVER STATUTES

The total count of states with some form of anti-takeover legislation is over 40. There are close to 10 types of statutes in use. Two-thirds of our largest corporations are incorporated in five states, all of which have anti-takeover laws (Delaware, New York, Ohio, Pennsylvania and Massachusetts). Delaware has two state anti-takeover laws: a business combination statute and a succession of labor contract provision. The other four states have some of the most extensive and innovative defensive takeover regulations in the country. Most states that have anti-takeover statutes have more than one type. Pennsylvania, for example, has a control share act, a business combination statute, a poison pill statute, a severance pay statute, a redemption statute and a disgorgement statute.

Most state legislatures attempting to regulate tender offers rely on one or more of four types of statutes: control share acquisition statutes, fair price statutes, redemption statutes and business combination statutes.

In a *control share* statute, a bidder not approved by the target board of directors cannot vote the newly-acquired shares without a favorable vote of the remaining shareholders. See, e.g., Ind. Code Ann. § 23–1–42 (Burns Supp. 1986); Minn. Stat. Ann. § 302A.671 (West 1985 & Supp.1987); Mo. Ann. Stat. § 351.407 (Vernon Supp. 1987); OGCL § 1701.831 (Anderson 1985). In a *fair price* statute, a bidder not approved by the target board cannot merge its firm into the target unless the remaining target shareholders are paid a fair price (the price paid any other shareholder for a period of time prior to the merger) or a majority of them approve. See, e.g., Md. Corps. & Ass'ns Code Ann. §§ 3–601 to 603 (1985 & Supp. 1986). In a *redemption* statute, also known as an *appraisal* statute, shareholders receive a put right for the fair value of their shares contingent on a triggering stock acquisition. See, e.g., Me. Rev. Stat. Ann. Tit. 13, § 910 (Supp. 1986); Utah Code Ann. § 16–10–76.5 (Supp. 1986). In *business combination* statutes, also known as *freeze-out* statutes, the acquirer may not engage in a back-end merger (or its equivalent) for a period of years after a triggering stock acquisition not approved by the target board. Ind. Code Ann. § 23–1–43 (Burns Supp. 1986); Ky. Rev. Stat. Ann. § 271A.397(3) (Baldwin Supp. 1986); Mo. Ann. Stat. § 351.459 (Vernon Supp. 1987); NYBCL § 912(b) (McKinney 1986).

Less popular statutes include Pennsylvania's *disgorgement* (or anti-greenmail) statute in which an unsuccessful hostile bidder, seeking to sell shares to a successful bidder, must give all profits back to the target firm. PBCL §§ 2573 & 2575; see also OGCL § 1707.043. One also sees *severance* statutes in which a successful hostile bidder must offer lucrative severance packages to terminated target employees. E.g., PBCL § 2582 (requiring minimum severance compensation to be paid to any employee terminated within two years of a control-share acquisition).

The U.S. Supreme Court has held that control share acts do not violate the commerce or supremacy clauses of the U.S. Constitution (*CTS Corp. v. Dynamics Corp.,* 481 U.S. 69 (1987)), and federal circuit courts have extended the reasoning of the opinion to cover the other popular statutes. See, e.g., *WLR Foods v. Tyson Foods,* 65 F.3d 1172 (4th Cir. 1995) (Virginia's four statutes).

The most important statutory reaction to takeovers is the business combination statute. First enacted by New York, and adopted in diluted form by Delaware, this type of statute prohibits certain business combinations between an interested shareholder and the target corporation for an extended period of time—five years in the case of New York's statute (NYBCL § 912(b)) and three years in Delaware's (DGCL § 203(a)). The statutes stop most leveraged or financial takeovers because a back-end merger (between the acquisition vehicle and the target) is necessary to secure control over the assets of the target. The purchaser needs to attach debt in the acquisition vehicle to the target's assets, to sell assets to generate cash and so on. Without a back-end merger in its plans, a purchaser cannot secure the financing necessary for an LBO. Moreover, the target board continues to owe fiduciary duties to the remaining minority shareholders.

Business combination statutes typically contain exceptions allowing for friendly bidders to consummate post-takeover transactions (e.g., second-step mergers). Common examples include pre-purchase board approval, or board approval plus a super-majority vote of the remaining shareholders. Business combination restrictions shield shareholders from the coerciveness of front-end loaded, two-tier offers by preventing the bidder from closing the second step of the offer unless the target's board of directors and, in some instances, the target's remaining shareholders, approve the transaction.

Delaware's statute deserves special mention. Its constitutionality upheld in *BNS Inc. v. Koppers Co., Inc.,* 683 F.Supp. 458 (D. Del. 1988), § 203 is triggered by an unapproved 15 percent or more stock acquisition and acts on a variety of transactions between a stockholder and the corporation. The statute, put simply, prevents business combinations, broadly defined, between an interested stockholder (basically a 15 percent or more owner of the outstanding voting stock of the corporation) and the target for a three-year period, unless one of the exceptions to the statute applies. As explained below, subsection (a) of § 203 sets forth three ways an interested stockholder otherwise subject to the section may escape its three-year freeze. Subsection

(b) lists circumstances in which the section does not apply at all.

Subsection (a) allows a bidder to consummate a second-step merger or other business combination when:

(1) the board approves the combination *prior* to the date the bidder becomes an interested stockholder—i.e., as part of a friendly, negotiated deal;

(2) the interested stockholder holds over 85 percent of the outstanding voting stock, excluding, for the purposes of calculating that percentage, shares owned by officers who are also directors of the target and those owned by certain employee stock plans. Thus, the tender offer price was so enticing that almost all target shareholders tendered;

(3) the board of directors approves the business combination *after* the bidder becomes an interested stockholder and the proposed combination is authorized by two-thirds of the outstanding voting stock *not owned* by the interested stockholder. This is not likely to happen, given that those still holding stock after a successful tender offer were obviously not impressed with the price offered. Thus, they are not likely to vote in favor of a second-step merger offering the exact same consideration.

Subsection (b) lists circumstances in which § 203 will not apply at all. Subsection (b)(1) permits newly-organized corporations to opt out of the statute. Subsection (b)(3) gives stockholders the power to amend the corporation's bylaws or charter to opt out. However, amendments are not effective for 12 months. Moreover, an interested stockholder is not covered by an amendment adopted after a hostile stock acquisition. Subsection (b)(4) exempts corporations that are not publicly traded. Subsection (b)(5) exempts persons who become interested stockholders inadvertently (e.g., through gift or inheritance). Subsection (b)(6), tipping its hat to the *Revlon* requirement of maximizing the target's sale price, releases all bidders from combination restrictions when another, competing bidder for more than 50 percent of the voting stock is approved by target management (let the bidding war begin!).

The Delaware statute, like most state anti-takeover statutes (except the appraisal statute in Pennsylvania perhaps), does not present a substantial additional deterrent to hostile takeovers over what firms had created through poison pill plans and other firm-specific defenses. However, the state statutes add yet another defensive weapon to an already potent arsenal of takeover defenses. The Delaware courts had been faced with supervising the decisions of target boards in creating and holding onto firm specific takeover defenses before the adoption of § 203; § 203 did not materially change the courts' task. The Delaware courts decide—under their increasingly intricate edifice of fiduciary duty case law—legal challenges both to a board's decision not to waive a firm-specific poison pill plan and its decision not to waive the statutory three-year cooling-off period under § 203 on similar standards.

§ 3. COURT REVIEW OF A BOARD'S DECISION TO BLOCK HOSTILE TAKEOVERS

When frustrated bidders or target shareholders contest a target's anti-takeover defenses in court, there is the preliminary legal issue of whether the defenses at issue are void *ab initio* (outside the power of the board of directors to adopt). Once the court decides that a board has the power to adopt a particular defense, the issue becomes one of proper use: Have the directors abused their discretion (breached their fiduciary duty to their shareholders) in deploying or refusing to defuse a defense on the facts of a particular case?

A. VOID DEFENSES: DEAD HAND PROVISIONS AND PRECLUSIONS OF PROXY CONTEXTS

There are two lines of Delaware cases that invalidate some defenses without regard to their specific use in a particular takeover. Both relate to the ability of a hostile bidder to wage a successful proxy contest for control of the target board.

In *Quickturn Design Sys., Inc. v. Shapiro,* 721 A.2d 1281 (Del. 1998), the Delaware Supreme Court held invalid a poison pill plan that could not be waived by a newly-elected board for six months after their election (a *delayed hand* provision). The court said the plan was an infringement of the board's statutory power to manage the business and affairs of the firm. DGCL § 141(a). The drafters of the plan intended to stop hostile proxy solicitations for control of the board as a prelude to an acquisition. Even if the acquirer took control of the board, the new board could not redeem the poison pill (and thus could not authorize an acquisition) for six months. Stronger versions of the defense, *dead hand* provisions that completely disable the new board from ever waiving a poison pill, are also presumably void. See *Carmody v. Toll Bros., Inc.,* 723 A.2d 1180 (Del. Ch. 1998).

The second line of cases, previously based on *Blasius Indus. v. Atlas Corp.,* 564 A.2d 651 (Del. Ch. 1988), but now presumably resting on *Coster v. UIP Cos., Inc.,* 300 A.3d 656 (Del. 2023), invalidates any takeover defense that impairs the right of target shareholders to vote unless the board meets certain stringent requirements. *Coster* is discussed in Chapter 12, § 3.E below. Any poison pill plan triggered by a hostile proxy solicitation (as opposed to a hostile stock acquisition), for example, should be considered a void defense.

B. THE BASIC STANDARD FOR EVALUATING THE USE OF TAKEOVER DEFENSES: THE *UNOCAL* TEST

As noted above, the general rule for evaluating the liability of directors sued by unhappy shareholders is the business judgment rule. Normally, the court will not substitute its judgment for that of the board. *Unitrin, Inc. v. American General Corp.,* 651 A.2d 1361 (Del. 1995). Indeed, business decisions should be made in the boardroom and not the court room with 20/20 hindsight. The business judgment rule in application means that the board is not liable for ordinary negligence. To get the benefit of the business judgment rule, a board (1) must not act primarily to protect their positions, (2) must act in good faith and free from conflicts of interest and (3) must have acquired an appropriate amount of information on the matters at issue with which to facilitate proper deliberation on those matters. See *Smith v. Van Gorkom,* 488 A.2d 858 (Del. 1985).

In *Unocal Corp. v. Mesa Petroleum Co.,* 493 A.2d 946 (Del. 1985), the Delaware Supreme Court fashioned a special application of the business judgment rule applicable to a target board's decision to implement takeover defenses, now called *enhanced judicial scrutiny.* The board's conduct must satisfy a two-part test *before* the business judgment rule applies to its decision to implement a takeover defense. The first part is the *reasonableness* test (the board must have reasonable grounds for believing an offer for the target represents a threat to corporate welfare before instituting defenses) and the second part is the *proportionality* test (the board's defensive response must not be draconian and disproportionate to the threat, that is, it must fall within a range of reasonableness). If the board does not satisfy either of the test's two parts, its conduct is evaluated under the stringent *entire fairness* standard.

In *Paramount Comm., Inc. v. Time Inc.,* 571 A.2d 1140 (Del. 1989), the high-water mark of takeover defenses, the court held that Time's defenses to a takeover by Paramount were reasonable because the board of Time reasonably believed that Paramount's offer threatened a previously-negotiated combination between Time and Warner Bros. Time also wanted to protect the "Time culture"—Time's history of editorial independence which would be threatened if Time became controlled by a single owner who, post-closing, could dictate editorial decisions if the new owner so desired (see, e.g., Rupert Murdoch and Jeff Bezos). The Time board, to protect its shareholders, disenfranchised them—the Time shareholders were not allowed to vote on the Time/Warner combination. The Time board turned the proposed statutory merger with Warner into an outright cash tender offer for Warner (thus ensuring that *Revlon* duties were not triggered) and blocked the Paramount offer. The court upheld the Time board's refusal to even entertain and discuss the Paramount bid with Paramount (the "*just say no*" defense). The result in the case is perhaps the most criticized of all the Delaware takeover cases.

In *Shamrock Holdings v. Polaroid Corp.*, 559 A.2d 278 (Del. Ch. 1989), the Polaroid board was anticipating a huge court judgment against a third party, Kodak, based on an alleged patent infringement on the part of Kodak. Therefore, Polaroid's board could not reveal to its shareholders all the information necessary for them to value accurately their stock in their decision on whether to accept the Shamrock bid. The threat to the company was an unwitting, bargain sale to a bidder and, according to the court, justified Polaroid's takeover defense (parking stock in an employee stock plan).

The court held, in essence, that if a firm has insider information that cannot be disclosed until it is less sensitive, then a takeover defense is in the best interests of current shareholders.

In *Unitrin, Inc. v. American General Corp.*, 651 A.2d 1361 (Del. 1995), the board repurchased its own stock to consolidate the voting power of insiders and take advantage of a super-majority voting provision in the firm's charter for business combinations with hostile acquirers. The board also adopted a poison pill plan. The Chancery Court upheld the poison pill plan but rejected the repurchase program. The Delaware Supreme Court remanded, asking the Chancery Court to reconsider its judgment on the repurchase program.

The perceived threat in *Unitrin,* which satisfied the first part of the *Unocal* test, was an underpriced tender offer. What split the trial and appellate courts, however, was the application of the second half of the threshold test—the proportionality test. Would the repurchase program preclude a successful proxy contest? If so, the defense might be draconian and thus void. The Chancery Court held that the bidder was chilled from buying stock to mount a proxy fight. The Delaware Supreme Court disagreed. It found that the bidder could, even after the repurchase program, solicit enough remaining shareholders to obtain control of the board and have the board waive a business combination charter provision. Indeed, the success of the proxy contest, although *highly improbable,* was still technically (mathematically) achievable. And this apparently was good enough for the Delaware Supreme Court.

The case is notable because of its proliferation of sub-tests under the two basic threshold tests. With respect to the reasonableness test, the Delaware Supreme Court highlighted three recognized threats posed by hostile tender offers:

(1) *Lost Opportunity.* A hostile tender offer may deprive the target's shareholders of the opportunity to select a superior alternative that may ultimately be offered up by target management or by a competing bidder;

(2) *Structural Coercion.* A hostile tender offer could be structured in a way where target shareholders tender their shares for reasons other than the merits of the tender offer (e.g., the structure of the deal itself will lead shareholders into tendering into the first-step tender offer because they would receive less in the deal's second-step merger); and

(3) *Substantive Coercion.* A hostile tender offer could result in target shareholders tendering into an underpriced offer that prevents them from receiving the true intrinsic value of their shares.

The court also parsed the proportionality side of the test. To assess proportionality a court first must decide whether a defense is *draconian.* A defense is draconian if it is either *coercive* or *preclusive.* "Coercive" in this context means a management-sponsored alternative to the hostile party's offer that target management crams down the throats of its own shareholders. "Preclusive" in this context covers target defenses that make a bidder's ability to wage a successful proxy contest and gain control of the target's board realistically unattainable. See *Air Products and Chem., Inc. v. Airgas, Inc.*, 16 A.3d 48 (Del. Ch. 2011). Even if not draconian, the defense must fall within a *range of reasonableness*. Assuming a given defense falls within that range, the business judgment rule will attach to the board's decision to implement it. In other words, if the target board satisfies the *Unocal* two-part test, the taint of self-interest is removed from the board's decision to implement the defense in question.

Although poison pill defenses have routinely been upheld by the Delaware courts under the *Unocal* test (e.g., *Moran v. Household Int'l., Inc.*, 500 A.2d 1346 (Del. 1985)), companies adopting them can go too far. In addition to *Quickturn Design Sys., Inc. v. Shapiro,* 721 A.2d 1281 (Del. 1998), discussed in the previous Section, *The Williams Companies Stockholder Litig.*, 2021 WL 754593 (Del. Ch.), presents another successful challenge to a company's adoption of a poison pill.

The Williams Companies ("Williams"), like many Delaware corporations, had a shareholders' rights plan (poison pill) that it could quickly adopt in the event a threat arose. Because of its ability to be quickly adopted, the pill was referred to as an "on-the-shelf" (or "morning after") poison pill. The pill was geared towards a traditional change in control situation and thus was a traditional, defensive poison pill.

What Williams was particularly fearful of—given the company's low stock price and the deleterious impact that COVID-19 had had on its business, were stockholder activists. Accordingly, the board approved an amended pill that had as its key benefit the prevention of an opportunistic party (i.e., an activist) from achieving a position of substantial influence or control without paying a control premium to other shareholders.

The plan the board approved would expire at the end of one year and had four key features: (i) a 5% trigger; (ii) a definition of "acquiring person" that captured beneficial ownership as well as ownership of certain derivative interests, such as warrants and options; (iii) an "acting in concert" provision that extended to parallel conduct and included a "daisy chain" concept (the "AIC Provision" (sometimes referred to as a "wolfpack" provision)); and (iv) a limited "passive investor" exemption.

The market reacted very negatively to the plan, and plaintiff-stockholders of Williams sued the Williams board for breach of fiduciary duty. Additionally, the plaintiffs sought declaratory and injunctive relief regarding the validity and enforceability of the plan. Utilizing a *Unocal* analysis, the Delaware Chancery Court held for the plaintiffs and issued a mandatory injunction requiring redemption of the pill.

With respect to Unocal's first prong—the *reasonableness* test (the board must have reasonable grounds for believing an offer for the target represents a threat to corporate welfare before instituting defenses)—the court highlighted that the plan was not adopted to protect against any *specific* threat at all. The board was not concerned about any specific activist threat. Nor was the Board acting to preserve any specific asset like a net operating loss. Rather, the board was acting pre-emptively to interdict hypothetical future threats. In fact, the plan was not even adopted in light of the company's prior experience with activism.

The court held that preventing these hypothetical threats did not present a legitimate corporate objective under Delaware law. The court highlighted that directors cannot justify their actions by arguing that, without their intervention, the stockholders would vote erroneously out of ignorance or mistaken belief in an uncoerced, fully informed election. Indeed, the notion that directors know better than the stockholders about who should be on the board is, according to the court, no justification at all. Thus, viewing all stockholder activism as a threat is an extreme manifestation of the proscribed "we-know-better" justification for interfering with the stockholder voting franchise. That is, categorically concluding that *all* stockholder efforts to change or influence corporate direction constitute a threat to the corporation runs directly contrary to the ideological underpinnings of Delaware law. According to the court, the broad category of conduct referred to as stockholder activism, therefore, cannot constitute a cognizable threat under the first prong of *Unocal*.

But the court did recognize as a cognizable threat the board's concern over so-called "lightning strike" stock accumulations by activists. These stem from the ability of an activist to keep acquiring stock in a target in an undetected fashion because, under SEA Rule 13d–1(a), an activist has 10 days (now changed to only five business days) after the time the activist acquires more than 5% of a target's equity securities to file its Schedule 13D disclosure schedule with the SEC. Therefore, a pill with a 5% trigger would stop an activist from engaging in a lightning strike accumulation. Such a pill would "fill the gap" in the federal securities laws, and thus in this regard such a pill is referred to as a "gap-filling pill."

However, the court then turned to the second part of *Unocal*—the *proportionality* test (the board's defensive response must not be draconian and disproportionate to the threat, that is, it must fall within a range of reasonableness). Is the board's adoption of a gap-filling pill proportional to the threat posed by the potential of lightning strike stock accumulations? Here, the court held that the Williams pill was not a reasonable response. Evidence had been presented that only 2% of all poison pills had a trigger lower than 10%, so Williams' pill was already in the extreme minority of pills. More importantly, the court found that the plan's other key features were extreme. Its "beneficial ownership," "acting in concert" and "passive investor" definitions all went far beyond federal definitions and concepts. Tongue in cheek, the court stated that the Williams' pill "increases the range of Williams' nuclear missile range by a considerable distance beyond the ordinary poison pill."

The court concluded by noting that the defendants bore the burden to show their actions were reasonable. However, they had failed to show that this extreme, unprecedented collection of poison pill features bore a reasonable relationship to their stated corporate objective. Because the defendants failed to prove that the plan fell within the range of reasonable responses, the court held that the plan was invalid.

C. THE BEST PRICE RULE VARIANT: THE *REVLON* ZONE

If a target board decides that the best defense may be a sale of the company to a favored bidder, a *white knight*, the target will attempt to close a sale to the favored bidder while blocking a sale to the unwanted bidder. In other words, it will play favorites regardless of the impact that doing so will have on the target's own shareholders. When a target pursues this tactic, a specialized application of the *Unocal* test may apply. First articulated in *Revlon, Inc. v. MacAndrews & Forbes Holdings, Inc.*, 506 A.2d 173 (Del. 1986), the Delaware Supreme Court held that the target board must act to sell the company at the *best price* for its shareholders on any changes of control. The change from the basic *Unocal* test is dramatic. Under *Unocal* a target board can successfully block an unwanted bidder; under *Revlon,* the target board must sell to the unwanted bidder *if* that bidder offers the best price to target shareholders. The success of a target board's efforts to block an unwanted bidder may depend, therefore, on which branch of the enhanced judicial scrutiny test applies, *Unocal* or *Revlon.*

The Delaware Supreme Court clarified when each test applies in the landmark case of *Paramount Comm. Inc. v. QVC Network Inc.,* 637 A.2d 34 (Del. 1994). Under the case, a court must determine whether a firm has "put itself up for sale." In *QVC,* the court found that Paramount had put itself up for sale and thus had to sell to the highest bidder. The court distinguished the situation of Time in the earlier case of *Paramount Comm., Inc. v. Time Inc.,* 571 A.2d 1140 (Del. 1989); Time had not put itself up for sale in agreeing to a negotiated merger with Warner. In fact, back then Time—not knowing whether its negotiated merger with Warner would trigger *Revlon* duties, completely restructured its deal *in media res* to be an outright acquisition of Warner by Time to make that crystal clear.

The court in *QVC* held that a corporation puts itself up for sale when it initiates an active bidding process, when it initiates a bust-up of the company's divisions or a sale of the company for cash, or when it initiates a transaction that otherwise results in a change in control. A change in control occurs in stock swap acquisitions when target shareholders take stock in a corporation dominated by a controlling shareholder, as in the facts of *QVC*. A change in control does not occur, however, if target shareholders take stock in a corporation owned by a diffuse body of shareholders, even if the target shareholders take a minority percentage of the stock, as occurred in *Paramount Comm., Inc. v. Time Inc.*, 571 A.2d 1140 (Del. 1989), and *Arnold v. Society for Savings Bancorp*, 650 A.2d 1270 (Del. 1994). For a change in control to occur, the acquiring firm that survives the acquisition must be controlled both before and after the acquisition by the same large-block shareholder.

If there is no control of change, the basic business judgment rule applies to the negotiation between the favored bidder and the seller. The *Unocal* test, however, applies to any deal protection covenants that deter the unwanted bidder. By applying the *Unocal* test to deal protection covenants generally, the Delaware courts recognize that those covenants can be used to deter other purchasers from materializing in the first place and/or provide compensation to the jilted suitor for the effort it put into finding a viable acquisition target. Covenants providing reasonable compensation to a jilted suitor will likely pass the *Unocal* test, while those designed to deter other purchasers will likely not.

If a firm has put itself up for sale or there is otherwise a control change, the firm must sell to the highest bidder for its voting shares. As demonstrated by the facts of the *Revlon* case itself, the directors must seek the highest value for shareholders regardless of whether it is in the best interests of other corporate constituencies. A board decision to protect the interests of debt holders at the expense of shareholders will not satisfy the test.

When in the *Revlon* zone, a board may not use takeover defenses to block the highest bidder unless the decision is related to economic value. For example, a board may turn down the highest offer only if it believes the offer needs to be discounted for financial reasons, i.e., a target board reasonably believes that the financial ability of the bidder to pay is suspect. Moreover, any one bidder may be offered deal protection covenants, but only if reasonably directed at the objective of getting the highest price. E.g., *Mills Acquisition Co. v. Macmillan, Inc.,* 559 A.2d 1261 (Del. 1989).

Target boards that have sold their companies can satisfy and have satisfied court review under *Revlon.* E.g., *In re Toys "R" Us, Inc. Shareholder Litig.,* 877 A.2d 975 (Del. Ch. 2005). The Delaware courts will defer to a board's decision on how to best sell the company if the board demonstrates that it is attempting to maximize shareholder value and takes reasonable steps to do so. In Delaware the duty to take reasonable steps to secure the highest value does not automatically require a board to conduct an auction or to do a market canvass; there is no "blue-print" for fulfilling the duty. *Barkan v. Amsted Indus.,* 567 A.2d 1279 (Del. 1989). The court decides whether the directors have made a reasonable decision on the sales price, not a perfect one. *Paramount Comm. Inc. v. QVC Network Inc.,* 637 A.2d 34 (Del. 1994).

A wonderful example of *Revlon* at work is found in *In re Mindbody, Inc., Stockholder Litig.*, 2023 WL 2518149 (Del. Ch. 2023). Vista Equity Partners Mgt., LLC ("Vista") acquired Mindbody, Inc. in 2019 via a merger for $36.50 per share. Prior to the sale, Mindbody's visionary founder, Richard Stollmeyer, had grown frustrated with his inability to monetize his holdings of Mindbody stock, fearful of the volatility and fickleness of the public markets, and uncertain about his ability to lead Mindbody through the next stage of its growth. A sale of Mindbody would solve his problems, and Stollmeyer decided it was a good time to sell.

After several positive interactions with Vista, Stollmeyer quickly became enamored with Vista as a potential purchaser. Vista's *modus operandi* was to leverage its ability to move quickly from an expression of interest, through confirmatory diligence, to a firm offer, thereby truncating the process and reducing interloper risk. While "sprinting," as Vista labeled its approach, was great for Vista, it was not great for a target company seeking to maximize stockholder value. Indeed, a truncated timeline limits the opportunity for the target to develop alternatives to promote purchaser competition and extract the best price. By sprinting to the finish line, Vista sought to prevent a target company from doing just that.

Stollmeyer did not adequately involve the Mindbody board in the sale process. Nor did he erect, much less adhere, to speed bumps to ensure a value-maximizing process. Rather, a Vista-smitten

Stollmeyer effectively greased the wheels for Vista by stalling the board process. Unaware of the full extent of the existing courtship between Stollmeyer and Vista, the board waited until late in the game to form a transaction committee to consider running a sale process.

Nevertheless, and to its credit, the transaction committee established guidelines to cabin management's communications with potential bidders. Stollmeyer, however, ignored them and tipped Vista that a formal sale process had begun. Moreover, the financial adviser that Mindbody employed at Stollmeyer's encouragement tipped Vista as to Stollmeyer's target price. By the time the committee had authorized the financial adviser to contact other financial bidders, Vista was already poised to pounce.

When Vista's firm offer arrived, the board asked other potential bidders to respond promptly with best-and-final offers of their own. Given that the others were still in the early stages of their due diligence, they were unable to respond in a timely manner. The committee countered Vista's offer, which resulted in Vista raising its final bid to $1 per share below where Vista's deal team thought the deal price would land. Rather than making another counter, the board approved Vista's final bid.

Plaintiff-stockholders brought suit claiming that Stollmeyer had breached his fiduciary obligations in connection with the merger and that Vista had aided and abetted those breaches. Plaintiffs advanced two main theories of breach. The first was that

Stollmeyer breached his fiduciary duties by tilting the sale process in favor of Vista. The second was that Stollmeyer committed disclosure violations by failing to disclose material facts about the sale process to the stockholders.

Pointing to *Revlon,* the Delaware Chancery Court stated that directors are generally free to select the path to value maximization, so long as they choose a reasonable route to get there. In this regard, the question to answer is whether the fiduciaries have exercised their powers in the service of a specific objective: maximizing the sale price of the enterprise. Generally speaking, to satisfy enhanced scrutiny under *Revlon,* defendants bear the burden of demonstrating both (i) the reasonableness of the decision-making process employed by the directors, including the information on which the directors based their decision, and (ii) the reasonableness of the directors' action in light of the circumstances then existing.

The court emphasized that when directors bias the sale process against one bidder and toward another not in a reasoned effort to maximize advantage for the stockholders, but to tilt the process toward the bidder more likely to continue current management, they commit a breach of fiduciary duty. This is also true even when just one board member causes the board to favor a particular bidder because of personal reasons. Indeed, the sins of just one fiduciary can support a viable *Revlon* claim. Thus, according to the court, the paradigmatic *Revlon* claim involves a conflicted fiduciary who is insufficiently checked by the board and who tilts the sale process toward his own personal interests in ways inconsistent with maximizing stockholder value.

Finding for the plaintiffs, the court held that Stollmeyer did not strive in good faith to pursue the best transaction reasonably available. Rather, he instead pursued a fast sale to Vista to further his personal interests. In this regard, the court highlighted that Stollmeyer suffered a disabling conflict because he had an interest in near-term liquidity, a desire to sell fast, and an expectation that he would receive post-merger employment accompanied by significant equity-based incentives. Because he tilted the sale process in Vista's favor for personal reasons, the process did not achieve a result that fell within the range of reasonableness.

On the disclosure claim, the court held that the plaintiffs proved that Stollmeyer breached his duty of disclosure by failing to disclose the full extent of his involvement with Vista, which was a material omission. The court noted that the plaintiffs also proved that *Vista* had aided and abetted Stollmeyer's fiduciary breach. According to the court, to prevail on an aiding and abetting claim, a plaintiff must demonstrate: (1) the existence of a fiduciary relationship, (2) a breach of the fiduciary's duty, (3) knowing participation in that breach by the defendants, and (4) damages proximately caused by the breach. Generally, a plaintiff bears the burden of proving a claim for aiding and abetting.

Here, the court found that the plaintiffs had proven that Vista had aided and abetted Stollmeyer's fiduciary breach by carrying their burden of proof on all three elements of an aiding and abetting claim, including the all-important third element. Vista did not correct the materially misleading proxy materials before they were sent to stockholders. Those materials failed to include a full and fair description of Vista's own interactions with Stollmeyer. Pursuant to the merger agreement, Vista was contractually obligated to review the proxy materials and inform Mindbody if there were material omissions in the proxy materials. Vista personnel who interacted with Stollmeyer reviewed the proxy materials, realized that they did not properly disclose Stollmeyer's interactions with Vista, and concluded that Stollmeyer had purposefully chosen not to disclose them. Thus, Vista knowingly participated in Stollmeyer's fiduciary breach by not speaking up.

The Delaware Supreme Court, in *Corwin v. KKR Financial Holdings LLC,* 125 A.3d 304 (Del. 2015), stated that when enhanced scrutiny under *Revlon* presumptively applies to a sale transaction, defendant fiduciaries can *lower* the standard of judicial review to an irrebuttable version of the business judgment rule. However, to lower the standard, (i) no controller must exist with respect to the target and (ii) the transaction must have been approved by a fully informed, uncoerced majority of the disinterested target stockholders. Importantly, a single disclosure deficiency will defeat *Corwin* cleansing. The plaintiff bears the initial burden of identifying alleged disclosure problems, but the defendant target directors bear the burden of proving at trial that the stockholder vote was fully informed.

In *In re Mindbody, Inc., Stockholder Litig.*, 2023 WL 2518149 (Del. Ch. 2023), discussed above, the defendants raised a *Corwin* defense. They were hopeful that the Delaware Chancery Court would lower the standard of judicial review of their actions to an irrebuttable version of the business judgment rule. However, because material facts concerning the sale-process breaches were not disclosed to Mindbody stockholders, the stockholder vote was not fully informed. As a result, the court held that this disclosure failure was more than enough to defeat the defendants' *Corwin* defense.

D. THE PRACTICAL EFFECT OF THE *UNOCAL/REVLON* DICHOTOMY

Outside the *Revlon* zone, the Delaware courts will evaluate the activities of the target board when favoring one bidder over another under the less rigorous and more deferential *Unocal* test. See *Paramount Comm., Inc. v. Time Inc.*, 571 A.2d 1140 (Del. 1989). Under the *Unocal* test, discrimination in favor of one bidder must be a reasonable response to a threat from other bidders and the decision must be proportional to the threat. The effect of the classification is dramatic: Target boards that discriminate against the highest bidder in the *Revlon* zone lose; target boards that discriminate against the highest bidder under a *Unocal* test may win.

Consider the effect of the *Revlon/Unocal* doctrinal dichotomy as explained in the *QVC* case. If one publicly traded company without a controlling shareholder acquires another in a stock-for-stock deal, the business judgment rule applies (and *Unocal* applies to test the deal protection covenants); if the same acquiring company pays in cash (or debt), the enhanced *Revlon* duties apply. If the transaction is structured to give target shareholders a choice of stock or cash, *Revlon* duties apply. See, e.g., *In re Lukens, Inc. Shareholders Litig.*, 757 A.2d 720 (Del. Ch. 1999) (62 percent of the consideration was cash and 38 percent stock in the acquirer).

The legal distinction based solely on *deal consideration* makes little sense. Moreover, empirical studies have shown that the post-acquisition performance of an acquirer is much better in cash deals than in stock swap deals; so the Delaware courts have penalized unwittingly the optimal form of large acquisitions. A doctrine that used an enhanced scrutiny test to evaluate whether, whenever a target board blocked potential bidders in any context, the board did so in an honest effort to enhance shareholder value, would work better. We doubt that many other states will follow Delaware case law on this point. Indiana, Ohio, and Virginia have, for example, by statute, eschewed the *Unocal/Revlon* line of cases.

Effect of Constituency Statutes. Note also that in those states that have adopted constituency statutes (and Delaware has not), a court could come to the opposite conclusion on the facts of the *Revlon* case. See Chapter 9, § 4.B. A court in New York, for example, could decide that the Revlon board's decision to support its debenture holders (at the expense of its shareholders) was within the board's authority under New York's constituency statute. See NYBCL § 717(b). The statutes relax the *shareholder primacy* principle for board actions. See, e.g., *Norfolk Southern Corp. v. Conrail* (E.D. Pa. 1996) (unpublished oral opinion) (supporting the decision of the board of a railroad corporation to favor one bidder over another in the national interest).

E. THE "MUSCULAR" *UNOCAL* TEST FOR DEFENSES THAT AFFECT PROXY CONTESTS

The decision of state courts and state legislatures to respect target boards' blocking power in tender offers aimed at target shareholders has led insurgents to fall back on a weapon of the 1960s, the proxy fight. An insurgent makes a tender offer (often called a *bear hug*) at an attractive price conditional on the support of the target board. If the target board resists, the bidder conditions its tender offer on winning a proxy fight for control of the target board. Once an insurgent wins control of the board, it has the board redeem outstanding poison pill plans and waive any applicable state anti-takeover laws. After board action, the bidder closes its tender offer.

The proxy fight, by itself expensive and hard to win because shareholders often see it as a personality dispute with everyone eventually tarred by the revelations, is focused by the tender offer: "Vote for the insurgents and receive X dollars." Shareholders can understand and vote on an offer of a premium sales price for their stock. Having said that, a combination tender offer/proxy fight is much more expensive and takes much more time than a mid-

1980s-style hostile tender offer. The Hilton takeover battle in 1997 lasted eleven months. *Hilton Hotels Corp. v. ITT Corp.,* 978 F. Supp. 1342 (D. Nev. 1997). The expense and time delay preclude financial purchasers from using the strategy; only strategic purchasers have the depth of resources and acquisitive desire to embark on such an attempt. The patience that Weyerhaeuser, a strategic purchaser, demonstrated (over 14 months!) during its successful takeover battle with Willamette Industries in 2001 provides a vivid example. Nevertheless, while combination tender offer/proxy fights will occur and receive the attention of the press, they are few and far between.

Target boards, intent on defending against combination tender offer/proxy fights, have found that an old trick, a staggered election of directors, has renewed vigor when coupled with a poison pill plan. Target boards have also attempted to use "delayed hand" poison pill plans, see *Quickturn Design Sys., Inc. v. Shapiro,* 721 A.2d 1281 (Del. 1998), and stock repurchase programs to deter proxy contests. See *Chesapeake Corp. v. Shore,* 771 A.2d 293 (Del. Ch. 2000).

A staggered board is authorized explicitly in the corporate codes of almost all states (e.g., DGCL § 141(d)), and courts usually leave them alone. But see *Hilton Hotels* (invalidating a director-approved (but not shareholder approved) bylaw amendment that installed a staggered board). Delayed hand poison pill plans and stock repurchase programs that are effective have not done well in court.

The Delaware courts, while tolerant of takeover defenses to tender offers, are much less tolerant of directorial actions that preclude proxy contests. Indeed, directorial actions that usurp stockholder voting power inspire those courts to apply enhanced scrutiny when reviewing stockholder challenges to those actions. The origin of that scrutiny is prominently found in two cases in particular: *Schnell v. Chris-Craft Indus., Inc.*, 285 A.2d 437, 439 (Del. 1971) (a board breaches its fiduciary duties when it "utilize[s] the corporate machinery" with the intent of "perpetuating itself in office" by interfering with a proxy contest), and *Blasius Indus., Inc. v. Atlas Corp.*, 564 A.2d 651, 661, 663 (Del. Ch. 1988) (directors' duty of loyalty is violated when directors take unilateral action that interferes with or impedes stockholder voting in director elections or touching on corporate control without a compelling justification for doing so).

Blasius' compelling justification standard of review became the most stringent standard of review under Delaware corporate law for over 30 years. When it was invoked, defendant directors would almost always lose the case against them. Of course, directors losing cases is not very "management friendly" to say the least, thus tarnishing Delaware's image as the leader in corporate law. Thus, the Delaware courts would seek ways to avoid applying that standard if at all possible.

In 2023, the Delaware Supreme Court decided to make a sea-change. In *Coster v. UIP Cos., Inc.*, 300 A.3d 656 (Del. 2023), the court folded the standards of review found in *Schnell* and *Blasius* into the "reasonableness" standard found in *Unocal Corp. v. Mesa Petroleum Co.,* 493 A.2d 946 (Del. 1985), the seminal case on the legality of a board's adoption of takeover defenses. *Unocal*'s two-part analysis applied by a court with sensitivity to the stockholder voting franchise is sometimes referred to as the "muscular" *Unocal* standard.

In *Coster,* UIP Companies, Inc. found itself in a so-called "deadlock" position. That is, the company ultimately was owned 50/50 by Marion Coster and Steven Schwat, and the two shareholders could not agree on who should be on the three-member board of directors. As a result, the three current directors of the company—Schwat, Bonnell, and Cox—remained UIP's directors as successors were unable to be chosen.

Coster ultimately filed a complaint in the Delaware Chancery Court seeking the appointment of a custodian under DGCL § 226(a)(1). That Section allows for the appointment of a custodian when, for among other reasons, the stockholders are so divided that they have failed to elect successors to directors whose terms have expired or would have expired upon qualification of their successors.

Coster's complaint mainly sought to impose a neutral tie-breaker to facilitate director elections. However, it also lodged allegations against Schwat about the lack of distributions and transparency into the company's affairs. Accordingly, Coster sought the appointment of a custodian with broad oversight and managerial powers. But the appointment of such a custodian rather than one specifically tailored to target the stockholder deadlock posed new risks to the company. Many of the company's most important revenue-generating contracts allowed the other contracting parties to terminate them upon the appointment of a UIP custodian with broad powers. Thus, such an appointment would throw the company's continued viability into question given that its business model was heavily dependent on those contracts.

In light of this threat to the company, the UIP board decided to issue shares of stock to Bonnell. Bonnell, a senior UIP executive and board member, had previously been promised stock in UIP on multiple occasions. The stock sale to Bonnell diluted Coster's ownership interest from one half to one third and thus negated her ability to block stockholder action as half owner of the company. The stock sale also mooted Coster's custodian action as there was no longer a deadlock.

Coster, in turn, cried foul and responded by filing suit seeking to cancel the stock sale to Bonnell. The Delaware Chancery Court, however, found for the defendants, noting that the stock sale met the standard of entire fairness—that is, both the process by which the stock sale was approved was "fair" to the company and the price at which the stock was sold was "fair" to the company.

In Coster's first appeal to the Delaware Supreme Court, the court did not disturb the lower court's entire fairness decision, but remanded the case with instructions for the lower court to review the stock sale under the *Schnell v. Chris-Craft Indus., Inc.* and *Blasius Indus., Inc. v. Atlas Corp.* precedents. In doing so, the Delaware Supreme Court explained that, in a vacuum, it might be that the price at which the board agreed to sell the one-third UIP equity interest to Bonnell was entirely fair, as was the process to set the price for the stock. But inequitable action does not become permissible simply because it is legally possible. If the board approved the stock sale for inequitable reasons, the lower court should have cancelled the stock sale. And if the board, acting in good faith, approved the stock sale for the primary purpose of thwarting Coster's vote to elect directors or reduce her leverage as an equal stockholder, it must demonstrate a *compelling justification* for such action to withstand judicial scrutiny under the *Blasius* precedent.

On remand, the lower court found that the UIP board had not acted for inequitable purposes under *Schnell* and had compelling justifications for the stock sale under *Blasius*. Turning to *Blasius* review, the lower court concluded that "[i]n the exceptionally unique circumstances of this case, Defendants have met the onerous burden of demonstrating a compelling justification." Importantly, the court's compelling justification analysis largely borrowed from *Unocal*'s reasonableness and proportionality test for defensive measures adopted by a board in response to a takeover threat.

According to the lower court, to satisfy the compelling justification standard, "the directors must show that their actions were reasonable in relation to their legitimate objective, and did not preclude the stockholders from exercising their right to vote or coerce them into voting a particular way." In this context, the lower court noted that the shift from "reasonable" to "compelling" requires that the directors establish a closer fit between means and ends.

Thus, the lower court jettisoned *Blasius*' compelling justification test in favor of a "muscular" *Unocal* approach (the "muscular" aspect relating to the "closer fit" demanded between means and ends). The court determined that the threat posed by the custodian action was an existential crisis that justified the UIP board's actions and that the stock sale was appropriately tailored to achieve the goal of mooting the custodian action while also achieving other important corporate goals.

On appeal again to the Delaware Supreme Court, the higher court agreed that a "muscular" *Unocal* approach should replace *Blasius*' compelling justification test. According to the court, "[e]xperience has shown that *Schnell* and *Blasius* review, as a matter of precedent and practice, have been and can be folded into *Unocal* review to accomplish the same ends—enhanced judicial scrutiny of board action that interferes with a corporate election or a stockholder's voting rights in contests for control." In a stockholder challenge to board action of that type, the board bears the burden of proof that the board action in question was legitimate.

According to the Delaware Supreme Court, the board must demonstrate two things in order to satisfy its burden of proof. First, the board must demonstrate that it faced a threat "to an important corporate interest or to the achievement of a significant corporate benefit." The court added that "[t]he threat must be real and not pretextual, and the board's motivations must be proper and not selfish or disloyal." Importantly, "the threat cannot be justified on the grounds that the board knows what is in the best interests of the stockholders."

Second, the board's response to the threat must be reasonable in relation to the threat posed and not be either preclusive or coercive to the stockholder voting franchise. That is, the board's response to the threat cannot deprive the stockholders of a vote or coerce the stockholders to vote a particular way. Indeed, according to the court, the board must tailor its response to only what is necessary to counter the threat.

Here, based on the lower court's additional factual findings, the Delaware Supreme Court agreed that the UIP board faced a threat. That threat was the "existential crisis" to UIP's existence that occurred through a deadlocked stockholder vote and the risk of a custodian appointment. According to the court, when faced with this threat, the UIP board responded reasonably and proportionately to the threat posed when it approved the stock sale. That sale "was appropriately tailored to achieve the goal of mooting the Custodian Action" while implementing an agreed upon succession plan and retaining

Bonnell. The Delaware Supreme Court also took note of the lower court's determination that there were more aggressive options that could have been pursued by the UIP board to break the deadlock, but were not, thus indicating that the stock sale was carefully tailored to the threat.

Moreover, the Delaware Supreme Court agreed with the lower court that the UIP board's response was neither preclusive nor coercive towards the company's stockholders. While the stock sale effectively foreclosed Coster from perpetuating the deadlock facing UIP, the new three-way ownership of the company presented a potentially more effective way for Coster to exercise actual control. As the court noted, Schwat and Bonnell were not bound to vote together, meaning Coster could cast a swing vote at stockholder meetings. As an equal one third owner with the two other stockholders, the court highlighted that Coster could join forces with either one of UIP's other owners "at some point in the future." According to the court, a realistic path to the control of UIP negates the preclusive impact of the stock sale.

CHAPTER 13

THE LIABILITY OF FINANCIAL CONSULTANTS IN ACQUISITIONS: INVESTMENT BANKERS

When an acquirer pays too much for another company and the combined company fails soon after the acquisition, ending up in bankruptcy, the bankruptcy trustee, looking for deep pockets to satisfy unpaid creditors, often sues the acquirer's investment banker. The failure is usually caused by the inability of the combined company to pay off the huge new debts incurred in the acquisition financing.

Investment bankers can play many roles in a transaction. On the facts of *In re Daisy Systems Corp.*, 97 F.3d 1171 (9th Cir. 1996), for example, the investment banker and the acquirer executed an engagement letter with two subsequent amendments. Initially the investment banker was an advisor on information gathered by the acquirer (with no independent verification by the bank) on the target. When the target refused to sell and the acquirer decided to make a hostile bid for cash, the investment banker then agreed to be the deal manager and help secure deal financing. Thereafter, the investment banker agreed to be an underwriter of debt securities sold to finance the acquisition and to provide a highly confident letter on the financing behind a tender offer. When other banks refused to lend money to finance the tender offer, the investment bank offered to be the primary lender.

When a deal turns friendly and the parties sign a merger agreement, an investment bank usually writes a fairness opinion for the seller on the adequacy of the deal price (the *Daisy* opinion is silent here). See Chapter 9, § 1.

In *Daisy* the bankruptcy trustee sued the investment bank alleging negligence (professional malpractice), negligent misrepresentation and a breach of fiduciary duty. The court granted summary judgment on the negligent misrepresentation claim but let the other two claims proceed to trial. The court held that the breach of fiduciary duty claim would depend on whether the investment bank understood that the CEO of the acquirer lacked sophistication and was relying heavily on the judgment of the bank. The dissent would have also granted summary judgment on the fiduciary duty claim.

In *Firefighters' Pension System of the City of Kansas City, Missouri Trust v. Presidio, Inc.,* 251 A.3d 212 (Del. Ch. 2021), Presidio, Inc. merged with an acquisition vehicle controlled by BC Partners Advisors L.P. ("BCP"). LionTree Advisors, LLC served as the financial advisor to Presidio. A plaintiff stockholder of Presidio alleged that, during the sale process, LionTree tipped off BCP regarding a competing bid by Clayton, Dubilier & Rice, LLC ("CD&R"). This allowed BCP to slightly outbid CD&R and put time pressure on CD&R to respond. While CD&R indicated that it could make a superior offer for the company, that offer would not be a binding one given the abbreviated timeframe. This was particularly unfortunate because, unlike BCP,

CD&R was a strategic purchaser. Given that CD&R could not proffer a binding higher offer in time, the Presidio board accepted BCP's lesser offer.

Among other claims, the plaintiff asserted aiding and abetting claims against both LionTree and BCP. The Delaware Chancery Court determined that those claims should survive the defendants' motion to dismiss. The court noted that LionTree's failure to inform the Presidio board of its tip to BCP created an informational vacuum that led the board to breach its duty of care. The court also highlighted that, with respect to the claims against BCP, viable aiding and abetting claims against a third-party bidder are rare. However, in this case the court emphasized that BCP knew that the tip it had received from LionTree was wrong. Finally, the court determined that the plaintiff had adequately alleged that the Presidio CEO was self-interested in the transaction. Indeed, he "tilted the sale process" toward BCP because it, unlike CD&R, promised to retain him and other current managers with a potentially lucrative compensation package. In addition, the plaintiff had sufficiently alleged that the CEO knew about LionTree's tip to BCP and failed to disclose that fact to the stockholders.

PART IV

OTHER REGULATIONS AFFECTING ACQUISITIONS

CHAPTER 14

ANTITRUST LEGISLATION ON ACQUISITIONS

Consumer protection in acquisitions has been a central part of the American legal landscape since the late 1800s. Industrial combinations after the Civil War demonstrated one form of opportunistic behavior in acquisitions: Two competing firms combine, creating a single firm that has enough market power to engage in noncompetitive pricing, or enough size to collude with other major firms to fix prices through express or tacit agreements. The surviving firm in such a combination may be more profitable than the two constituent firms standing separately, but this occurs at the expense of consumers, who pay higher prices. The firms, in bargaining over the merger price, simply split the expected gains created by monopolistic or oligopolistic pricing behavior.

A federal antitrust statute known as the Clayton Antitrust Act of 1914 ("Clayton Act"), 15 U.S.C. § 12 *et seq.*, and state antitrust statutes modeled after the Clayton Act, are designed to deter such acquisitions.

§ 1. THE CLAYTON ANTITRUST ACT OF 1914

The Clayton Act (as amended by the Celler-Kefauver Anti-Merger Act of 1950) expands on the general prohibitions of the Sherman Act of 1890. The Clayton Act is intended to stop anti-competitive problems in their incipiency by regulating acquisitions. Section 7 of the Clayton Act prohibits any merger or acquisition of stock or assets "where in any line of commerce or in any activity affecting commerce in any section of the country, the effect of such acquisition may be substantially to lessen competition, or to tend to create a monopoly." Section 15 of the Clayton Act empowers the Attorney General, and § 13(b) of the Federal Trade Commission Act (FTC Act), empowers the Federal Trade Commission (FTC) to seek a court order enjoining consummation of a merger that would violate § 7. In addition, the FTC may seek a cease and desist order in an administrative proceeding against a merger under either § 11 of the Clayton Act or § 5 of the FTC Act, or both. Private parties may also seek injunctive relief under § 15 of the Clayton Act.

There is a special statute for research and development joint ventures, the National Cooperative Research and Production Act, that relaxes Clayton Act standards for R&D combinations. 15 U.S.C. § 4301 *et seq.*

Congress designed the Clayton Act language to be preemptive—to prohibit acquisitions that "may . . . substantially lessen . . . competition." The government may stop acquisitions even if they do not in fact lessen competition. E.g., *U.S. v. Phila. Nat'l Bank,* 374 U.S. 321 (1963).

The case law on the Clayton Act analyzes mergers in three categories: *horizontal* (between competitors), *vertical* (between suppliers and those they supply), and *conglomerate* (between firms in unrelated markets). The law is the most developed on horizontal mergers, has recently picked up steam on vertical mergers, and is uncertain when applied to conglomerates.

The Department of Justice (DOJ) and the FTC have struggled with the general language of the Clayton Act and with judges who do not follow their views on the meaning of the language. As a result, they first issued formal guidelines on enforcement policy for horizontal mergers in 1992. New iterations have been issued periodically. See DOJ and FTC, Merger Guidelines, Dec. 18, 2023 (hereinafter "Guidelines").

The Guidelines start with a formula and soften (i.e., mitigate) its results with selected market considerations. The formula uses the Herfindahl-Hirschman Index (HHI) of concentration. To apply the formula, one (a) defines a market, (b) calculates the market shares of the parties to an acquisition and all the other competitors, and (c) then sums the squares of the individual market shares of all the participants. This is done twice, once assuming no acquisition and then assuming consummation of the acquisition at issue.

The HHI number is low when there are many small firms and grows larger as the market becomes more concentrated, reaching 10,000 in a market with a single firm. Markets with an HHI greater than 1,800 are highly concentrated, and a change of more than 100 points due to a merger between two firms operating in that market would be a significant increase. A merger that creates or further consolidates a highly concentrated market that involves an increase in the HHI of more than 100 points is presumed to substantially lessen competition or tend to create a monopoly. The DOJ and FTC also may examine the market share of the merged firm: a merger that creates a firm with a share over thirty percent is also presumed to substantially lessen competition or tend to create a monopoly if it also involves an increase in HHI of more than 100 points. See Guidelines. Importantly, this thirty percent market share metric was not in any prior guidelines and is taken from a 1963 U.S. Supreme Court case, *U.S. v. Phila. Nat'l Bank,* 374 U.S. 321, 364 (1963). For an example of the new thirty percent market share metric in action, see *F.T.C. v. IQVIA Holdings, Inc.,* 378 F.Supp.3d 329, 378–79 (S.D.N.Y. 2024).

The Guidelines present the following table relating to HHI and market concentration:

Indicator	**Threshold for Structural Presumption**
Post-merger HHI	Market HHI greater than 1,800 AND Change in HHI greater than 100
Merged Firm's Market Share	Share greater than 30% AND Change in HHI greater than 100

When exceeded, these concentration metrics indicate that a merger's effect may be to eliminate substantial competition between the merging parties and may be to increase coordination among the remaining competitors after the merger. This presumption of illegality can be rebutted or disproved. The higher the concentration metrics over these thresholds, the greater the risk to competition suggested by this market structure analysis and the stronger the evidence needed to rebut or disprove it.

The soft information that the DOJ and FTC use to soften or mitigate what the HHI numbers otherwise indicate includes recent market conditions (Is the market growing?), the ease of entry of new firms into the market, the health of the parties to the acquisition (Is one of the parties otherwise likely to go belly up?), and the efficiencies in operation generated by the acquisition (Are product price reductions due to reduced production costs due to synergies between the two firms?).

The cases on the Clayton Act demonstrate that the factual definition of the relevant product market often determines the result. The plaintiff (typically the Government) attempts to narrow the size of the relevant market, making it more likely that the defendants have an antitrust problem. The defendants, by contrast, attempt to expand the market. Once the product market is defined, the market concentration figures follow mathematically.

F.T.C. v. Whole Foods Market, Inc., 548 F.3d 1028 (U.S. App. D.C. 2008), provides a useful insight into determining the appropriate market for antitrust scrutiny. Whole Foods sought to acquire a competitor, Wild Oats. When the deal was challenged by the government, a food fight broke out over the relevant market. Was the relevant market "all supermarkets" (i.e., a huge market), as Whole Foods argued? If yes, the deal with Wild Oats would pose no antitrust problems. Or was the market "premium, natural, and organic supermarkets" (PNOS) (i.e., a small market), as argued by the FTC? If yes, the deal was problematic from an antitrust perspective. In reversing the District Court, the Court of Appeals held that the relevant market was, indeed, the PNOS market. The court's determination caused the deal to be scuttled.

The saga of unrequited love between Staples and Office Depot is also demonstrative of the market issue. In the first round, *F.T.C. v. Staples, Inc.*, 970 F.Supp. 1066 (D.D.C. 1997), the merger between the two companies was enjoined. The market was defined as "office supply superstores" (rather than all office supply stores), and Staples and Office Depot were two of the three biggest competitors. The District Court granted the preliminary injunction the government requested despite the fact that Staples and Office Depot had only a 6–8 percent market share of the *overall* market for office supplies. If the market had been defined as "big," the constituent corporations would have won. Here, the market was defined as small.

In round two, *F.T.C. v. Staples, Inc.*, 190 F.Supp.3d 100 (D.D.C. 2016), the District Court enjoined Staples' and Office Depot's second attempt at a merger. Between rounds one and two, the market had changed. Now the market was defined as the "business-to-business" (B-to-B) market, and Staples and Office Depot dominated this market. They argued that Amazon Business was beginning to eat their lunch, and that they needed to combine to compete. However, the District Court determined that Amazon Business was not *presently* a threatening competitor (although it was clearly on its way!) and refused to include it in the HHI calculation.

Could competing bidders for a given target company violate antitrust law by colluding in an effort to avoid a bidding war in the first instance? Such was the allegation in *Finnegan v. Campeau Corp.*, 915 F.2d 824 (2d Cir. 1990). Both Macy's and Campeau Corp. went after the same target, Federated Department Stores. However, to avoid a bidding war, the two bidders agreed that Campeau would buy Federated, while Macy's would be allowed to purchase two Federated divisions from Campeau after the deal closed. Macy's then dropped its $75.51 per share bid for Federated and allowed Campeau's $73.50 per share bid to succeed.

A disappointed shareholder of Federated brought a lawsuit against Campeau alleging illegal collusion. Specifically, he alleged that Campeau and Macy's, in violation of § 1 of the Sherman Act, conspired to refrain from bidding against each other in order to suppress and eliminate competition in the market for Federated common stock. The Second Circuit, however, disagreed. It held that the federal securities laws (specifically the Williams Act) took precedent over the antitrust laws in this situation. Because *disclosure* is the means by which Congress sought to protect target shareholders in the context of the federal securities laws, once information regarding an agreement between rival bidders has been revealed in a securities filing (which Campeau and Macy's had done), Federated's shareholders had received the protection Congress and the SEC had designed for them.

Most proposed acquisitions survive or fail antitrust scrutiny at the agency level. Nonetheless, Clayton Act scrutiny does not necessarily end even if the transaction in question has closed. In *Midwestern Machinery, Inc. v. Northwest Airlines, Inc.*, 167 F.3d 439 (8th Cir. 1999), the Department of Transportation had approved the merger between Northwest Airlines and Republic Airlines but had not granted antitrust relief to the deal. After the merger closed, some "frequent travelers" on Northwest sued claiming that the merger violated § 7 of the Clayton Act. The Eighth Circuit noted that § 7 prohibits acquisitions of the "whole or any part of the stock" or assets of a company, where the effect may be to substantially lessen competition or tend to create a monopoly. The language of § 7 expressly provides for a claim even when all ("whole") of the stock or assets are acquired. Thus, although the merger of Republic and Northwest had closed (i.e., Northwest had acquired *all* of Republic's stock and assets), the court held that it did not cut off a § 7 claim.

§ 2. THE HART-SCOTT-RODINO ANTITRUST IMPROVEMENTS ACT OF 1976

The Hart-Scott-Rodino Antitrust Improvements Act of 1976 (HSR Act) grew out of the frustration of the Department of Justice in its attempt to enjoin mergers in lawsuits that lasted over five years. Often the mergers had been long closed and were impossible to unscramble. So Congress passed a notification act that requires all parties involved in sizable acquisitions to notify the DOJ and the FTC of any pending merger plans. Note the double dipping: The Clayton Act proscribes mergers that may lessen competition and HSR requires notification of mergers that might violate the Clayton Act. After notification, there is a mandated waiting period before any deal closes.

The notification requirements include a size-of-transaction test and size-of-person test. Based on applicable 2025 numbers (which numbers are adjusted for inflation each January), if the size of the transaction is greater than $505.8 million, the size-of-person test is inapplicable and the parties must file HSR forms unless their transaction is otherwise exempt. Exempted transactions include goods or realty transferred in the ordinary course of business, acquisitions of 10 percent or less of the voting securities of a seller solely for the purpose of investment, acquisitions by institutional investors and specified acquisitions of foreign issuers.

For transactions with a value between $126.4 million and $505.8 million, the parties must file HSR forms if the size-of-person test is met—to wit, either

(1) a person with total assets or net sales of $252.9 million or more is acquiring voting securities or assets of a person with total assets, or net sales if a manufacturer, of $25.3 million or more; or (2) a person with total assets or net sales of $25.3 million or more is acquiring voting securities or assets of a person with total assets or net sales of $252.9 million or more.

To implement the statutory standards the FTC has, by administrative rule, created "notification thresholds." The thresholds require filings for acquisitions of assets and voting securities valued at greater than $126.4 million but less than $252.9 million, $252.9 million or greater but less than $1.264 billion, and $1.264 billion or greater. There are separate thresholds for acquisitions of 25 percent but less than 50 percent of voting securities if valued at $2.529 billion or more, and voting securities amounting to 50 percent or more if valued at greater than $126.4 million. The acquiring party identifies which of these acquisition thresholds it intends to meet and has five years to acquire stock or assets that do not exceed any upper limit on the threshold. 16 CFR § 801.1(h).

An HSR filing starts a mandatory 30-day waiting period. For most transactions, the federal agencies have 10 days to review the materials if the deal is a cash tender offer and 30 days to review the materials in all other offers. The HSR thus favors cash tender offers in contested acquisitions. There is a substantial penalty for each day a party is late making a required filing. For 2025, the maximum daily penalty is $53,088. If either the DOJ or the FTC issues a request for additional information (the dreaded *second request*), the request tolls the waiting period.

Consider the poor fit of the HSR with § 13(d) of the Williams Act. Under the Williams Act, an acquirer has five business days after the date of purchase to file a notice with the target (which allows the acquirer to purchase significantly more than the 5 percent triggering amount before notice). See SEA Rule 13d–1(a). Under the HSR, an acquirer must notify the target at least thirty days (fifteen if the purchase is through a cash tender offer) *before* it can purchase stock that triggers the Act.

Jumping the gun *before* receiving antitrust approval is a big no-no, and *U.S. v. Computer Assoc. Int'l, Inc.*, 67 FR 41472-01 (DOJ Antitrust Div. 2002), provides a vivid example. Computer Associates and Platinum, bitter competitors, agreed to merge. *Prior* to receiving antitrust clearance, however, Computer Associates assumed operational control of Platinum. While normal "ordinary course" covenants in merger agreements do not raise red flags, Computer Associate's exercise of operational control of Platinum "went far beyond ordinary and reasonable pre-consummation covenants and constituted a violation of the HSR Act." As part of a settlement with the DOJ, Computer Associates agreed to pay a $638,000 civil penalty.

Private causes of action under federal antitrust laws are also available. For example, in *California v. American Stores Co.*, 495 U.S. 271 (1990), two grocery store chains made HSR filings in anticipation of their merger. The FTC conducted an investigation. Ultimately, a settlement was reached whereby the two parties agreed to modify the terms of their merger to comport with the Clayton Act. The settlement agreement called for the two parties to divest several stores post-merger. Until they did, they could not integrate their operations.

Despite the FTC settlement, the State of California initiated an independent lawsuit against the merger based on antitrust grounds. The U.S. Supreme Court held that the FTC settlement did not preclude future suits. Indeed, the government always reserves the right to sue if it should change its mind, and negotiated settlements between the federal government and constituent parties to a merger prompted by an HSR filing do not divest private plaintiffs from suing to set aside a merger. American Stores finally settled with the State of California by agreeing to divest itself of most of its Southern California stores—something not required by its settlement with the FTC.

CHAPTER 15

ACQUISITIONS OF UNITED STATES CORPORATIONS BY FOREIGN COMPANIES

§ 1. THE EXON-FLORIO AMENDMENT OF 1988 AND CFIUS

Congress passed the Exon-Florio Amendment to stop acquisitions of U.S. companies in defense-related industries. Exon-Florio authorizes the U.S. President to block acquisitions in the name of "national security." Treasury Regulations have created an interagency committee, The Committee on Foreign Investment in the United States (CFIUS), to aid the President in exercising his or her discretion. 32 C.F.R. §§ 800 *et seq.* (1998).

The purpose behind CFIUS's review of a proposed transaction is solely to determine the effect of that transaction on the national security of the United States. The key term "national security" is undefined. The only guidance offered regarding the interpretation of national security appears in the commentary to the proposed regulations. The commentary adopts the interpretation found in the Congressional Conference Report to the Omnibus Trade and Competitiveness Act, which states simply that the "term 'national security' is intended to be interpreted broadly without limitation to particular industries." This allows the President or his or her designee to review transactions on a case-by-case basis. The commentary, also incorporated in the amendment's preamble, states that the "intent of the regulations is to indicate that notice . . . [is] clearly appropriate when, for example, a company is being acquired that provides products or key technologies essential to the U.S. defense industrial base." The lack of a proper definition irks foreign governments who view the Act as a potential government licensing system for foreign direct investment in the U.S. Indeed, Japan, in trade negotiations, continually requests that the U.S. make the term specific.

Exon-Florio was substantially amended by the Foreign Investment and National Security Act of 2007 ("FINSA"). FINSA broadened the concept of national security. *Homeland security,* including critical infrastructure, is now also covered.

Dramatic substantive changes were made to CFIUS review through the Foreign Investment Risk Review Modernization Act of 2018 (FIRRMA). FIRRMA is part of the John S. McCain National Defense Authorization Act for Fiscal Year 2019 (H.R. 5515), which President Trump signed into law on August 13, 2018. Final FIRRMA implementing regulations became effective in 2020. FIRRMA caused fundamental changes in the foreign investment review process overseen by CFIUS, including a broad expansion of CFIUS's jurisdiction. Although China is not identified in FIRRMA, Congressional desire to expand CFIUS's ability to review additional types of Chinese investment in the U.S. was the main catalyst for these changes.

Before FIRRMA became law in 2018, CFIUS's jurisdiction was limited to acquisitions, investments and joint ventures that could result in foreign control over any U.S. business, direct or indirect (referred to as "*covered control transactions*" in FIRRMA's 2020 final regulations). FIRRMA expanded the range of transactions subject to CFIUS jurisdiction to include, among other transactions, certain *non-controlling*, non-passive investments by foreign persons in U.S. businesses that involve critical technology, critical infrastructure, or the maintenance or collection of sensitive personal data of U.S. citizens (referred to as "*TID U.S. businesses*" in FIRRMA's 2020 final regulations).

Non-controlling, non-passive investments in TID U.S. businesses are referred to as "*covered investments*" in FIRRMA's 2020 final regulations. In order to fall within CFIUS's jurisdiction, a given investment must afford a foreign person one of the following: (i) access to any material nonpublic information in the possession of the TID U.S. business; (ii) membership or observer rights on the board of directors or equivalent governing body of the TID U.S. business or the right to nominate an individual to such a position; or (iii) any involvement, other than through voting of shares, in substantive decision-making of the TID U.S. business regarding (a) the use, development, acquisition, safekeeping, or release of sensitive personal data of U.S. citizens maintained or collected by the TID U.S. business, (b) the use, development, acquisition, or release of critical technologies, or (c) the management, operation, manufacture, or supply of covered investment critical infrastructure.

Two specific transactions are not considered to be covered investments even if they meet the criteria set forth in the previous paragraph: (i) a non-controlling investment in an air carrier; and (ii) a non-controlling investment by a so-called "excepted investor." In order to qualify as an excepted investor, a foreign person must, among other things, be able to meet several criteria demonstrating substantial connections to a country that CFIUS has identified as an "*excepted foreign state.*" A foreign state can qualify as an "excepted foreign state" if it has established and is effectively utilizing a robust process to analyze foreign investments for national security risks and coordinates with the United States on matters related to investment security. Currently, only four countries are considered "excepted foreign states": Canada, the United Kingdom, Australia and New Zealand. That status is deemed indefinite until CFIUS determines otherwise.

Long form (formal) CFIUS notice filings (pre-FIRRMA) by transactional parties had always been *voluntary*. FIRRMA, however, introduced a new category of short-form filing called a "declaration," which, in theory, is designed not to exceed five pages in length. By filing a "declaration" with CFIUS rather than a long-form (formal) notice, transaction parties ostensibly have a faster and less costly mechanism for obtaining CFIUS's reaction to a transaction that appears to fall under CFIUS's jurisdiction.

FIRRMA now requires a *mandatory* filing of a declaration with CFIUS when a transaction would result in the acquisition of a "substantial interest" in a sensitive U.S. business by a foreign person in which a foreign government has, directly or indirectly, a substantial interest. FIRRMA's 2020 final regulations define "substantial interest" to mean (i) a voting interest, direct or indirect, of 25 percent or more in a U.S. business by a foreign person and (ii) a voting interest, direct or indirect, of 49 percent or more in a foreign person by the national or subnational governments of a single foreign state. Failure to comply with this new foreign government-linked mandatory filing requirement could lead to a civil penalty against both the purchaser and the seller of up to $250,000 or the value of the transaction, whichever is greater. "Excepted foreign states," discussed above, are excepted from the mandatory filing requirement.

Apart from certain transactions that are subject to the mandatory filing requirement authorized under FIRRMA, parties typically submit short-form declarations or long-form (formal) notices of transactions to CFIUS on a voluntary basis. By law, CFIUS must treat as confidential any information provided to CFIUS by parties to a transaction, including the fact that parties have submitted a transaction for review in the first place. CFIUS also has the authority to review pending or completed transactions even absent a voluntary filing by the parties if a member of the Committee has reason to believe that the transaction is subject to CFIUS jurisdiction and may raise national security concerns.

CFIUS is required to complete a "review" of a long-form (formal) notified transaction within 45 days. Assuming CFIUS does not clear the transaction during this review period, CFIUS may initiate an "investigation" that could last up to 45 additional days if CFIUS determines that it needs additional time to complete its assessment of the transaction. The investigative period can be extended for another 15 days at the discretion of the Secretary of the Treasury and the head of the lead agency on a given CFIUS case (acting together), but such an extension must be based on "extraordinary circumstances."

Instead of submitting a voluntary long-form (formal) notice, transaction parties may choose to file a short-form declaration with CFIUS. FIRRMA provides that CFIUS is required to respond to a declaration within 30 days of its filing. It is possible that CFIUS's response to a declaration may be to clear the proposed transaction entirely. CFIUS will clear a proposed transaction if it determines that the transaction does not pose any unresolved national security concerns, that any national security concerns are adequately addressed by laws other than Section 721 and the International Emergency Economic Powers Act (IEEPA), or that mitigation measures agreed to by the transaction parties or imposed on those parties by CFIUS address any unresolved national security concerns.

While CFIUS may choose to clear a transaction based on a declaration, it is also empowered to (a) ask the transaction parties to file a long-form (formal) notice or (b) choose not to make a decision with respect to the transaction at all (the dreaded "shoulder shrug"). Thus, while the time it takes to submit a declaration is shorter and the overall process is less invasive, filing a declaration rather than a long-form (formal) notice is, at best, a high-risk, high-reward proposition. Indeed, a CFIUS "shoulder shrug" with respect to a declaration leaves the parties in the awkward position of having to decide for themselves whether to file a long-form (formal) notice with CFIUS voluntarily or live in fear of a potential future action brought by CFIUS against them. Thus, in situations where a transaction implicates identifiable national security issues, prudence dictates that the transaction parties file a long-form (formal) notice given that CFIUS is unlikely to clear such a transaction based on a short-form declaration and, therefore, would request that the parties file a long-form (formal) notice in any event.

If CFIUS determines that the transaction poses unresolved national security concerns, it will refer the transaction to the President of the United States unless the parties choose to abandon the transaction. The President may suspend or prohibit the transaction, including by requiring divestment. By law, the President has to make a decision no later than 15 days after the completion of CFIUS's investigation or the date on which CFIUS otherwise referred the transaction to the President. The President must publicly announce his or her decision. While the findings and actions of the President are supposed to be immune to judicial review (see 50 U.S.C. § 2170(e)), *Ralls Corp. v. CFIUS*, 758 F.3d 296

(D.C. Cir. 2014), discussed *infra,* represents a rare instance of successful litigation *against* the U.S. government.

CFIUS will seek mitigation measures or refer a transaction to the President only after such action is justified in a detailed written analysis of the national security risk posed by the transaction. CFIUS's determinations must be confirmed at senior levels by CFIUS member agencies. With limited exceptions, a given transaction will receive a "safe harbor" (a.k.a. a green light) if (a) the transaction is submitted to CFIUS for its review, (b) CFIUS determines that the transaction is subject to its jurisdiction, and (c) CFIUS concludes all of its action relative thereto. In the case of a transaction afforded a "safe harbor," CFIUS and the President will not subject it to review again absent certain exceptional circumstances (e.g., discovery of a material misstatement by the parties in their filings).

In November 2024, the Treasury Department, acting in its position as Chair of CFIUS, approved a final rule to enhance certain CFIUS procedures and sharpen its penalty and enforcement authorities. The final rule is the first substantive update to the monitoring and enforcement provisions of the CFIUS regulations since the implementation of FIRRMA. The final rule reflects and builds upon enhancements CFIUS had made to its compliance and monitoring capabilities in the years leading up to the rule's approval. The rule also helps CFIUS in its ability to identify and investigate transactions that were not notified to CFIUS. Specifically, the rule enhances

CFIUS's authority through the following key changes:

- Expanding the types of information CFIUS can require transaction parties and other persons to submit when engaging with them on transactions that were not filed with CFIUS;
- Allowing the CFIUS Staff Chairperson to set, as appropriate, a timeline for transaction parties to respond to risk mitigation proposals for matters under active review to assist CFIUS in concluding its reviews and investigations within the time frame required by statute;
- Expanding the circumstances in which a civil monetary penalty may be imposed due to a party's material misstatement and omission, including when the material misstatement or omission occurs outside a review or investigation of a transaction and when it occurs in the context of CFIUS's monitoring and compliance functions;
- Substantially increasing the maximum civil monetary penalty available for violations of obligations under the CFIUS statute and regulations, as well as agreements, orders, and conditions authorized by the statute and regulations, and introducing a new method for determining the maximum possible penalty for a breach of a mitigation agreement, condition, or order imposed;

- Expanding the instances in which CFIUS may use its subpoena authority, including in connection with assessing national security risk associated with non-notified transactions; and
- Extending the time frame for submission of a petition for reconsideration of a penalty to CFIUS and the number of days for CFIUS to respond to such a petition.

CFIUS's Enforcement and Penalty Guidelines (the "Guidelines") require CFIUS, prior to taking an enforcement action, to send the target of the action a notice of penalty. The notice must include a written explanation of the violation, the amount of the proposed monetary penalty, and any aggravating and mitigating factors that CFIUS has considered. The recipient of a notice of penalty may, within 15 business days of receiving the notice, submit a petition for reconsideration to the CFIUS Staff Chairperson, including any defense, mitigating factors, or explanation. CFIUS must then consider the issues raised and issue a final penalty determination within 15 business days following the receipt of a petition for reconsideration.

According to the Guidelines, when determining any appropriate penalty in response to an identified violation, CFIUS must engage in a "fact-based analysis in which it weighs aggravating and mitigating factors." The Guidelines set forth a non-exhaustive list of potential aggravating and mitigating factors that CFIUS may consider, depending upon the facts and circumstances of a given violation. These include:

- Accountability for the violative conduct (the impact of the enforcement action on protecting national security and/or holding violative parties accountable for their actions and motivating future compliance with CFIUS regulations);
- Harm (whether and the extent to which the violative conduct impacted U.S. national security);
- Negligence, awareness, and intent (the extent to which the conduct was the result of simple negligence, gross negligence, intentional action, or willfulness as well as whether there were any efforts to conceal the violation or delay the sharing of relevant information regarding the violation with CFIUS);
- Persistence and timing (the length of time that a violative party had been aware, or had reason to be aware, of a potential violation prior to CFIUS becoming aware of the violation);
- Response and remediation (whether the violative party self-disclosed the violation, whether the violative party cooperated fully in the CFIUS investigation, and whether the violative party performed a root cause analysis regarding the violation and took appropriate remedial actions to prevent future violations); and

- Sophistication and past record of compliance (including the violative party's history and familiarity with CFIUS, its past compliance with CFIUS mitigation, and its internal and external resources dedicated to compliance).

In the past, CFIUS has recommended that the President block very few takeovers and has threatened to block a few others (the threats stopped the deals). In 2005, Exon-Florio made front page news when a state-owned Chinese oil company made an offer to purchase an American oil company. The Chinese withdrew after Congress passed a joint resolution demanding that the President block the deal. Given the vigor that FIRRMA infused into CFIUS, it is likely that CFIUS will challenge more deals going forward, particularly those directly or indirectly involving the Chinese government and Chinese nationals.

One such challenge focused on Nippon Steel's proposed friendly deal to acquire U.S. Steel for $14.1 billion, which was announced in late 2023. The proposed deal between Japan's fourth largest steel company and the iconic U.S. Steel was met with brutal condemnation by the United Steelworkers Union, as well as politicians on both sides of the aisle. President Biden, Vice President Harris and former President Trump all expressed their disdain for the deal, highlighting their belief that U.S. Steel should continue to be domestically owned and operated. Given that 2024 was a presidential election year, Biden, Trump and ultimately Harris were all too eager to condemn the deal on the campaign trail. In response, executives from both Nippon Steel and U.S. Steel went on a charm offensive in both Washington, D.C. and Pittsburgh, Pennsylvania.

CFIUS, of course, actively reviewed the proposed transaction. According to correspondence between the Committee and Nippon Steel, some Committee members were concerned about Nippon Steel's immense size and foreign steel mills. Others viewed the proposed deal as a potential threat to U.S. Steel's production as well as to steel output in the U.S. generally. Nippon Steel, in response, offered to engage in mitigation measures. In particular, it offered to provide the federal government with broad oversight over U.S. Steel's operations. Moreover, it promised not to reduce steel production capacity at U.S. Steel's plants for 10 years without the permission of the federal government.

Nippon Steel's promises did not win over enough CFIUS members to carry the day. On December 23, 2024, the Committee notified President Biden that its members had deadlocked over whether to recommend the deal. The ball, therefore, was in Biden's court. Given that Biden had already expressed his disdain for the deal, it was no surprise when, on January 3, 2025, Biden signed (autopenned?) an executive order blocking the deal. Making matters worse, the merger agreement between Nippon Steel and U.S. Steel contained a $565 million reverse break-up fee payable by Nippon Steel to U.S. Steel if their deal did not receive regulatory approval.

In response, Nippon Steel and U.S. Steel sued the U.S. government claiming that Biden's executive order was signed for "purely political reasons" and was a "clear violation of due process."

Newly-elected President Donald Trump then entered the picture. After vociferously denouncing the tie up between the two companies on the 2024 campaign trail, President Trump announced on May 23, 2025, that Nippon Steel and U.S. Steel would enter into a "partnership" in which Nippon Steel would invest heavily in U.S. Steel. It was unclear, however, how much equity Nippon Steel would be allowed to own in U.S. Steel. The transaction would be subject to a national security agreement between Nippon Steel and the U.S. government. Nippon Steel would name a separate board to oversee its North American business operations, and a majority of the board would be U.S. citizens and the operations' top managers would be U.S. citizens as well. A federal monitor would be appointed to oversee the board's compliance with the national security agreement outlining spending commitments and other requirements of Nippon Steel.

Can an effective legal challenge to a President's decision to block an acquisition based on national security concerns be brought? *Ralls Corp. v. CFIUS*, 758 F.3d 296 (U.S. App. D.C. 2014), provides a rare successful challenge to the authority of CFIUS and the President. Ralls Corp. purchased four limited liability companies (the "Project Companies") formed to develop windfarms in Oregon. While Ralls was a U.S. corporation, its two owners were Chinese nationals. CFIUS determined that Ralls's acquisition of the Project Companies threatened national security and issued temporary mitigation orders restricting Ralls's access to, and preventing further construction at, the Project Companies' windfarm sites. The matter was then submitted to President Obama, who also concluded that the transaction posed a threat to national security. He issued a Presidential Order that prohibited the transaction and required Ralls to divest itself of the Project Companies.

Ralls challenged the final order issued by CFIUS and the Presidential Order in the District Court in the D.C. Circuit. It alleged, *inter alia,* that the orders violated the Due Process Clause of the Fifth Amendment to the U.S. Constitution. To support its allegation, Ralls highlighted that neither CFIUS nor the President provided Ralls with the opportunity to review and rebut the evidence upon which they had relied.

The District Court dismissed Ralls's due process challenge. It noted that Ralls could have sought CFIUS's permission to buy the Project Companies *prior* to completing the purchase. Ralls, therefore, assumed the risk that the completed transaction would be prohibited by CFIUS and the President *post hoc.*

The Court of Appeals, however, sided with Ralls. According to the court, due process requires, at a minimum, that an affected party be informed of the official action, be given access to the unclassified evidence on which the official actor relied and be afforded an opportunity to rebut that evidence. Ralls was not given any of these procedural protections at any point. The court added that the government's substantial interest in national security supports withholding only *classified* information but does not excuse the failure to provide notice of, and access to, the *unclassified* information used to prohibit a transaction. The court noted that the fact that Ralls had the opportunity to present evidence to CFIUS and to interact with it was not enough to satisfy due process, because Ralls never had the opportunity to tailor its submission to CFIUS's concerns or rebut the factual premises underlying the President's action. The court thus held that the lack of due process afforded Ralls constituted a clear constitutional violation, notwithstanding the government's substantial interest in national security and the court's own uncertainty that more process would have led the President to make a different decision.

§ 2. "REVERSE" CFIUS

In August 2023, certain *outbound* U.S. investments (as opposed to the inbound investments potentially scrutinized by CFIUS) drew the attention of the U.S. government. That month President Biden issued Executive Order 14105 directing the Treasury Department to restrict or monitor outbound U.S. investment in the Chinese semiconductor and microelectronic, quantum information technology, and artificial intelligence sectors. The order also covers Chinese-controlled territories outside of mainland China. The program is referred to as the

U.S. Outbound Investment Security Program ("OISP") or, more affectionately, as "reverse CFIUS."

On October 28, 2024, the Treasury Department issued a final rule (the "Outbound Investment Rule" or "OIR") implementing President Biden's executive order and creating a regime restricting investment by U.S. persons in targeted sectors in "countries of concern" (currently limited to China). The Outbound Investment Rule applies to: (a) equity investments by U.S. persons and entities they control, (b) made directly or indirectly in companies based in China, owned by Chinese interests, or with a majority of their revenue or expenses in China, and (c) that are conducting targeted activities in one of the following three sectors: (i) semiconductors and microelectronics, (ii) quantum information technologies, or (iii) artificial intelligence (AI) models above specified thresholds of computing power or developed for specified end uses. Not all investments in the three aforementioned sectors are restricted; however, the Outbound Investment Rule provides detailed criteria to determine whether an investment is notifiable or prohibited.

Importantly, the Treasury Department will not provide guidance on a particular proposed transaction in advance. Rather, the Outbound Investment Rule places the burden on U.S. investors to identify transactions that are subject to prohibition or notification requirements. Violators are subject to civil or (in the case of willful violations) criminal penalties. Not only will investors' actual knowledge of a company's activities be held against them, but so too will any information that they could have obtained through "reasonable and diligent inquiry" (an "after the fact" Treasury Department determination based on facts and circumstances). Moreover, given that many of the critical elements of the Outbound Investment Rule are broadly defined, the Treasury Department will have considerable discretion in the way in which it enforces the Rule.

On February 21, 2025, newly-elected President Trump issued a national security presidential memorandum (a "NSPM") outlining his "America First Investment Policy." The NSPM predominantly focused on the recently implemented OISP. The NSPM provides a clear policy statement that "economic security is national security." Further, the NSPM defines "foreign adversaries" to mean China (including Hong Kong and Macau), Iran, North Korea, Russia and the "regime of Venezuelan politician Nicolas Maduro." Despite references to countries other than China, the primary focus of the NSPM is clearly on China. Moreover, the Outbound Investment Rule's prohibitions are expanded to cover new sectors, including biotechnology, hypersonics, aerospace, advanced manufacturing, directed energy, and other areas.

§ 3. FEDERAL LEGISLATION SPECIFIC TO FOREIGN ACQUISITIONS IN PARTICULAR INDUSTRIES OR OF PARTICULAR ASSETS

The U.S. Congress has passed a series of laws that regulate foreign ownership (and therefore foreign acquisitions of domestic businesses) in specific industries. Some states, notably California, Iowa, New Mexico and Pennsylvania, may also restrict foreign ownership of certain types of property and the exploitation of natural resources by foreign investors.

The following list of federal acts focuses only on those that restrict not only the activity of foreign entities but also the activity of domestic entities (those incorporated in the U.S.) owned by foreign citizens or entities. The list is not exhaustive.

The *Foreign Bank Supervision Enhancement Act* of 1991 establishes special clearance and oversight criteria for foreign-owned banks that do business in the U.S. 12 U.S.C. § 3105(d). The *Federal Communications Act* of 1934 bars foreign persons, entities or governments and U.S. entities controlled by foreign interests from possessing a broadcast or common carrier license unless the FCC determines it will serve the "public interest." 47 U.S.C. § 310(b). The *Communications Satellite Act* of 1962 restricts foreign ownership of wireless satellite communications networks. 47 U.S.C. §§ 201–04. The *Merchant Marine Act* of 1920 provides that merchandise moving between U.S. ports must be transported on U.S. built, owned and registered vessels. 46 U.S.C. § 55102(b). The *Coast Guard Authorization Act* of 1989 limits direct or indirect foreign investment in our commercial fishing industry. 46 U.S.C. § 12103(b). The *Mineral Lands Leasing Act* of 1920 allows the Secretary of the Interior to grant federal leases to develop natural resources in the U.S. to companies with larger than 10 percent foreign ownership only if U.S. citizens can obtain similar licenses or leases from the home governments of the foreign interests. 30 U.S.C. § 181. The *Atomic Energy Act* of 1954 effectively bars foreign ownership of companies that operate in the nuclear power industry, 42 U.S.C. § 2133(d), and foreign ownership of companies that mine uranium on public lands. 42 U.S.C. § 2097.

Numerous federal laws also establish specific disclosure requirements for foreign investors. Again, the following list is not exhaustive. The *International Investment and Trade in Services Survey Act* of 1976 requires U.S. corporations to report to the Department of Commerce within 45 days of the acquisition by a foreign person or entity of a 10 percent or larger voting equity interest if the stock acquired is valued at more than $1 million or if the corporation has annual sales, assets or net income of greater than $10 million. 22 U.S.C. §§ 3101–3108; see also 15 C.F.R. 806 (Commerce Department regulations). The Act also requires reports when an existing U.S. company that has a foreign investor who holds 10 percent or more of its voting stock acquires additional U.S. businesses. The *Foreign Investment and Real Property Tax Act* of 1989 gives the Secretary of the Treasury the power to require reporting by foreign persons or entities holding direct investments in U.S. real estate having an aggregate fair market value in excess of $450,000. 26 U.S.C. § 6039C. The *Agricultural Foreign Investment Disclosure Act* of 1978 requires foreign persons or entities or domestic entities in which a foreigner holds 10 percent or more of the equity to file a report within 90 days before purchasing an interest in U.S.

farming, ranching or timberland. 7 U.S.C. §§ 3501–3508.

INDEX

References are to Pages